ASCD

Supervision of Teaching

Prepared by the ASCD 1982 Yearbook Committee
Thomas J. Sergiovanni, Chairperson and Editor.

Association for Supervision and Curriculum Development
225 N. Washington St., Alexandria, Virginia 22314

Editing:
   Ronald S. Brandt, ASCD Executive Editor
   Nancy S. Olson, Senior Editor

Stock number: 610-82262
Library of Congress Catalog Card Number: 81-71400
ISBN 0-87120-112-7

Contents

Foreword

WE OFTEN SPEAK OF THE SCIENCE AND ART OF TEACHING. If we accept that supervision is teaching, we are comfortable to consider the science and art of supervision as well. The characteristics of both include planning of instruction, self-actualization, quality performance, facilitation of learning, and evaluation.

This Yearbook is an attempt to provide a current benchmark of thinking about supervision and deals with its three faces: the artistic, the clinical, and the scientific. Early in the book these faces are discussed separately, and then are integrated within the description of the personal helping relationship role of the successful supervisor.

These authors are not offering answers, as of course there are no panaceas. Rather they deal with the varied facets of supervision and give perspective on its history, organizational framework, strategies, models, and future prospects. The point is made that though educational supervision has developed concurrently with economics and technology that we must never lose sight of the human aspects of its responsibilities.

In regard to future efforts to strengthen the supervisory role as a way to improve instruction and the image of public education, there are several appropriate changes suggested: collaboration between classroom teachers and supervisors is vital even though bureaucratic structures discourage it; they both need to identify their strengths and weaknesses and to plan perscriptive staff development opportunities; and solving new problems is more important than perfecting ways to accomplish standard routines. New sets of standards for certification should include high level intellectual skills; expertise in observation, data collection, and analysis; and evidence of successful leadership activities.

Business and industrial leaders count heavily on a strong supervisory staff to ensure quality performance. Hence their representatives relate to specific descriptions of responsibility as school personnel needs are expressed. As we lessen ambiguity and sharpen the focus of responsibility for educational supervisors, it is expected that they will perceive their roles more realistically and will therefore perform more effectively.

The bottom line then can be professional satisfaction, budgets sufficient to ensure job security, and administrative and lay support for the role of the educational supervisor.

Lucille G. Jordan
President, ASCD, 1981-82

Introduction

Supervision and the Improvement of Instruction

THIS YEARBOOK ON SUPERVISION IN SCHOOLS is a straightforward attempt to provide a modest benchmark of thinking in the field as of 1982. The word modest is key for supervision is a field broadly conceived, as a general school activity that encompasses a number of school roles and that includes virtually all of the activities of administrators and supervisors involved in the improvement of instruction. Though the chapters in this book acknowledge this broad base, our perspective is limited primarily to the task of helping teachers, working in classrooms with students, to be more effective.

Embedded in the concept of supervision are certain principles and ways of operating that are often taken for granted. Supervision as authority stemming from superordinate and subordinate relationships and supervision as quality control are but two examples. These ideas become increasingly fallible as their origins are discovered and understood.

Part I of the Yearbook provides a brief historic sketch of supervision in the United States. This sketch is particularly important to supervisors who seek to understand why so many contemporary supervisory structures and practices are taken for granted.

From this brief exploration into our past, the book moves directly to the issue of evaluating and understanding teaching. One's view of the world of teaching and the process of supervision depends largely on one's vantage point or perspective. In education and other human sciences vantage point and perspective are more than topographical. They emerge from values, assumptions, and points of view each of us holds dear. Like colored lenses, different perspectives and vantage points provide persons viewing the same teaching with entirely different realities of this teaching. These differences provide us with important issues yet to be resolved.

Supervision, then, has many faces, three of which — the scientific, the artistic, and the clinical — are discussed in Part II. Though these faces can be viewed as competing, they can also be viewed as images of "truth" in their own right which, when applied *alternately* and *integratively*, provide a more useful view of reality than any one alone. A theory of supervisory practice proposed in the final chapter of Part II seeks to integrate the scientific, artistic, and clinical views, around the theme of helping teachers to be more effective.

Part III of the Yearbook is concerned with the human factor in supervision. Simply stated, supervision is a human enterprise which seeks to help teachers provide high quality classroom experiences for students. Personal and professional growth are key here. Such growth aspirations are not likely to be achieved in schools, conceived as organizations, which hinder rather than help learning. Such aspirations are not likely to be achieved in schools where growth goals apply only to teachers. Such aspirations are not likely to be achieved in settings where teachers are objects of supervision and where the emphasis is on evaluating teachers rather than teaching. Such aspirations are not likely to be achieved under the shroud of prejudice, whatever its source and whomever its target. These are the themes considered in the four chapters which comprise this important part of the book.

Teaching is not easily separated from teaching arrangements or from the curriculum. Teaching and structural arrangements and teaching and curriculum interact and modify each other. The *curriculum in use* is a hybrid born of the stated curriculum on the one hand and the inclinations, biases, and beliefs of teachers on the other. With respect to structural arrangements, teaching might be viewed as an elderly river that seeks to follow its own course but bends as well to topographical contours. Organizational structure and bureaucratic requirements are two such contours affecting teaching.

Part IV examines the impact of the curriculum and the impact of the school's bureaucratic structure on the process of supervision. Curriculum and bureaucratic structure are hidden dimensions that act as powerful determinants of classroom life. They are, in fact, a surrogate system of supervision. Included in Part IV is an analysis of political and social forces that affect educational policy. Particular attention is given to the long and short term effects on supervision of emphasizing scientific rationality now in vogue.

Part V assesses the possibilities and new directions, given progress to date, in developing the field of supervision and evaluation. A state of the art summary is provided and from this summary comes a statement of possibilities and some basic coordinates to help us begin to realize the future we desire in supervision.

The Association for Supervision and Curriculum Development membership is vast and heterogeneous. A Yearbook such as this is not likely to please everyone. There is no sensationalism here. There are no quick answers and sure-fire cures. Those who seek an encyclopedic survey of the field will not find it here. We concentrated on key aspects of supervision bearing on the improvement of classroom life: models of supervision we implicitly and explicitly hold, an integrative framework for putting these models to work to help teachers, some human issues that impinge on the process of supervision, surrogate forms of supervision implicit in curriculum and organizational designs which we believe are often overlooked, and some analysis of future prospects for supervision as a field of inquiry and practice.

What is to become of our efforts? We hope they will open up new avenues of inquiry of interest to scholars and practitioners alike. More important for the present, we hope to provide practitioners with better (more intellectually reasoned and sensitive) cognitive maps from which strategies of supervision can be developed. We seek not to replace the intuitions of supervisors with a set of practices for them to imitate, but to improve the intuitions of supervisors so they might refine present practices and develop better ones.

Fifteen authors prepared the yearbook chapters and we are indebted to many others from the professional and academic communities. The Council of Professors of Instructional Supervision devoted a major portion of their fall 1980 conference to reviewing the yearbook chapters and to this group we owe a special debt. The yearbook committee is particularly indebted to the seven authors who accepted our invitation to help us prepare this Yearbook.

Thomas J. Sergiovanni

Part I.
The Genesis of Supervision

THE AGE-OLD DEBATE OVER THE EXACT MIX of influence between society and school remains unresolved. Nonetheless, most will agree that societal influences on schooling have historically been and remain strong. It is no accident, for example, that schools throughout the states and territories of the United States share a remarkable resemblance in organization and structure. The requirements of accrediting agencies and state education departments for program and licensing approval, for example, provide certain uniformity in thought and practice about education in general and teaching and supervision in particular that overrides any diversity assumed by public commitments to state and local control. This uniformity occurs in reaction to certain societal forces and expectations. Standards and practices are ideologies that reflect the pressures dominant in our society. To understand fully present practice in supervision, therefore, historical analysis is necessary.

In the tradition of ''Roots,'' Clarence Karier provides a sense of our history in the first chapter of this book. In ''Supervision in Historic Perspective'' he argues that the ''precise form supervision will take at any given time is directly related to a number of historically determined facts.'' The facts analyzed by Karier are the goals of education considered most important at the time, the nature and distribution of educational authority, and the generally accepted means for achieving educational goals. As these dimensions change, so does the nature of supervision.

In any given period, however, competing views of supervision exist among those within the scholarly and professional education communities. Teaching as science, for example, and supervisory strategies based on technical rationality are dominant today. But these views and related practices coexist with more aesthetic and humanistic views and practices. The genesis of these supervisory emphases and their fate over the years is part of the story Karier tells.

Chapter 1.
Supervision in Historic Perspective

Clarence Karier

IF WE DEFINE EDUCATION AS LAWRENCE A. CREMIN DOES "as the deliberate, systematic, and sustained effort to transmit, evoke, or acquire knowledge, attitudes, values, skills, or sensibilities, as well as any outcomes of that effort," [1] and we define supervision as "the direction and critical evaluation of instruction," [2] then the form supervision takes is directly related to a number of historically determined factors. The first factor is the goal of education, the second is the locus of educational authority, and the third is the socially acceptable means for implementing the educational goal. Viewed historically, all three dimensions of the supervisory process have changed considerably.

While many goals of education have remained fairly constant, others have undergone considerable change. Although it is difficult to specifically articulate the goals of American education at any given time, they do exist, if only implicitly in our action. However defined, the goals of American education are a composite picture of the hopes, expectations, and possibilities any generation has with respect to the future generation. In this sense, education is a cultural renewal process in which the economic, social, religious, and cultural values of one age are systematically reconstituted for the next. As values shift so eventually does educational practice. The goals of education of seventeenth century Puritan New England were thus quite different from those of the nineteenth century settler on the western frontier and vastly different from those of the corporate-minded twentieth century American.

Not only have the goals of American education changed over time but the locus of educational authority has also changed. Who is responsible for the education of the young? For the Puritan, that responsibility rested with the parent in cooperation with the church which helped define the larger community. In the context of the family unit most of the economic, social, religious, and cultural values were transmitted. To be sure, there were institutional forms of education such as the col-

---

[1] Lawrence A. Cremin, *Traditions of American Education* (New York: Basic Books, 1977), p. viii.
[2] *Webster's New Collegiate Dictionary,* p. 852.

Clarence Karier is Professor of the History of Education and Chairperson of Educational Policy Studies at the University of Illinois, Urbana-Champaign.

lege, Latin grammar school, district school, and dame school, each in its own way institutional legacies of Medieval, Renaissance, and Reformation cultures, but the center of authority did not rest in state or public hands. The educational authority in colonial America rested mainly with the parents who expressed that authority in a variety of private forms of education.

Private education remained the dominant form throughout the colonial era, even while governmental authority increased. By the constitutional period, a wide variety of private educational institutions served a very literate population.[3] As the nineteenth century dawned in the grips of a strong nationalistic fervor, public power at both the federal and state levels grew. By the third and fourth decades of that century, state authority had grown especially in the northeast and middle Atlantic states to such an extent that a public school could be clearly defined as a school that was publicly controlled and publicly financed. By the common school era (1830-1850) this distinction as to what constituted a public school as opposed to a private school was largely accepted. Prior to that time the difference was often blurred.[4]

Although the major authority over the education of the child still rested with the parent in the family unit, the common school movement led by Horace Mann in Massachusetts, Henry Barnard in Connecticut, Calvin Stowe in Ohio, Caleb Mills in Indiana, and John P. Pierce in Michigan extended state authority at the expense of what had been parent-family authority. The common school movement itself was spurred on by the passions of nationalism and the social and economic instability resulting from immigration and industrialization. By the Civil War period America had greatly extended state authority in education.

What began as a trickle of state authority in education became by the end of that century a raging torrent. Underlying the declining educational role of the family was its changing function from being both a producing and consuming unit to being solely a consuming unit. When the first artisan cobbler laid down his pegs and awl and left his household for the power-driven machines of the factory, the decline of the family as a vocational educator began. At virtually every turn in the nineteenth and twentieth centuries the educational authority of the parent gave way to the growing authority of the state.

Not only have the goals of education and the locus of authority changed, but also the acceptable means for implementing those goals. The idea that schooling is necessarily the main course of one's education is of relatively recent origin. In the age of Benjamin Franklin and Thomas Jefferson formal schooling was not critical in the education of the young. Thus, when Jefferson argued that the average citizen must

---

[3] For example, see Cremin's discussion of this in *Traditions of American Education*, pp. 39-89.

[4] See Clarence J. Karier, *Man, Society, and Education* (Glenview, Ill.: Scott, Foresman, 1967), p. 59.

be educated so as to "recognize tyranny and be able to revolt against it," and then suggested in his *Bill for the Diffusion of Knowledge*[5] that the average citizen would need only three years of publicly supported schooling, he was thinking in terms of the self-taught individualism of his age. Jefferson believed that in three years of schooling one could learn enough of the essential tools to become an educated citizen. Thus one might learn art, architecture, law, medicine, navigation, surveying, engineering, and languages in a variety of ways. For example, one could become accomplished in any of these areas by self-study, by apprenticing oneself to a person practicing the art, or by responding to any of the newspaper advertisements promising to teach an art for a fee.

In that pre-modern world, Jefferson, Franklin, and others could become knowledgeable in a variety of fields. But by the early decades of the nineteenth century that world began to change. As new knowledge increased, requests for extended formal training and state licensing and credentialing in some fields appeared.[6] The beginning signs of the modern practice of making education synonymous with schooling were evident in the nineteenth century.

As the idea of education as synonymous with schooling grew, the locus of authority shifted from parent to state. In this context, a cadre of state representatives emerged who, working within the growing corporate structure, claimed expertise in the techniques of implementing institutionally-derived goals. As the system became more bureaucratic, the primary values became standardization and efficiency. As means became evaluated more on efficiency grounds, the role of the professional teacher and supervisor entered the highly-charged, problematic modern world of social engineering.

Given, then, the changing nature of the supervisory process with respect to goals, means, and authority over time, it might be helpful to keep these dimensions of the process in mind as we scan two significant periods of educational reform and briefly analyze one of the problems of the professional supervisor in the mid-twentieth century. Our first period under consideration will be that of the common school era (1830-1850) when the state system of publicly controlled elementary schools took shape. The second period will be that of the progressive liberal reform era (1890-1920). This was the period when our secondary schools not only underwent fantastic expansion, but it was also the period when they were effectively reorganized within the framework of a centralized bureaucratic system that has remained the dominant model of school governance throughout the twentieth century.

---

[5] See Gordon Lee, *Crusade Against Ignorance* (New York: Classics Series, 1967), p. 83.

[6] I do not mean to imply that all skill training was wide open or that it had been previously. The Medieval guild system was not an open system. However, in the transition from the feudal system to the capitalist system, there was a weakening of the guild system even as the apprenticeship system was derived from that system, making room for a more competitive, possessive individualism as reflected in the bourgeoisie class. Once this class was in place, new institutional structures were created that were equally as controlling.

The Common School Era

The common school, as many have noted, was not a school for commoners but was a school that taught the common elements of American culture. The integrative purpose of such a school loomed large in the minds of Horace Mann and others who led the common school movement. To Mann and others the new American society seemed to be disintegrating before their eyes as they observed the social, religious, and economic conflicts of the day. As the family began to lose its producer function to a factory system of employment and poverty-stricken Irish Catholics flooded Protestant Boston providing cheap labor and undercutting the native workers, the potential for social disintegration seemed alarmingly clear. As Horace Mann put it:

The mobs, the riots, the burnings, the lynchings, perpetrated by the men of the present day, are perpetrated because of their vicious and defective education. We see and feel the ravages of their tiger passions now, when they are full grown; but it was years ago when they were whelped and suckled. And so too, if we are derelict in our duty in this manner, our children in their turn will suffer. If we permit the vulture's eggs to be hatched, it will then be too late to take care of the lambs.[7]

As a whig politician opposed to Jacksonian democracy and as a strong advocate of industrial expansion, Mann saw the possibilities of social class conflict. He argued that, "Property and labor, in different classes, are essentially antagonistic; but property and labor, in the same class, are essentially fraternal." [8] Mann's solution to the social class conflict that surfaced on the first wave of industrialization in America lay in the development of the common school and a more highly educated populace. It "never can happen," Mann argued, "that an intelligent and practical body of men should be permanently poor." [9] The more formal education a population had the less chance it had of being poor.

The argument Mann set forth in his Twelfth Annual Report to the Massachusetts Board of Education assumed not only that education would prevent poverty and thus reduce class conflict through the process of dividing the wealth, but that the pool of wealth to be distributed would steadily increase as a consequence of a more highly educated populace. Horace Mann believed education to be the "balance-wheel of the social machinery," [10] which disarmed the poor of their hostility toward the rich by preventing "being poor." As Mann put it:

Beyond the power of diffusing old wealth, it has the prerogative of creating new. It is a thousand times more lucrative than fraud; and adds a thousand fold more to a nation's resources than the most successful conquests. Knaves and robbers can obtain only

---

[7] As quoted by Karier, *Man, Society, and Education,* p. 60.
[8] As quoted by Lawrence A. Cremin, *The Republic and the School: Horace Mann on the Education of Free Men* (New York: Teachers College Press, 1957), p. 87.
[9] *Ibid.*
[10] *Ibid.*

what was before possessed by others. But education creates or develops new treasures, treasures not before possessed or dreamed of by anyone.[11]

Mann had clearly conceptualized a theory of human capital. He wrote to Abbott Lawrence that "Education has a market value. . . . It may be minted and will yield a larger amount of statutable coin than common bullion." [12]

The same year Karl Marx wrote *The Communist Manifesto* (1848), Horace Mann penned his last Annual Report to the Massachusetts Board of Education. In that report was embedded a theory of human capital that conceptually linked schooling to economic and social growth within a meritocratically-organized social and economic class system. Here, then, was the rationale for public schooling that would sustain the American nation for the next century. Implicit in that rationale was an ideology of competitive and possessive individualism packaged in the context of equal opportunity for all within a system of schools locally managed under state authorization.

The whig political-educational platform of Mann combined the earlier Hamiltonian respect for property with the Jeffersonian concern for equality, all nicely set within the institutional framework of a meritocratically governed public school system. The end product was a school system that taught not only how to read, write, and cipher but also Horatio Alger stories from which children learned that material rewards and riches came to those who played the competitive games of business life. As the nineteenth century wore on, the religious and moral values expressed in the educational literature of an earlier period were frequently overshadowed by business values.

The common elements of American culture were woven into the fabric of children's books and teaching manuals throughout the nineteenth century. As Barbara Berman, Monica Kiefer, and others have shown, these strands consist of considerable Protestant moral precepts intertwined with business values interspersed with military modeling. The Mexican War, the Civil War, the Indian Wars, and the Spanish-American War left their imprint on the rhetoric and practice of the common school.

It was not only the line and staff method of organization that school people borrowed from the military, the military model clearly entered the literature on classroom teaching and supervision of instruction as well. As the *Michigan Teacher* in 1873 attests, "A good school, like a great army, must be drilled to precise, prompt, and well-ordered movement." [13] In 1887, Gabriel Compayrés in *Lectures on Pedagogy, Theoretical*

---

[11] *Ibid.*, p. 88.

[12] As quoted by Richard H. deLone, *Small Futures: Children, Inequality, and the Limits of Liberal Reform* (New York: Harcourt Brace Jovanovich, 1979), p. 43.

[13] As quoted by Barbara Roesch Berman, "A Method of Progress: Social Mission in Nineteenth-Century Teacher Training Literature, 1830-1890" (Ph.D. dissertation, University of Rochester, 1978), p. 257.

and Practical wrote, "A child of our common schools is not only a future workman, but a future soldier." [14]

The Progressive Era

By 1900 only ten percent of American youth 14 to 17 attended a secondary school. Fifty years later approximately ninety percent of that age group was in secondary schools. This massive system of schooling was economically based, to a large extent, on the rising development of corporations which profoundly shaped American life.

The phenomenal growth of the corporation was critical in establishing the mass system of American production, distribution, and consumption in the twentieth century. Charles Forcey points out that:

. . . in 1897 the total capitalization of all corporations individually valued at a million dollars or more came to only 170 million. Three years later the same figure for total capitalization stood at five billion, and in 1904 at over twenty billion.[15]

Massive accumulation of capital was now underwriting the creation of mass production systems.

As Lawrence Cremin in 1961 correctly concluded, industrialization, urbanization, and immigration were the central problems of the era.[16] The political progressives' solution to these problems was found in the idea of the regulatory state. This concept of state, as it was fashioned by such Wisconsin progressives as Robert T. Ely, John R. Commons, and Robert M. LaFollette and later instituted by the national government, was itself historically rooted in the paternalistic Bismarckian state that utilized government to rationalize and regulate the political-social economy.

The Wisconsin idea as expressed in progressive legislation at both the state and national level was modeled after its German counterpart. The corporate liberal state that emerged in America was, like the Bismarckian state, designed to ameliorate fundamental conflict between competing economic and social interests. As the state became a regulatory agency, it also became a protective welfare agency which, in exercising its power, extended its compulsory authority to nearly all aspects of life. The larger corporations as well as unions found it to their financial advantage to support greater governmental regulatory authority in many areas of life.[17] That same state authority that regulated commerce also came to regulate drugs, alcohol, tobacco, food, clothing, work, leisure time, communications, news, knowledge, research, medicine, child labor, social welfare, and education.

---

[14] *Ibid.*, p. 258.

[15] Charles Forcey, *The Crossroads of Liberalism* (New York: Oxford University Press, 1961), p. xiv.

[16] Lawrence A. Cremin, *The Transformation of the School* (New York: Knopf, 1961).

[17] See Gabriel Kolko, *The Triumph of Conservatism: A Reinterpretation of American History* (New York: Free Press and Glencoe, 1963); and James Weinstein, *The Corporate Ideal in the Liberal State* (Boston: Baron Press, 1968).

Within this rising tide of state power, child labor laws as well as compulsory education laws began to be seriously enforced. The new immigrants from southeastern Europe who flooded into our urban centers now had to be Americanized quickly and trained for the workplace. With the Haymarket Riot, the Ludlow Massacre, and the Pullman Strike in the background, more and more voices could be heard calling for order, control, and social efficiency. Political and social reform was intimately tied to educational reform. Within that milieu of ethnic and racial conflict and economic and social dislocation, there emerged a workable coalition of business and professional elites, new school managers and university people who organized to reform the schools. As David Tyack put it, these elites:

. . . planned a basic shift in the control of urban education which would vest political power in a small committee composed of "successful men." They wished to emulate the process of decision making used by men on the board of directors of a modern corporation. They planned to delegate almost total administrative power to an expert superintendent and his staff so that they could reshape the schools to fit the new economic and social conditions of an urban-industrial society. They rejected as anachronistic, inefficient, and potentially corrupt the older methods of decision making and school politics. Effective political reform, said one of their leaders, might require "the imposition of limitations upon the common suffrage." They ridiculed "the exceedingly democratic idea that all are equal" and urged that schooling be adapted to social stratification.[18]

Raymond E. Callahan in his work *Education and the Cult of Efficiency* very well documented the efficiency craze of the new administrative bureaucracy. He however mistakenly laid the cause of the problem on the vulnerability of schoolpeople to business pressures. Paul Violas in *The Training of the Urban Working Class* and Joseph Cronin in *Control of Urban Schools*, as well as David Tyack in *The One Best System*, have clearly shown that school leaders were not so much victims of business influence and pressure as they were exponents of it. These works further document that even though there was some opposition, on the whole, school leaders were clearly successful in achieving their goal.[19] One such leader, Ellwood P. Cubberley, for more than three decades not only dominated the field of history of education, but profoundly shaped the thinking of the administrative cadre of public schools in the twentieth century. Cubberley argued that the ward system of organizing urban schools was not only inefficient and unwieldy, but it allowed the less intelligent and less successful people to rule the board. As Cubberley put it:

The writer once knew a ward board composed of one physician, two businessmen, one good lawyer, two politician lawyers with few clients, one bookkeeper, one blacksmith, one saloon-keeper, one buyer of hides and tallow, one butcher, one druggist, one worker in a lumber yard, one retired army officer, one man of no occupation except general opposition to any form of organized government, and one woman. The result

[18] David Tyack, *The One Best System* (Cambridge: Harvard University Press, 1974), p. 126.
[19] For an analysis see *Ibid.*, p. 137.

was a board divided into factions, members from the better wards having but little influence with those from the poorer wards. The constant danger was that the less intelligent and less progressive element would wear out the better element and come to rule the board.[20]

The schools, Cubberley argued, must be governed by the "better" people of the community and this could be accomplished by changing from a ward system of school board representation to a five to seven member board elected at large. As he put it:

One of the more important results of the change from ward representation to election from the city at large, in any city of average decency and intelligence, is that the inevitable representation from those "poor wards" is eliminated, and the board as a whole comes to partake in the best characteristics of the city as a whole.[21]

School board reorganization during the progressive era proceeded with the clear intent of getting our "best elements" to control the school system. Board members elected at large would no longer represent their own respective wards where they were accountable at the neighborhood level but would be supposedly more representative of ". . . the best characteristics of the city as a whole."

Reformers also insisted that politics be removed from the schools. This was to be done first by electing school board members at large so that the "better elements" of the community would control the board and, second, by holding school board elections separate from political elections, thus freeing them from the taint of party affiliation. The progressive liberal drive for a "nonpartisan" school board elected at large, effectively disenfranchised the poorer classes. School boards in the progressive era moved more under the control of business and professional leaders, and the disproportionate representation of these classes on school boards remains to the present day.[22]

Amidst these changes emerged a professionalization of the superintendency which came in the wake of the growth of cities. As late as 1870, Cubberley reports 29 city superintendents of schools, but by 1876 there were 142 cities of 8,000 inhabitants or more which had a city superintendent.[23] The population growth in the metropolitan centers stimulated both the bureaucratization of management as well as the professionalization of school administrators. By the beginning of the century courses in school administration could be taken at the university level.

Throughout the early decades of the twentieth century, school management was increasingly recognized as a job for professional experts trained at the university level. For the most part, these experts

[20] Ellwood P. Cubberley, *Public School Administration* (New York: Houghton Mifflin, 1922), p. 93.

[21] *Ibid.*, p. 95.

[22] See George Sylvester Counts, *The Selective Character of American Secondary Education* (Chicago, 1922).

[23] Cubberley, *Public School Administration*, pp. 58-59.

were drawn from the middle class. By the 1920's most city school systems were governed by boards drawn primarily from business and professional classes and managed by middle-class professional administrators who in turn tended to hire lower middle-class teachers who had just moved from a social position of lower class. It is little wonder, then, that most American public schools by mid-twentieth century were so thoroughly middle class.

While the nineteenth century witnessed the rise of the common school, the first half of the twentieth century witnessed the rise of the secondary school. For example, during the 70 year period from 1870 to 1940 the population of the United States increased three times over, while the population of our secondary schools increased 90 times over. This astonishing growth in schooling set the conditions for reorganizing schools from a committee system to the more efficient military line and staff system. The new organization allowed for greater centralized control and yet considerable specialization of function.

As the overall school systems became larger, the role of the superintendent became more specialized. As this occurred, the work of supervision of instruction was delegated to a new cadre of administrators. By February 1921, the National Conference on Educational Method was organized as an independent society, and by 1929 the organization changed its name to the Department of Supervisors and Directors of Instruction and became a separate department of the National Education Association. This department maintained its separate identity until 1943 when it merged with the Society for Curriculum Study to become the Department of Supervision and Curriculum Development of the NEA.

Thus by 1929 the trend toward professionalizing supervision as a separate field had advanced far enough to warrant a separate department in the NEA. Although it is impossible to describe all the concerns of supervisors and directors during the next two decades within this short space, it is clear that the problems they struggled with were problems of ends as well as means, very much influenced by the historic circumstances of their time.

The Depression

The new Department of Supervision and Curriculum Development of the NEA was hardly organized when the country was overwhelmed by a severe depression. Many supervisors and administrators believed their role during that time was to lead the new generation to social adjustment and to what little happiness might be wrested from the "dull and sordid years" that they believed lay ahead for that generation. While Franklin Delano Roosevelt spoke of this generation having a rendezvous with destiny, public school administrators more often spoke in sadder, less uplifting terms. E. W. Butterfield, State Commissioner of Education for Connecticut, expressed this view when he said,

Our schools face this new task. While children are still pupils, the schools are to educate all, to lead to social adjustments, to train for a mechanical age, and to give, thru club activities, thru music and art and moving picture appreciation and home-making and beauty culture, the interests that will carry happiness thru many dull and sordid years.[24]

Throughout the next few decades the overall view of education was to help the younger generation adjust to the real world of pain and suffering which lay ahead. As Butterfield continued,

Blessed is the boy or girl who, for fifty years, will meet in turn pain, worry, poverty, loss of friends, hard work, generous in amount and monotonous in nature, and all of the woes and ills that flesh is heir to, and yet will search for no escape thru the door of despair, suicide, or insanity.[25]

While a few educators paused momentarily to listen to George S. Counts' clarion call — "Dare the Schools Build a New Social Order?" — most continued on in the more secure role of adjusting the younger generation to the social and economic necessities of what they perceived to be the real world. Meeting the needs of children in such a world called for "individualizing instruction," which often meant tracking the young back into the social and economic class from whence they came.

The world of technological change continued to impress supervisors. Some spoke of cultural lag, while others spoke of scientific management, social efficiency, and scientific measurement. Still others spoke of cooperative curriculum revision, the whole child, pupil-teacher planning, democratic supervision, and life adjustment curricular goals. While efficiency and scientific management continued to occupy the attention of many, toward the closing years of the 1930s such words as democracy, cooperative living, and group thinking became increasingly commonplace. While a few educational leaders sought to change the social order through the schools, many more thought in terms of social harmony and life adjustment. All seemed to agree that educational supervisors ought to avail themselves of the new techniques emerging from the new sciences of psychology and sociology for analyzing, shaping, and controlling human behavior so as to become more efficient social engineers or, at least, more effective educational leaders.

The interrelationship of ends and means, as John Dewey never tired of repeating, was inevitably transactionally related. Social science methodology was never socially neutral, although many educators liked to treat it as if it were. Dewey correctly warned that undemocratic methods, no matter how objective, were still likely to produce undemocratic ends.

---

[24] *National Education Association Proceedings,* Vol. 72, 1934, p. 684.
[25] *Ibid.*

By the end of the 1930s a crucial philosophical discussion was taking place among professional educators which proved highly significant in terms of the role the profession would take in the decades ahead. That discussion centered on the changed meaning of the word democracy and what was meant by democratic method. While in retrospect some have dismissed these discussions as rhetorical flourishes, they were, indeed, substantive critical arguments.

In the minds of Dewey and others the argument over democracy centered on the question of method. The question of whether social science methods would or could contribute to a more democratic society troubled the young professor of education, Kenneth D. Benne at the University of Illinois. In a 1949 edition of *Progressive Education* devoted to social engineering,[26] Benne argued that educational leaders must become "change-agents skilled in inducing, directing, and stabilizing those changes in persons, groups, and organizations which intelligent development of educational situations today requires."[27] Such social engineering, Benne argued, "will serve democratic aims and observe democratic scruples and standards only if it is guided by a methodology which incorporates basic democratic values as procedural norms."[28]

Benne, along with R. Bruce Raup, George E. Axtelle, and B. Othanel Smith, further developed these ideas in the 1943 Yearbook of the National Society of College Teachers of Education under the title, *The Discipline of Practical Judgment in a Democratic Society,* later published as *The Improvement of Practical Intelligence* in 1950. Although Dewey did not entirely agree with the work of these authors, their study is a landmark attempt to explicitly deal with the practical linkage between the use of social science methodology and the possible consequences for a democratic social order. That the book failed to reach a large audience makes it no less significant. It may have fallen on deaf ears because it was originally published during war time when other concerns were obviously more significant. Perhaps it was the fact that it did not represent the wave of the future. For most educational administrators and supervisors in the post-World War II period the wave of the future lay in indiscriminate borrowing and use of new social science techniques, devoid of philosophic and social concerns. The demise of philosophy of education as a significant component in the education and training of administrators and supervisors parallels the rise in the use of social science disciplines. Since World War II, educational leaders have tended to worry most about the efficiency of means and to treat the ends as something given.

[26] For example see David H. Jenkins, "Social Engineering in Educational Change: An Outline of Method," *Progressive Education* 26, 7 (May 1949): 193-197; Max R. Goodson, "Social Engineering in a School System," *Progressive Education* 26, 7 (May 1949): 197-301; Kenneth D. Benne, "Democratic Ethics in Social Engineering," *Progressive Education* 26, 7 (May 1949): 201-207.

[27] *Ibid.,* Benne, p. 201.

[28] *Ibid.,* p. 207.

World War II demonstrated the useful application of social science methods to practical problems of change. Systems analysis of budgets as well as personnel found its way into the lexicon of educational leadership. "Group Dynamics" was another technique with direct application to educational engineering.

Funded by the Office of Naval Research, the first National Training Laboratory on Group Development took shape under the joint directorship of Leland P. Bradford of the NEA and Dorwin Cartwright of MIT with a selected cadre of trainees, among whom were Kenneth Benne of Teachers College, Columbia, and Ronald Lippitt of MIT's Research Center for Group Dynamics. The stated intent of this laboratory was to help leaders and groups "achieve maximum human productivity" while bringing their "behavior into line with the difficult demands of democratic ideology."[29] The laboratory was further initiated:

(1) to provide research scientists with an opportunity to communicate scientific knowledge of group dynamics to key education and action leaders, (2) provide an opportunity for observing, experiencing, and practicing basic elements of the democratic group process which are relevant to educational and action leadership, and (3) to provide an experimental laboratory for further research explorations of basic problems of assessment and improvement of efficiency of group growth, group thinking, and group action.[30]

Thus the National Training Laboratories gave birth to sensitivity training. Over the next three decades it was used by government, business, education, and religious institutions under the rubric of "democratic group process" to achieve efficiency in "group growth, group thinking and group action." While one might seriously take issue as to whether or not this process was democratic, it is clear that it was a highly manipulative series of techniques whereby individual thought, identity, and freedom were overcome in order to serve the bureaucratic "group" in thought and action. In the end it proved to be a highly effective apparatus to be used in any corporate structure from the military, which originally funded it, to the religious, economic, and educational institutions which used it. From its origins it promised efficiency in maximizing "human productivity" within an institutionalized framework.

The problem that emerged in the NTL experiment was one that emerged over and over again in the field of education in the post-World War II period. While administrators and supervisors repeatedly turned to the social sciences for more effective methodology and efficient techniques for predicting and controlling human behavior, their role in goal determination was diminishing. As this occurred the function of the humanities in the education of such leaders became more and more irrelevant, if not a bit anachronistic. The older self conception of the

[29] *Preliminary Report of the First National Training Laboratory on Group Development* (Mimeographed) Bethel, Maine, June 16 to July 4, 1947, p. iii.
[30] *Ibid.*

supervisor as participating in goal determination, which often appeared in the earlier pre-war literature, seemed to fade as the more technocratic model predominated. Under the circumstances the question of moral and ethical ends of education found little place in the professional literature.

For the most part educators did not take the lead in social reform movements. Although some educators in the late 1930s and early 1940s participated in intercultural programs which struggled against racism and sexism so inherent in this culture, by and large, the limited progress made in the post-war years in these areas was a consequence of the educational bureaucracy being forced to react from outside the system.

Over the last century as the idea of education became equated with schooling, and the locus of educational authority shifted from parent to teacher and then to bureaucratic authority, the locus of educational decision-making became increasingly obfuscated. Within this kind of framework, lacking any significant philosophical rationale for judgment, the means of education tend to be seriously evaluated solely in terms of efficiency criteria. Under such circumstances the end of efficiency justified the means of electrical shocks, group psychological manipulation, time-out boxes, sensitivity training, and drugs. Thus these devices became part of the repertoire of educational training techniques in the 1980s.

Perhaps Max Weber was correct when he argued that, "the fully developed bureaucratic mechanism" has characteristics similar to that of a machine when he said,

Precision, speed, unambiguity, knowledge of the files, continuity, discretion, unity, strict subordination, reduction of friction and of material and personal costs — these are raised to the optimum point in the strictly bureaucratic administration. . . .[31]

It was clear to him that,

The decisive reason for the advance of bureaucratic organization has always been its purely technical superiority over any other form of organization. The fully developed bureaucratic mechanism compares with other organizations exactly as does the machine with the nonmechanical modes of production.[32]

Early on Weber pointed out that such an organization in its fullest development carried with it a thoroughly rationalized fundamental disrespect for life.

When fully developed, bureaucracy also stands, . . . under the principle of *sine ira ac studio* (without scorn and bias). Its specific nature, which is welcomed by capitalism, develops the more perfectly the more the bureaucracy is "dehumanized," the more completely it succeeds in eliminating from official business love, hatred, and all purely personal, irrational, and emotional elements which escape calculation. This is the specific nature of bureaucracy and it is appraised as its special virtue.[33]

[31] H. H. Gerth and C. Wright Mills, *From Max Weber: Essays in Sociology* (New York: Oxford University Press, 1958), p. 214.

[32] *Ibid.*

[33] *Ibid.*, pp. 215-216.

The driving force of the Kafka-like bureaucratic world of profit and efficiency in which we live when carried to its rationalized extreme becomes irrationally devoid of human purpose and dignity. Unexamined, unchecked, and uncontrolled, the criteria of efficiency cut deeply into our traditional views of the dignity of life, knowledge, the meaning of words, and the overall political process by which we govern ourselves. In such a world, words like democracy and freedom lose their traditional meanings as they take on a propaganda function. Margaret Mead reflected this when she spoke to an earlier generation of progressive educators who in 1935 were involved in the task of creating a new social studies curriculum for what is now our present adult generation:

. . . that for a society to operate efficiently, there must be a great number of words and phrases which will set up immediate responses in the minds of any group which is appealed to act or to refrain from action. Without such rallying words as ''Democracy,'' ''The Constitution,'' ''Americanism,'' it would be impossible to organize masses into sufficiently integrated groups to produce social action. One definite task of the social studies teaching is to build up the *tone* of certain words, to place them in a series of contexts so that they have come to have a fixed stimulus value in the mind of the listener. The tale of the martyr, the patriot, the hero, the narration of events as traitorous or despicable — all of these have this function.[34]

The extent to which social studies teachers accepted Mead's analysis of the political process and the extent to which they were successful in effectively reaching the younger generation with such ideas is the extent to which they, in part at least, significantly helped shape the political life of the America of 1984.

[34] Margaret Mead, ''Report of the Committee on the Social Studies of the Commission on the Secondary School Curriculum,'' October 26, 1935, Section 3, Rockefeller Archive Center. As quoted in Russell Marks' unpublished manuscript, ''The Idea of I.Q.,'' Indiana University, Bloomington, Indiana, p. 162.

Part II.
The Many Faces of Supervision

THIS SECTION INCLUDES CHAPTERS THAT PRESENT several alternative models or ways of knowing in supervision. John D. McNeil leads off with a chapter analyzing "A Scientific Approach to Supervision." Noreen Garman follows with a chapter promoting "A Clinical Approach to Supervision." To complicate matters, these very different views are followed by yet a third view articulated by Elliot W. Eisner in his chapter "An Artistic Approach to Supervision." Not only do these analyses provide certain explicitly formulated assumptions or postulates in support of the advocated view but they provide as well background assumptions that reveal the philosophical perspectives and epistomological beliefs of these authors. Each, therefore, is able to argue a point of view as true because the standards used to determine truth are suited to the view argued. Truth, in this sense, is not determined by an external set of standards but by criteria implicit to the view being argued.

McNeil, for example, argues convincingly for a scientific view of supervision based on beliefs that teaching is or can be a science and on assumptions that technical rationality correctly characterizes human thinking and behavior. Eisner, on the other hand, argues convincingly as well for an artistic view of supervision based on beliefs that teaching is a form of art and on assumptions that tacit knowledge, intuition, and particularistic rationality correctly characterize human thinking and behavior. Noreen Garman avoids this debate directly but provides nevertheless a view of humankind and a framework for supervision with unique background assumptions: faith in individuals to share, to problem solve, to trust, and to relate to each other in some authentic fashion given a proper climate.

On first reading the chapters one can conclude that each of the authors is talking past the others and that the views themselves are not reconcilable. Stuck with this predicament one must either choose a particular point of view and thus reject others or give up on the whole affair as another argument of interest only to academics. But a careful reading of the McNeil and Eisner chapters will reveal that the views proposed are sensitive to a variety of ways of knowing. McNeil, for example, points out that not enough scientific information exists about teaching and that a research base for supervision is still wanting. Though he believes that developing this scientific base is important, he concludes nevertheless that scientific supervision should be viewed as only one of many methods for improving instruction. Caution and a balanced perspective are evidenced in Eisner's paper as well. He seeks not to throw out scientific reasoning with its abuses but to broaden the concept to allow a more sensitive, particularistic, and meaningful rendering of the actual and possible in teaching. If one judges each point of view not as true or correct in a universalistic sense, but as true or correct given certain background assumptions, then perhaps each of the supervisory perspectives can be viewed as alternative and overlapping lenses, none of which alone provides an adequate view of supervision and evaluation of teaching.

Chapter Five, "Toward a Theory of Supervisory Practice" concludes Part II of the book by attempting to bring together scientific, artistic, and clinical views of supervision in an integrated framework designed to help understand and improve teaching. It is in this improvement sense that a theory of supervisory practice is proposed rather than a theory of measurement or evaluation.

Chapter 2.
A Scientific Approach to Supervision

John D. McNeil

WE ARE APPROACHING ANOTHER FIN DE SIECLE. Scientific supervision began with the optimistic promise to deliver both a more just authority for teacher improvement and great gains in student achievement. Forty years later, in the early 1960s, scientific supervisors were denigrated for not having determined teaching effectiveness nor the methods by which pupils best learn. Consequently, and again with optimism, professional researchers — behavioral scientists — took over responsibility for discovering scientific knowledge that would make teaching more effective and supervisors were relegated to implementing their findings. A highly supported R and D effort aimed at strengthening the research basis for teacher effectiveness followed. However, in the early 1980s, this effort is viewed pessimistically. The behavioral scientists are criticized as having had little impact on what or how students learn or, even worse, that their research is reinforcing inadequate goals of education. Nevertheless, the conduct of research as an underpinning to supervision will continue albeit in differing directions: (a) theoretical research to explain what occurs in classrooms and to get better ideas about what is involved in teaching and (b) practical action research whereby practitioners and researchers together try to resolve limited problems in particular school situations and to search for procedures that work in the hands of teachers.

Scientific Supervision as Part of the Scientific Management Movement

Early in this century, scientific supervision was viewed as an answer to the lack of clearly defined standards, a lack that made it difficult to determine which methods were proving best and which teachers were doing the best work. Franklin Bobbitt, for example, saw scientific supervisors as addressing two initial tasks: guiding teachers in the selec-

John D. McNeil is Professor of Education at the University of California at Los Angeles.

tion of methods and preparing and renewing teachers.[1] Supervisors themselves were to discover the best procedures for performing teaching tasks and to help teachers acquire these methods in order to ensure maximum pupil achievement. Basic to this early concept of scientific supervision was the need for a research basis for teaching — a replacement for supervision that appeared to be personal and arbitrary.

Examples of the kinds of information sought in deriving appropriate methods are seen in these questions regarding the teaching of addition in arithmetic: At what age should the 45 addition combinations be taught? What are the combinations that require much, medium, and little drill? Should the drill be oral or written? Is it best performed with abstract examples or in connection with concrete problems? What is the value of using exercises that involve vocational or civic motives?

Teacher preparation and renewal were to be undertaken only after identifying the teacher's weaknesses by measuring the teacher's knowledge of subject matter, understanding of methods and teaching processes, ability to see teaching in academic and social perspectives, endurance, and energy.

Scientific Supervision as Drawing on Research Studies and Applying a Problem Solving Method

By 1930, the difficulty of separating scientific supervision from the scientific study of education itself was apparent. Data generated from early investigations — experimental and statistical — aimed at yielding knowledge of optimum methods to be employed by teachers were deemed inadequate. Instead supervisors were to be familiar with the broad range of educational research and to use this knowledge in the appraisal, training, and improvement of teachers. Supervisors were to draw implications from research undertaken by educational psychologists interested in mental measurement, individual differences, and the psychology of learning; they were to construct, understand, and use new types of tests suggested by educational measurement experts; and they were to see that teachers formulated objectives in accordance with the curriculum experts' new techniques.

At this time, the concept of scientific supervision changed from that of regarding research findings as fixed conclusions, formulated into a pattern for all to follow, to that of regarding such findings as data for sharpening observation and directing further thinking. The influence of John Dewey's *The Sources of a Science of Education*[2] was apparent. Accordingly, the object of scientific supervision was the development of

---

[1] Franklin Bobbitt, "The Supervision of City Schools," in *The Twelfth Yearbook of the National Society for the Study of Education* (Chicago: University of Chicago Press, 1913).

[2] John Dewey, *The Sources of a Science of Education* (New York: Horace Liveright, 1929).

teachers who would attack their classroom problems scientifically, free from the control of tradition, and activated by the spirit of inquiry (the forerunner of action research). Supervisors and teachers together were to adopt an experimental attitude, trying out new procedures and studying the effects of each newly introduced means of improvement until satisfactory results were attained. An underlying assumption was that the efficiency of teachers would be increased through the guidance of a supervisor who would translate aims of the school into terms which the teachers understand, gain teacher acceptance of the aims and objectives, help teachers adapt the curriculum in light of community and individual factors, analyze teaching, and judge the quality of instruction and the efficiency of the results.[3]

Scientific Supervision as Democratic Ideology

In the early 1940s, scientific supervision took a new turn in response to political concerns and the climate of war. Principles associated with democracy — widespread participation, respect for personality, and the importance of eliciting the contributions of many in reaching a common goal — tempered the earlier admonitions that teachers should act in accordance with facts and principles that were reasonably well established by the process of science.

Indeed, supervisors were to help teachers apply scientific methods and attitudes only in so far as those methods and attitudes were consistent with the social values of the day. The formulating of hypotheses, the selecting of appropriate research designs, and the statistical analysis found in action research centered on instructional problems of importance to the participating teachers. Such scientific methods were to help teachers and supervisors collect data and draw conclusions that would be more sufficient and systematically organized than the facts and conclusions they would derive from their uncontrolled opinion. Although supervisors continued to study and relate the generalizable findings from research that seemed to have implications for school practice, they tended to cite only those studies that were consistent with the political ideology of the time. For example, a limited study comparing the effects of autocratic, democratic, and laissez-faire leadership by Lewin, Lippitt, and White, indicating the superiority of the democratic role over autocratic and laissez-faire roles, was taken as the defining answer regarding the most appropriate teaching style for the classroom.[4] This study had a more far reaching effect on practice than any other single piece of research, although it was faulty as an experimental study.

---

[3] A. S. Barr, *An Introduction to the Scientific Study of Classroom Supervision* (New York: Appleton and Company, 1931).

[4] K. Lewin, R. Lippitt, and K. White, "Patterns of Aggressive Behavior in Experimentally Created 'Social Climates,'" *Journal of Social Psychology* 10(1939):271-299.

The End of Scientific Research by School Supervisors

By the 1960s supervisors were no longer engaged with teachers in action research. Action researchers were criticized for their lack of quantitative methods and their failure to conceptually grasp the problems undertaken.[5] Educational science did not cement teachers into a self-governing expert group. Instead, research on teaching was about to be relegated to technically professional researchers, not supervisors and teachers.

The *Handbook of Research on Teaching* published in 1963 signaled an effort to put research on classroom behavior into contact with the behavioral sciences. The content of the book emphasized methodology for conducting research on teaching — theories, paradigms, statistics, and experimental designs. In focusing on the methods and concepts of the behavioral sciences, the authors of the handbook sought causal interpretation and explanation in contrast to the earlier positivist conception of science which limited inquiry to simple investigation into facts, such as experimental design to determine the relative effectiveness of phonics versus whole word method in the teaching of reading. The handbook both set the direction for future research on teaching and revealed the limited knowledge derived from previous research.

The paucity of knowledge about teaching variables and student achievement attained in the previous era was apparent. Little was known about the practical productivity and unexpected effects of given teaching methods. A research basis for guiding supervisors was still lacking. The following conclusions by experts who reviewed the status of knowledge regarding teachers are testimony to this uncertainty:

Procedures for Assessing Teachers. Ratings of teaching effectiveness have no discernible relationships to student gains. After 40 years of research on teacher effectiveness, one can point to few outcomes that supervisors can safely employ in hiring a teacher or in granting tenure.

Effects of Classroom Practices. There is a lack of both a formal system of pedagogical theory and knowledge about the relationship between particular classroom procedures and their educational consequences. Different kinds of teachers get varying amounts of achievement from different kinds of children.

Programs for Teacher Improvement. It is hard to find evidence that patterns of teacher behavior are generated by teacher training. Teaching behavior has little to do with scientific knowledge of learning. Instead, most teaching patterns are influenced more by tradition and the personal needs of teachers than by research on teaching. The teacher is formed by the social situations imposed by the job, especially by the teacher's relationship with students. A teaching method cannot be designed in terms of a set of laws of learning alone. It must also include a

---

[5] H. L. Hodgkinson, "Action Research — A Critique," *The Journal of Educational Sociology* 31, 4(1957):137-153.

set of laws that characterize the consequent behavior of the teacher. We have no such laws.

Teacher Characteristics. The relationship between psychological malfunctioning and teaching effectiveness is low. There are inconsistent findings regarding the relationship of the teacher's intellectual power and success in teaching. Little is known about the relationship between teaching personality and teaching effectiveness.

Teaching in Nursery Schools. The body of knowledge regarding nursery school teaching is spotty and unorganized. Statements about teaching method are so tentative that they are of little value.

Teaching in Higher Education. When one is asked whether lecture is better than discussion, the appropriate counter is "For what goals?"

Teaching Reading. There is considerable difference of opinion among experts on reading methods. Research has not given much help in identifying developing skills, appropriate attitudes, or flexibility necessary when reading for different purposes and reading different kinds of materials. There seems to be no "best" method for all children learning to read.

Teaching Science. Research on the relationship between the behavior of science teachers and other variables, such as the behavior of their pupils, is meager.

Teaching Math. Evidence about the consequences of tell-and-do methods versus heuristic methods is not conclusive. One should be wary of adopting one method or another on the basis of the evidence available.

Teaching Composition. The transfer value of grammar to the writing of compositions depends on the particular grammatical ability involved. We do not know what specific items of grammatical knowledge hold the greatest promise for improving composition skills.

Teaching Social Studies. Research on the outcomes of any given technique has yielded conflicting results.

Teaching Visual Arts. Those in this field do not seek a single set of procedures for teaching art. There is no theoretical base that is correct to the exclusion of other points of view.

Teaching Foreign Language. There is no adequate classroom experimentation. There is no research from which to draw useful conclusions for teaching grammatical habits. The problem of optimal methods of teaching pronunciation is practically untouched. There is a dearth of evidence on methods of teaching reading in a foreign language.

Similarly, A. S. Barr's summary of studies related to the measurement and prediction of teacher effectiveness indicated little was known.[6] During a period of nearly 40 years beginning with his experience as director of supervisors in the public schools, Barr sought to apply the

---

[6] A. S. Barr et al., "Wisconsin Studies of the Measurement and Prediction of Teacher Effectiveness — A Summary of Investigations," *Journal of Experimental Education* 30, 1(September 1961):1-153.

scientific approach to objectifying teaching. Under his direction, teachers, supervisors, and 75 doctoral candidates carried out studies of teaching effectiveness. Almost every conceivable aspect of teaching ability and evidence of efficiency was explored: interests, attitudes, behaviors, knowledges, skills, and personality traits. In looking back over these investigations, Barr asked, "What progress has been made?" His answer was that some progress had been made in clarifying the problem. He correctly saw that the problem that needs clarifying before all others is the criterion of teaching effectiveness. Different people employ different criteria and approaches to the evaluation of teachers. Some prefer to approach effectiveness from the point of view of personal prerequisites; some from teacher-pupil behaviors; some from basic knowledge, attitudes, and skill; and some from the point of view of results or products. These different approaches give different answers to the question, "Is this teacher an effective teacher?"

Other problems include the difficulties of (a) isolating teacher influence from the influences of home, peers, and environment and (b) relating the specific teaching acts to larger ends. (Supervisors tend to infer significance of specific acts to larger purposes, but they have not established the validity of their inferences according to the canons of science.) A number of unresolved problems are associated with the need for assessing how teachers make decisions with respect to pupil needs, means of instruction, rewards, punishments, and standards. Supervisors themselves should be tested by demonstrating their ability to improve a teacher's effectiveness through the manipulation of variables thought to be associated with effectiveness. One of Barr's most important conclusions is that the constituents of effectiveness are not found in teacher, pupil, or in situation, but in the relationships that exist among the three at any given time and place.

Current Teacher Effectiveness Research

A Technology of Instruction Based on Learning and Behavior Theory

Behavioral scientists thought that the problem of effective instruction could best be met by applying psychological theories of learning and the results of experiments involving controlled manipulation of specific factors. The development of teaching machines and programmed instruction became the vehicle for generating ideas about critical instructional variables and for testing their effects. B. F. Skinner, in connection with the design of teaching machines, drew attention to the importance of such instructional variables as active overt responding, elicitation of covert responses, reinforcement, and knowledge of results. Psychologists, such as A. A. Lumsdaine[7] and R. M. Gagné,[8] who had been engaged in training research for the military in World War II, sought to develop an instructional technology by which a teacher could be aided and made more effective.

Lumsdaine stressed the need for controlled experiments showing the influence of specific factors that consistently influence the outcomes of instruction. Some of his conclusions were that overt responding is less important in meaningful context learning than in rote learning and that such responding is likely to be greatest with very young children and with difficult material; there is value in prompting or cueing student responses in learning a procedural skill; and that learning may be enhanced by repetition, pacing, example, review, and opportunity to repeat missed items. He urged better definitions of variables and analysis of their interactions as well as empirical demonstration of the effects of these variables in particular instructional programs.

Gagné stressed the idea that achievement of the objectives of an instructional program depends on whether or not the learner has attained the learning prerequisites to the task that the program is designed to teach. Accordingly, the teacher would have to decide on the ultimate goal and determine the subskills necessary to progress smoothly to the goal, keeping in mind the methods and materials to be used. Knowing the components of a logical and hierarchal sequence and the use of this sequence in preparing diagnostic tests to assess the learners' preparation offers considerable possibility for improving instruction.

J. B. Carroll presented a conceptual model of the learning process that proposed that the success of learning is a function of five elements[9]:

1.   Aptitude — basic characteristics that influence the time sequence for one to attain mastery of a task

2.   Intelligence — the ability to understand the task to be learned and the procedures to follow in learning the task

3.   Perseverance — the amount of time during which one will engage in active learning of the task

4.   Quality of instruction — the degree to which elements of the task are well presented, explained, and ordered

5.   Opportunity for learning — the amount of time allowed for learning reflected in the pacing of instruction relative to the students' capacity to profit from it.

While the first three elements reside in the learner, the latter two reside in the teaching.

[7] A. A. Lumsdaine, "Educational Technology, Programed Instruction, and Instructional Science," *Theories of Learning and Instruction*, 63rd Yearbook of the National Society for the Study of Education, Part I, 1964, pp. 371-401.

[8] R. M. Gagné, *The Conditions of Learning* (New York: Holt, Rinehart and Winston, 1967).

[9] J. B. Carroll, "A Model of School Learning," *Teachers College Record* 64 (1963):723-733.

The technology of instruction emanating from the work of these behavioral scientists had a great impact on both school practice and the conduct of research on teaching effectiveness. Government supported agencies such as regional laboratories for research and development created curriculum materials that followed the technologists' demands for specification of objectives; measures that match the objectives to use in evaluation; delineation of the component skills requisite for achievement of the objectives; prototype development and tryout; and testing of the learning sequences in both laboratory and field situations to find out to what extent they attain desired results. Publishers of instructional materials also adopted features of the new educational technology, such as specific objectives, continua of skills, criterion-referenced tests, and provision for immediate feedback.

The application of technology to the development of instructional products constitutes an indirect form of supervision, that is, product developers external to the classroom determine objectives of instruction and provide the means to attainment. Although it has been more popular to focus on teachers as the way to affect instructional improvement, behavioral scientists with a product development orientation assumed that by improving materials, they would improve educational practice.

Technology of instruction was not only applied in the development of products. Instructional procedures associated with mastery learning, personalized teaching (The Keller Plan),[10] individually-guided instruction, and other popular innovations are based on the concepts and work of the behavioral scientists. Indeed, one can make the case that present trends in competency-based education and performance testing are dependent on the technologists' notions of prespecified objectives, criterion measures, and direct practice with important skills.

Criticism of learning theory as a basis for guiding teaching practice was forthcoming. W. J. McKeachie attacked Skinner and programmed instruction as well as the laws of learning themselves as applied to human learning.[11] He challenged the usefulness of the concept of reinforcement by citing incidents when children do less well in learning when materially rewarded, and the concept of knowledge of results by citing evidence showing that knowledge of results does not always produce better learning and that feedback and praise do not always lead to improvement. McKeachie attributes the popularity of psychological principles and the technology of teaching to their simplicity; the basic ideas are simple to apply and they work often enough to maintain enthusiasm for them.

[10] F. S. Keller, *The Keller Plan Handbook* (Menlo Park, Calif.: W. A. Benjamin, 1974).

[11] W. J. McKeachie, "The Decline and Fall of the Laws of Learning," *Educational Researcher* 3, 3 (March 1974): 7-11.

The Process-Product Paradigm

N. L. Gage is a representative proponent of an approach by which investigators search for teaching processes (teacher behavior and characteristics) that predict or cause student achievement and attitude. This approach is similar to that followed by A. S. Barr and others in a prior era of criterion of effectiveness studies. As stated previously, this approach as carried out in the past failed to produce conclusive knowledge for a variety of reasons: failure to control for the intervening events between teaching behavior and outcomes; failure to get at the meaning behind teacher behavior; failure to attend to the variables that are unstable but important in bringing about learning; and failure to recognize that the relation between teacher practice and results need only be better than chance. Gage sees some ways of overcoming these failures and holds that the approach will lead to a scientific basis to teaching.[12] He does not look for a science whereby good teaching is attainable by following laws that yield predictability and control. Instead, he aims at scientific findings that will allow teachers to know that certain teacher behaviors are likely to have an effect on what students learn.

Inasmuch as the number of variables referring to teacher behavior, pupil behavior, and classroom environment number in the hundreds, Gage recommends instructional treatments that combine teacher variables found to correlate with pupil achievements into combinations of components. Should the combination improve achievement, further analysis can show the relative influence of the individual components.

By testing the significance of combined results through an estimation of the "nonchanceness" of a number of independent findings related to a process variable, Gage has been able to find effects that were masked in isolation. This situational technique is aimed at overcoming the failure to find significant correlations due to small sample size. After sifting several hundred variables in teacher behavior, Gage developed a set of inferences as to how third-grade teachers should work if they wish to maximize achievement in the basic skills. Most of these call for optimizing academic learning time:

• Establish classroom rules that allow pupils to attend to personal and procedural needs *without* having to check with the teacher

• Move around the room a lot, monitoring seatwork and attending to academic needs

• When pupils work independently, ensure that assignments are interesting and worthwhile, yet easy enough to be completed without teacher direction

• Spend little time in giving directions and organizing the class

• Call on a child by name *before* asking questions to ensure that all have opportunity to respond.

[12] N. L. Gage, *The Scientific Basis of the Art of Teaching* (New York: Teachers College Press, 1978).

D. M. Medley claims to have overcome other limitations of process-product research by summarizing the results of studies of teacher behavior that used pupil gain after several months of instruction as the criterion of effectiveness.[13] He concluded that the following three kinds of teacher behavior have strong enough relationships to effectiveness that they can be considered dependable:

Learning environment — the effective teacher has a classroom that is orderly and psychologically supportive.

Use of pupil time — the effective teacher devotes more time to academic activities with the class organized in one large group. Although effective teachers devote less time to pupil seatwork than ineffective ones, they supervise pupils engaged in seatwork more closely.

Method of instruction — contrary to popular opinion, teachers who use more low-level questions and whose pupils initiate fewer questions and get less feedback or additional amplification of their questions are associated with higher pupil gains.

Medley's research is consistent with the findings from a number of process-product researchers. For example, B. V. Rosenshine found that of ten promising variables two that showed the highest correlation with achievement are those related to content covered (opportunity to learn what is being tested) and task orientation or academic focus.[14] The work of D. C. Berliner and others at the Far West Laboratory for Educational Research and Development; the research of J. E. Brophy and C. M. Evertson further supports the value of teachers giving direct supervision to pupils in order to ensure academically engaged time.[15]

Impact of Process-Product Research on Supervision

The impact of this process-product research has been great. Supervisors now emphasize staff development programs aimed at getting teachers to apply a method called "direct instruction," a method derived from research findings regarding the apparent importance of academically focused teacher-directed classrooms. In accordance with direct instruction, teachers are expected to make goals or objectives clear to students, to allocate time for instruction in sufficient and continuing amounts, to match the content presented to that which will be measured on tests of achievement, to monitor the performance of pupils, and to keep questions at a low level so that pupils have a high success rate while learning and to give immediate feedback to students. Unlike the teaching model of the 1950s, the "good" teacher is neither

[13] Donald M. Medley, "The Effectiveness of Teachers," in *Research on Teaching,* ed. P. L. Peterson and H. J. Walberg (Berkeley, Calif.: McCutchan, 1979), pp. 11-27.

[14] B. V. Rosenshine, "Academic Engaged Time, Content-Covered, and Direct Instruction," paper presented at AERA, New York, 1977.

[15] D. C. Berliner et al., *Phase III of the Beginning Teacher Evaluation Study* (Far West Laboratory for Educational Research and Development, 1976); J. E. Brophy and C. M. Evertson, *Process-Product Correlation in the Texas Teacher Effectiveness Study* (Austin, Tex.: University of Texas, 1974).

laissez-faire nor democratic but controlling. The teacher controls the instructional goals, chooses materials appropriate for the student's ability, and paces the instructional sequence.

Action research has been reintroduced as a way to sensitize teachers to the importance of time-on-task. Supervisors in the San Diego City Schools, for instance, involved teachers and researchers to determine what keeps teachers from giving more time to direct academic instruction. They found that organizational and management problems within the classroom were the chief obstacles, not external interruptions. Teachers often did not have the solutions for the problem of a productive classroom climate.

B. S. Bloom points out that although supervisors have always recognized time as a central factor in learning, they are now giving more attention to improving instruction so that pupils will give more time-on-task. The key is that pupils comprehend what is being taught and what they are to do.[16] Identification of specific knowledges, abilities, or skills that are essential prerequisites for the learning of a particular task and teaching these prerequisites accounts for much of the success attributed to mastery learning. Bloom is also concerned that teachers are frequently unconscious of the fact that they do not provide equal opportunity for learning to all students. Thus, he recommends that supervisors help teachers secure an accurate picture of their interactions with students.

In the 1920s, supervisors stressed time-on-task and student attention from a preoccupation for efficiency, effectiveness, and productivity. In the 1940s, they downplayed time-on-task as being too mechanistic and authoritarian for democratic classrooms. Now, partly as a result of the process-product studies and the studies of mastery learning, supervisors are looking to this variable as the answer to improvement of teaching and learning. Therefore, supervisors encourage teachers to be aware of their allocation of time in class, to the manner in which pupils utilize that time, and to how meaningful the task is to the pupil.

In her workshop for supervisors, Madeline Hunter, for example, has influenced staff development in the direction of clear indications of lesson objectives, expected work patterns, criticizing assignments — all of which represent proactive rather than reactive teacher behavior.[17] Her prescriptions for teachers are as follows:

1. *Diagnosis* — Identify a major objective and the status of learners in relation to this objective.

2. *Specific objectives* — On the basis of the diagnosis, select a specific objective for a particular group's daily instruction.

[16] B. S. Bloom, ''The New Direction in Educational Research: Alterable Variables,'' *Phi Delta Kappan* 61, 6 (February 1980): 282-305.
[17] Doug Russell and Madeline Hunter, *Planning for Effective Instruction* (Lesson Design) (Los Angeles: University Elementary School, 1980).

3. *Anticipating set* — Focus the learners' attention, give brief practice on related learning previously achieved, and develop a readiness for the instruction that will follow.

4. *Perceived purpose* — Inform the learners of the objective, indicating why its accomplishment is important and relevant to present and future situations.

5. *Learning opportunities* — Select learning opportunities that promise to help learners achieve the objective.

6. *Modeling* — Provide both a visual example of what is to be attained (product or process) and a verbal description of the critical elements involved.

7. *Check for understanding* — Check for learners' possession of essential information and skills.

8. *Guided practice* — Circulate among students to see that they can perform successfully before being asked to practice independently.

9. *Independent practice* — Once learners can perform without major errors, they should be given opportunities to practice the new skill or process with little or no teacher direction.

The Process-Product Paradigm and Practices that Follow From It

Some of the limitations of the process-product paradigm are overcome by applying newer statistical techniques, such as meta analysis,[18] and by conducting experimental studies in which the variables identified through correlation studies are manipulated — acted on by teachers — to determine if they have a causal influence. However, serious problems remain. Chief among them are those mentioned by Barr long ago — the difficulty of getting agreement on the criterion of effectiveness and the problem of implementing the implications of research findings into unique classroom situations.

Process-product researchers use controversial definitions of achievement. Their definitions are chiefly mastery of narrowly defined skills in arithmetic and reading, a closed set of performance and information. Mastery is usually measured by an achievement test measuring low levels of understanding, such as recall and comprehension, rather than application and evaluation. We do not know that the education of pupils is advanced by teachers who follow the newly prescribed processes, only that certain skills are attained. There is no validation of these prescribed processes to other definitions of literacy, such as critical thinking and invention.

The use of a questionable criterion for effectiveness might account for some of the unexpected findings from process-product research. Consider the low correlations between the asking of high level questions

---

[18] G. V. Glass, "Integrating Findings: The Meta Analysis of Research," in *Review of Research in Education,* 5. ed. L. S. Schulman (Itasca, Ill.: Peacock, 1978).

by teachers and achievement of pupils. Inasmuch as achievement tests demand low level responses, it follows that high level questions are less appropriate. Also, findings showing the superiority of direct instruction whereby teachers exercise control are unacceptable to those who value self-directed learning and the student's own sense of personal control.

In her examination of studies that seem to favor direct instruction, P. L. Peterson found that only small effects were attributable to such instruction.[19] Indeed, the data on effect size suggested that while the average student tended to achieve more with direct instruction, the difference between this instruction and an individual or open approach was only one-tenth of a standard deviation. Further, Peterson found the non-direct rather than the direct instruction to be more associated with creativity and problem solving.

Teacher difficulties in acting on research findings are numerous. By way of example, teachers are confronted with the dilemma of following a set of teaching procedures designed to attain high levels of pupil time-on-task by concentrating on whole class settings, while at the same time pursuing a path aimed at maximizing the individual meaningfulness of instruction requiring individualized activity. Consider, too, the relative difficulty of getting active learning time in a classroom where pupils are motivated to learn as opposed to one where pupils view school tasks as aversive stimuli. The dependable finding that effective teachers have orderly classrooms may be only an artifact. Orderly pupils may just as well produce an effective teacher as an effective teacher cause an orderly class.

Acquiring an understanding of the reasons for the considerable day-to-day fluctuation in pupil engagement is unlikely to come from reliance on process-product research. There is a need for action research in widely different classroom contexts whereby participants attend to variables outside of those offered by the behavioral scientists. No matter how well planned a lesson, effective teaching will remain difficult because of the many changing cues to which teachers and students must respond. Supervisors and teachers sense the uselessness and absurdity of some of the conclusions from product-process research.

G. D. Fenstermacher[20] offers the view that behavioral scientists err in believing that what teachers do is more important than what teachers think. He would have supervisors give more attention to helping teachers think and feel differently about what makes teaching worthwhile. Getting knowledge about teaching and getting teachers to be effective are two different activities. Instead of asking: "Do these teachers' behaviors produce x effect?", supervisors should ask, "Why do these

---

[19] P. L. Peterson, "Direct Instruction Reconsidered," in *Research on Teaching and Concepts, Findings and Implications,* ed. P. L. Peterson and H. J. Walberg (Berkeley, Calif.: McCutchan, 1979), pp. 57-69.

[20] G. D. Fenstermacher, "A Philosophical Consideration of Recent Research on Teacher Effectiveness," *Review of Research in Education* 6 (1978): 157-186.

teachers perform as they do?'', looking for relationships between performance and teacher intentions. The relation between thought and action may be the critical issue in research on teaching.

The Future of Scientific Supervision

One of the United States' great strengths is the extraordinary development of science and technology which is a direct consequence of the freedom of investigation and criticism. Also, the American national character is rooted in optimism — ''A sense of efficacy.'' Our problems can be solved. We shall make life better. It is not surprising then that a scientific approach to supervision — that we can find out why some people are more effective teachers than others and that we can use this knowledge to help teachers become effective — is a central dimension in the supervision field. There are other reasons as well. Supervisors want a knowledge base to free them from charges of personal arbitrariness in their supervisory practice. Teachers, even though they at times distain the results of scientific inquiry into teaching, see the need for such activity, if only to strengthen the myth that teaching is a profession as evidenced by the use of scientifically validated procedures which are not possessed by and which cannot always be judged objectively by the general public.

On the other hand, the case for scientific supervision has not been won. Just as there is an erosion in the American's faith in science, so there is a lack of confidence that research in teacher effectiveness will ever fulfill its promise. The search for effective teaching methods and teachers is like the search for the Holy Grail. Not all teachers can be successes because we are dealing with an art, and there are no formulas for art.

Limitations to the Scientific Approach to Teaching Effectiveness

Future scientific research into supervision will probably follow the direction of social research in general.[21] This means that scientific supervision will be seen as only one among several analytical methods for improving instruction. Other forms of information and analysis, including the ordinary knowledge of supervisors and teachers, may be more effective than the results of scientific inquiry. Ordinary knowledge is not won by the methods of science but by common sense, empiricism, and thoughtful speculation. Such knowledge is highly fallible, but, nevertheless, knowledge to anyone who takes it is a basis for action.

[21] C. E. Lindblom and D. K. Cohen, *Usable Knowledge* (New Haven: Yale University Press, 1979).

The Limited Contribution of Research to Improving Teaching

Research has been limited in its contribution to teaching practice for a number of reasons:

1.   The number of propositions produced by a scientific approach is tiny compared to the judgments and guidelines employed in teaching.

2.   Researchers of teaching refine ordinary knowledge more than they create new knowledge. The researchers' newly found alterable variables of time-on-task, prerequisites to learning, pupil opportunity to participate, home environment, teachers' attitudes toward children, feedback and corrective procedures have circulated as part of teachers' and supervisors' ordinary knowledge for generations.

3.   Researchers refine knowledge in a highly selective fashion. Only a few of the propositions from ordinary knowledge are tested by researchers, and of these only a few are given a high degree of verification.

Indeed, Walter Doyle has called for a fundamental conceptual reorganization of research on teaching on the grounds that present variables found to be associated with achievement, such as time-on-task, may be leading to spurious interpretations.[22] These teaching variables are assumed to cause student behavior when it may be that the student behavior, such as specifying time in learning, is a factor of teacher adaptation to students or students' need for authority. Doyle would reorganize research so that less attention is given to teacher behavior as the treatment variable and more attention is given to the nature of the tasks students are trying to accomplish. Examples of task variables are degree of risk and ambiguity. Other variables of importance are the meanings students give to the objects and events they encounter in instruction. Admittedly, research conducted along this reconstructed line would not increase knowledge about effective teaching patterns, but might provide an analytical framework for helping teachers interpret the problems they meet in their specific classrooms.

4.   There is little hope that research will bring authoritativeness to supervision. Research does not cover the whole terrain of classroom problems. Also, many of the scientific findings will be rejected on other grounds — political, economic. Further, teachers and supervisors will not agree that any finding is sufficiently established to serve as the final word of authority. The most authoritative knowledge is that which has been confirmed by research *and* corresponds to the ordinary knowledge of teachers. Ordinary knowledge that children achieve more when they engage in appropriate learning tasks, that learning opportunities should not be frustrating, and that low teacher expectations preclude pupil

---

[22] Walter Doyle, "Learning the Classroom Environment: An Ecological Analysis," *Journal of Teacher Education* 28 (1977): 51-55.

progress are more authoritative statements than some of the findings from the behavioral scientists' process-product research.

5.   Many scientific findings regarding teaching effectiveness are divergent. When there are divergent views — teacher praise and criticism, class size, open structure, value of drill, pupil choice, concurrent versus transference methods in bilingual education — then supervisors and teachers take only the view that is consistent with their ordinary knowledge as authoritative and act on it. The other view is dismissed as being incorrectly defined or the research design and sample are said to be faulty.

Optional Directions in the Scientific Approach

In view of the lack of authoritativeness of educational research regarding methods and effective teaching, how should it be redirected? One option is for researchers to forsake the search for practical solutions to well-defined problems and instead attend to the functions of fundamental enlightenment of thought as achieved by those such as Dewey, Piaget, Chomsky, and Freud. Members of the National Academy of Education in their recent review of instances of research that have influenced educational practice credited theoretical ideas as having the greatest impact, not hard-core statistical demonstrations.[23] Accepting the goal of enlightenment rather than social engineering sets new tasks for researchers on teaching. Instead of aiming at authoritativeness and testable scientific propositions, they would try to clarify understanding of the classroom and its problems. Conceptualization which might include alternative ways to enhance learning would be an example of such activity.

A second optional direction is for researchers to return to the earlier practice of action research and limit themselves to highly selective but restricted questions of importance to a local community. The argument for this direction is that problems of teaching require a wide range of outlooks and participants, not just problem solving. The interactive problem solving of action research is an alternative to solving problems, understanding, thought, or analysis from the viewpoint of a particular source of knowledge. Researchers using forms of human interaction for the purpose of reducing a problem have the advantage of implementing knowledge as well as finding it.

A third direction is to pursue the ideal of objective experiments on children, attempting to modify them by the process in question. Such efforts to improve the science of pedagogy will be difficult because they involve entanglements with questions of both ends and means. The sciences from which pedagogy draws, particularly psychology, often limit the inquiries undertaken.

[23]   P. Suppes, ed., *Impact of Research on Education: Some Case Studies* (Washington, D.C.: National Academy of Education, 1978).

A fourth direction is to improve teaching through fact-finding studies, adding to knowledge about teaching problems: who are the achievers, non-achievers, where are they, and what do they lack. Although reporting may seem insignificant compared to other dimensions of scientific undertakings, researchers have a higher success rate in this activity than in achieving scientific generalizations. Further, the facts uncovered may contribute to solving problems of teaching.

Chapter 3.
The Clinical Approach to Supervision

Noreen B. Garman

IN THE CLINICAL APPROACH TO SUPERVISION, the supervisor provides the practitioner with a service that is concerned with the quality of his/her practice. The supervisor is competent, compassionate, professional; however, it should be emphasized that supervision represents a good deal of effective tinkering. Supervisors are itinerant, working in one place and then another, seeing no beginning, no middle, no end. They must be knowledgeable and skillful enough to have "the courage not to know" and yet to function confidently. This is the clinical supervisor's legacy.

The clinical approach to supervision takes the name and assumptions from the landmark works of Cogan[1] and Goldhammer[2] and others who have interpreted clinical supervision for their own practice and writing. In this chapter I will develop key concepts related to the clinical approach to supervision and will posit that clinical supervision as a construct is different from the procedural orientation popularly described in the literature. In other words the classic eight phase process known as "the cycle of supervision"[3] is useful under limited conditions, but does not define the practice itself. During the last decade, meaningful features have developed that provide a conceptual framework from which to derive alternative methods appropriate to the broad circumstances of clinical practice. A substantive knowledge base from the collected experiences of supervisor practitioners has begun to generate a language for intellectual study. The concepts, *colleagiality, collaboration, skilled service,* and *ethical conduct,* have become the imperatives that, when explicated, stake out the domain of the clinical approach to supervision.

---

[1] Morris L. Cogan, *Clinical Supervision* (Boston: Houghton-Mifflin, 1973).

[2] Robert Goldhammer, *Clinical Supervision* (New York: Holt, Rinehart and Winston, 1969).

[3] Both Cogan and Goldhammer describe the operational procedures of clinical supervision as a cycle that emphasizes the ongoing involvement of the process. Cogan's eight phases are: 1. Establishing a relationship; 2. Planning with the teacher; 3. Planning for observation; 4. Observing instruction; 5. Analyzing the data from the observation; 6. Planning for the conference; 7. The conference; 8. Renewed planning — thus the resumption of another cycle.

Noreen B. Garman is Professor of Curriculum and Supervision at the University of Pittsburgh.

A Knowledge Base

A little over a decade ago educators had no effective way to describe a clinical supervisor. It was in the early 1970s that a new language was introduced by Cogan and Goldhammer. In 1972, Lewis and Miel devoted one page to the nascent field in *Supervision for Improved Instruction*; Mosher and Purpel in *Supervision: The Reluctant Profession* devoted one chapter. In 1976 *The Journal of Research and Development in Education* featured, as the central theme, *Clinical Supervision,* as did *Contemporary Education* in 1977. By 1980 bibliographies reflected the state of the art.[4] To date, the literature has established a recognizable construct[5] and delineated a method that researchers have tried and found generally, "it works."[6] A number of enthusiasts and sceptics continue to debate the future of the method as well as the semantic dissonance caused by the term clinical.[7]

Discourse about clinical supervision generally reveals two dispositions toward the process, the itinerant and the clinical. Itinerant supervisors often report, "We are *doing* clinical supervision in our school" (meaning we are following the plan of the method) or more direct, "I am using the cycle on a group of teachers." Itinerants are generally competent leaders who find the clarity of the method refreshing and are guided by the texts. Sometimes they wish for more time to work through compelling issues. They regret the demands of their jobs, reminding themselves of the "real world" of supervision.

The clinical disposition, by contrast, imagines that the "real

---

[4] Perhaps the most complete explication of the state of the art to date is found in Robert H. Anderson and Robert J. Krajewski, *Clinical Supervision: Special Methods for the Supervision of Teachers* (New York: Holt, Rinehart and Winston, 1980), pp. 186-199. See also Cheryl Granade Sullivan, *Clinical Supervision, A State of the Art Review* (Alexandria, Va.: Association for Supervision and Curriculum Development, 1980); and Charles A. Reavis, *Teacher Improvement Through Clinical Supervision* (Bloomington, Ind.: Phi Delta Kappa, 1978).

[5] Not only have a growing number of publications focused on clinical supervision in the past few years but there seems to be evidence that the construct is becoming internationally recognized. Example: Project CLINSUP '80 (acronym for clinical supervision) is currently a joint venture by the School of Education and schools in the Colac Inspectorate, Deakin University, Victoria, Australia, 3217. The project co-ordinator is W. John Smyth.

[6] Charles A. Reavis, "Research in Review/Clinical Supervision: A Review of the Research," *Educational Leadership* 35 (April 1978):580-584.

[7] See Robert J. Krajewski and Robert H. Anderson, "Goldhammer's Clinical Supervision a Decade Later," *Educational Leadership* 37, 5 (February 1980): 420-423, for details of the label, *clinical*.

I personally find the etymology of the term interesting: In the 1600s a "clinic" was described in church history as one who was a bedridden patient, "one who deferred baptism until the death bed in the belief that there could be no atonement for sins committed after that sacrament." The clinical physician became the one who administered "at the bedside" and often gave the last rites. The physician became known as the clinic (clinicus). In 1752 Chambers reported: " 'Clinicus' is now seldom used but for a quack, or for an empirical nurse who pretends to have learned the art of curing diseases by attending on the sick." Thus, from the earliest roots, *clinical* has been associated with the act of administering to the patient in close proximity and the curative process was "empirical," based on actual observation and treatment. A contemporary definition of clinical includes as one notation, "extremely objective and realistic."

world'' is the clinic (wherever that may be). It is a time and place where special involvements will eventually be meaningful. At present there are a number of clinicians in the field of supervision who share a common knowledge base; that is, they have had a residency-like experience for a prolonged period of time when their primary activity centered on working with teachers in classrooms. They were there to learn about their own supervision.

The cycle of supervision was fashioned by Goldhammer and Cogan out of long, arduous searching as they lived with supervisors and teachers in the collaborative world of Harvard-Lexington and Newton MAT programs. Ironically, taken together their texts remind us about the essential knowledge that can come from intense introspection under pressure. What we don't read about is that as a supervisor encounters the awesome universe of teaching and learning and becomes committed to the challenge, there is no place to retreat from the ignorance. The processes implicit in the cycle of supervision can become inquiry methodology for one to generate theory. The empirical qualities of observation and analysis, two of the phases of the ''cycle,'' help the novice to quantify events in order to be free from judgmental preconceptions. Personal empowerment releases one's senses to savor the aesthetics of teaching and learning. Freedom is won through patience and devotion, through careful documentation of accumulated experiential knowledge (Goldhammer developed detailed case studies; Cogan wrote insights and information on file cards, hundreds of file cards). Somewhere, in the rigor of inquiry, the clinical spirit is born.

Constructs and Concepts in Supervision

To understand the nature of the clinical approach to supervision, it is necessary to recognize the importance of concept formation as a rational way to communicate. Any terms used to describe the events under consideration deal with aspects of the events, not the events themselves. Thus a construct or concept is an abstraction of some aspect of an event given from a particular point of view. For the educator there are at least two characteristics of operational concepts that can be used as criteria for their value. One is reliability, that is the degree to which the same event, observed by other colleagues, would be recognized or described in the same way by them. The other criteria for a good construct or concept is its utility for a given purpose. Therefore, as one attempts to understand a particular point of view of supervision (or teaching), one would not necessarily ask ''What is supervision (or teaching) really?'' or ''What are the true aspects of supervision?'' Rather, concept formation addresses the question, ''What is a *reliable* and *useful* way to describe people and events so that we can understand why we perform as we do in regard to various skills?''

If a construct is explicated well through key concepts and subconcepts, the terms can provide explanation and interpretation. More important, concepts guide our actions in supervisory practice. Julian Rotter discusses the nature of concepts in the field of clinical psychology: "In all sciences, terms that have been used at one time to describe the events of nature have later been discarded as poor or erroneous conceptions. The belief that a term of long standing is necessarily accurate or useful is mistaken."[8] If educational practice has integrity, the practitioner recognizes that concept formation is necessary for renewing the life of the practice, and searches for unifying principles which connect the past to the present. Twenty years ago Morris Cogan and his contemporaries groped for terms to describe what they perceived to be the critical features of the events they encountered. "In these new roles and processes, and especially in these new relationships we found some cause for optimism and we began to refer to our basic procedures as 'the cycle of supervision.' "[9] By 1973 he had recognized the inevitable: "It should be noted at once that certain phases of the cycle may be altered or omitted or new procedures instituted depending upon the successful development of working relationships between the supervisor and the teacher."[10]

As a tribute to my beloved Colleague, Morris Cogan, and to my other colleagues — the clinicians who have been transformed by the baptism of fire, the itinerants who have effectively tinkered with sacred words, and especially the teachers and supervisors who are part of my own clinical practice — I offer the conception of clinical supervision that follows.

The Clinical Approach: Twenty Years Later

The concepts offered here are not necessarily exclusive of the clinical approach. It is the explication of each, the referents and the relational aspect of the four together that help to describe and guide the events of clinical practice. For instance, to contrast colleagiality and collaboration helps illuminate each. *Colleagiality* refers to the posture of the persons who become involved in supervision; that is, their state of being, their prevailing tendencies — more direct, the "mental baggage" they bring with them as they work together. *Collaboration* addresses the nature of the involvement of the persons during the supervisory alliance. *Skilled service* suggests that the supervisor is able to offer competent accommodation and activities required by the supervisee as a result of prolonged and specialized intellectual training and practice. *Ethical conduct* refers to constant discretion and judgment in one's actions through standards of behavior so that those involved can be confident that this professional attitude will provide trust and protection.

[8] Julian B. Rotter, *Clinical Psychology*, 2nd ed. (Englewood Cliffs, N.J.: Prentice-Hall, 1964).
[9] Morris L. Cogan, *Clinical Supervision* (Boston: Houghton-Mifflin, 1973), p. 7.
[10] Cogan, p. 12.

Colleagiality: A Frame of Mind

Colleagiality, defined here as an internal state, depends on the way (or ways) one identifies with the world of teachers and learners and supervisors in a self-conscious sense. It is the particular frame of mind one brings to educational encounters. In this section the notion of "frame of mind" is embodied in the alienated critic, the neutral observer, the connected participant, and the organic member. Each represents a special set of attitudes associated with colleagiality.

Alienated Critic

As a clinical supervisor encountering the everyday world of teachers and students, I have the vantage of looking again at the place where I used to live. In Maxine Greene's words,

It is like returning home from a long stay in some other place. The homecomer notices details and patterns in his environment he never saw before. [One] finds that [one] has to think about local rituals and customs to make sense out of them once more. For a time he [she] feels quite separate from the person who is wholly at home in the in group and takes the familiar world for granted.[11]

Because I have an emotional investment in the educational environment, it is easy for me to become an alienated critic, unable to accept the imperfections I now see. Because I care about kids and learning, I can find the faults, describe the absurdities, and offer suggestions based on what could have been done in the past or what might be better in the future. Yet I can only deny the present, unable to deal effectively with the here and now because of the displaced feelings of frustration. In this professional disequilibrium I cannot identify with "them." I have no disposition toward colleagiality until I can understand the source of my attitudes.

Similar reactions are reflected in Goldhammer's first chapter, "A Context for Supervision." The reader is able to sense how he comes to terms with his own denial and alienation. In the beginning pages he says, ". . . if I am forced to exist in an environment filled with insanity, in time my own behavior will begin to incorporate the insanities that have surrounded me."[12] For 50 pages he describes with eloquence and passion the typical school world as he sees it. By the end of the chapter he is resigned, "For better or for worse, that school and others like it, represent the context in which constructive supervision must occur, if it is to occur at all."[13] His chapter serves as a kind of self-relief. The burden is discharged. The emotional pressure is reduced to a manageable level through the aesthetic expression which objectifies his

[11] Maxine Greene, *Teacher as Stranger* (Belmont, Calif.: Wadsworth, 1973), pp. 267-268.
[12] Robert Goldhammer, *Clinical Supervision* (New York: Holt, Rinehart and Winston, 1969), p. 2.
[13] Goldhammer, p. 52.

private sensations by making them into a shareable entity.

Similar feelings were expressed by a group of teachers in the Reynolds School District in Pennsylvania after a prolonged, intense experience.[14] While six of them were taking part in a field-based team sabbatical, they talked about their temporary alienation and frustration at being disconnected from the familiar world they had taken for granted. With a mixed sense of sadness and joy, they realized that they might never return as the same people. One of their favorite concepts was described as a metaphoric affliction called R_2 — *ressentiment* — a state of mind more permeating than R, simple resentment. In their words, "R_2 has been described as a subconscious, free floating illtemper which penetrates the personality causing a chronic negativism toward most situations."[15] Once the condition was labeled, the Reynolds teachers began to deal with their own symptoms. In addition, they said they could empathize with colleagues who showed signs of severe, perhaps terminal, cases.

Neutral Observer

The first inclinations toward colleagiality come when I am able, as a neutral observer, to think about the events of my professional world in a detached dispassionate way. As one novice supervisor said, "I may not be doing any good, but at least I'm not doing too much damage." It is when I have developed mental techniques for quantifying my judgments, when I can easily tell the difference between high inference and low inference, that I begin to understand the importance of descriptive data as the basis for a rationale. It is when I know I am being "judgmental" by my unverified and unbending normative responses to events that I can struggle to make careful judgments based on stable data.[16] The mathematical knowledge that allows me to understand "approximations" of perfection and "probabilities" of success also provides me with a way to derive reasonable expectations for myself and others. It is then that I recognize the humaneness of an empirical approach.

I feel obliged to comment here on a condition that leads to the deterioration of colleagiality. Many supervisors get stuck somewhere between alienated critic and neutral observer. They have developed the facile skills and language associated with scientific-like techniques and can assume a neutral, descriptive position for a period of time only to

---

[14] A. Collins and others, "The Reynolds Model for Professional Development," interim Report to the Members of the School Board, Reynolds School District, Greenville, Pa., March 8, 1978.

[15] See Reynolds Interim Report p. 19 for a more detailed description of the characteristics of R_2.

[16] Noreen B. Garman, "Objectivity and Clinical Supervision: A Study of the Supervisor's Use of Stable Data During Classroom Observation and His/Her Awareness of Selective Perception," Faculty Research Grant, 1979.

return, even more articulate, to the comforts of the *alienated critic,* not wanting the responsibility for action and accountability. They have learned to put aside temporarily their expectations for perfection. Lack of compassion for those with whom we differ locks the mind and spirit. It is the combined flaws of ignorance and lack of compassion that prevent us from making meaningful connections with those whom we find disagreeable.

Connected Participant

Genuine colleagiality is possible when I can become the connected participant. It is that spirit that allows me to "connect" with another person so that both of us are aware of the connectedness. I am able to identify with the other at a level of respect and affection, I am not "at odds" with my colleague, even though I may not agree with him or her. I accept the image of myself as a participant in an educational alliance and I share some of the responsibility. I have faith that together we can discover the kind of contributions we make to each other.

Another form of connectedness is manifested when at some point I am able to identify with the community of teachers and especially with the heritage of teaching-learning and schooling. The "we" of colleagiality is articulated when we accept the richness of our common mythology and folklore of teaching. We may, indeed, carry around with us some forms of pedagogical archetypes, as well as images of universal traits of the typical teacher, such as vitality, dedication, self-sacrifice, intellectual sharing, nurturance, arrogance, pomposity, absurdity, punishment, and love. Cogan mentions that "powerful social and cultural forces not only press us into the form and behavior of teacher but also generate in us the evaluative ambience surrounding the role of teacher."[17]

I am convinced that it is in the appreciation of our mythology that we can address our educational myths. Contrary to the popular notion that a myth is a widely held belief that is not true,[18] I find Campbell's definition of myth, "the symbolized facts of the mind,"[19] an important one. The myth is a conscious representation of our past identity. It is the source and nature of our culture within the educational institution. Campbell reminds us that the life supporting nature of myths allows us to recognize, analyze, and interpret the present. We can evolve techniques for retaining these images in health and, as the old, often

[17] Morris L. Cogan, "Rationale for Clinical Supervision," *Journal of Research and Development in Education* 9, 2 (1976): 7.

[18] See Arthur W. Combs, *Myths in Education* (Boston: Allyn and Bacon, 1979). It is at this point that I disagree with Arthur Combs' approach to the notion of myth as an insidious belief which has "hampered progress and frustrated human goals through history." He says "We must break ourselves loose from the myths that bind us." He confounds the term *myth* with the dysfunctional aspects of tradition.

[19] Joseph Campbell, *Myths to Live By* (New York: Bantam, 1978), p. 11.

dysfunctional traditions of the past fade, we can, through knowledge and appreciation, assist in the rearrangement of pedagogical culture patterns. To reject our heritage is to sever our connections to the past, a form of collective denial that can only lead to professional alienation. Perhaps a properly functioning mythology (one that we, as supervisors, recognize) can help us relieve our professional anxiety. As I engage in a supervisory relationship with a teacher, the appreciation or denial of the rich culture of teaching will inevitably become a force in establishing mutual colleagiality.

Organic Member

A heightened sense of colleagiality is possible when I can imagine myself as a member of an organic unit,[20] when the distinction between supervisor and teacher is less discernable and I can transcend my conventional role status. While in the frame of mind of the connected participant I remain conscious of my unique self in relation to another; the emphasis is often on the quality of the relationship and the nature of the interaction. As the organic member I'm aware of the individual and collective possibilities when members are involved in the flow of the experience toward common goals. As a member of an organic unit I am active and reactive, inductive and productive during the life of the experience. I can be most effective when I imagine how other members might contribute. I'm able to see that much of the activity and results of the involvement will unfold in a manner that will lead to new and unpredictable states. I can be energized by seeing others and myself make important contributions, discovering potential we never imagined in ourselves.

Colleagiality as a Face-to-Face Encounter

In clinical supervision there is an implicit assumption that the face-to-face situation is the basis for practice. When two or more people come together for this special kind of supervisory encounter, the amount of time they are together may not be the most important factor. It is the quality of the time spent that makes the specialness. Those who bring a particular collegial frame of mind to the situation will inevitably set the mood for the quality of the experience.

In their treatise on the sociology of knowledge, Berger and Luckman emphasize the unique reality level of the face-to-face situation and, in particular, the importance of the shared reality with "others."

The most important experience of others takes place in the face-to-face situation which is the prototypical case of social interaction. All other cases are derivations of it, . . . My and his "here and now" continuously impinge on each other as long as the face-to-

[20] See the Reynolds Interim Report for a comprehensive definition of *organic team*, p. 19.

face situation continues . . . no other form of social relating can reproduce the plenitude of symptoms of subjectivity present. . . . only here are the other subjectivity emphatically "close." All other forms of relating to the other are in varying degrees "remote." In the face-to-face situation the other is fully real.[21]

The above statement may seem obvious and yet, as supervisors, we need to remind ourselves that we are engaged in both immediate and remote interactions. Others can become progressively anonymous the farther we get from face-to-face working situations. The disposition and skills of collaboration are fashioned through prolonged and intense collegial encounters.

Collaboration: Toward Educational Alliances

The following discussion of collaboration addresses the nature of involvement between or among the people working in an educational alliance. If we consider four types of involvements and the conditions of each, we might better understand the notion of "educational alliance." Because clinical practice depends on face-to-face interactions, we can assume that, for whatever motives, there are verbal interchanges in the types of involvement presented here.

Non-working Involvement

The non-working involvement is characterized by feelings of resistance on the part of one or more of the people. Resistance may take the form of conflict or open hostility, in which case the involvement would be a short one. Defensive behaviors are more subtle, less abrasive, and take a bit longer to discharge; albeit, most supervisors are well versed in the wide range of defenses, from negativism, silence, oververbalization, self-deprecation ("I'll tell you my faults before you do") to unmitigated charm and ebullience (including flattery for the supervisor's cleverness). Even more subtle are the protective devices supervisors cultivate to keep themselves intact. There is an insidious, compelling urge (called "zap the teacher") ever-present as one develops the empirical skills of the neutral observer. The more data one has, the more one can verify one's prejudgments. In the non-working involvement those involved have intuited that not much good will come from the efforts and therefore "it is not working very well."

Working-Acceptance Involvement:

The term working-acceptance is borrowed from Erving Goffman's insightful essays on face-to-face behavior, *Interaction Ritual*.[22] This type

---

[21] Peter L. Berger and Thomas Luckman, *The Social Construction of Reality* (New York: Anchor, 1967), pp. 28-29.

[22] Erving Goffman, *Interaction Ritual: Essays on Face-to-Face Behavior* (New York: Anchor, 1967).

of involvement is concerned primarily with the ritual aspect of supervisory encounters. A key assumption is that within the ritualistic interchanges there is an acceptance of customary modes of operating. The prevailing mood is that of politeness. Goffman describes the rule of self-respect and the rule of considerateness as it relates to interaction ritual in the following passages:

Just as the member of any group is expected to have self-respect, so also he is expected to sustain a standard of considerateness; he is expected to go to certain lengths to save the feelings and the face of others present, and he is expected to do this willingly anc spontaneously because of emotional identification with the others and with their feelings. In consequence, he is disinclined to witness the defacement of others. The person who can witness another's humiliation and unfeelingly retain a cool countenance himself is said in our society to be "heartless," just as he who can unfeelingly participate in his own defacement is thought to be "shameless."

The combined effect of the rule of self-respect and the rule of considerateness is that the person tends to conduct himself during an encounter so as to maintain both his own face and the face of the other participants. This means that the line taken by each participant is usually allowed to prevail, and each participant is allowed to carry off the role he appears to have chosen for himself. A state where everyone temporarily accepts everyone else's line is established. This kind of mutual acceptance seems to be a basic structural feature of interaction, especially the interaction of face-to-face talk. *It is typically a "working" acceptance, not a "real" one since it tends to be based not on agreement of candidly expressed heart-felt evaluations, but upon a willingness to give temporary lip service to judgments with which the participants do not really agree.*[23] (The emphasis is mine.)

The "working" aspects of ritual and custom in supervision have not been closely examined, perhaps because we assume they are barriers to productive results. Blumberg's examination of supervisors and teachers in a private cold war[24] details many of the incidents that are related to the non-working as well as the ritualistic working-acceptance situations. In my opinion, ritualistic activity may be viewed as marginal aspects of educational alliances. There is considerable ritual behavior in any culture that supports the life of the institutional organism at the ordinary, day to day level. At another level, certain ritual can reaffirm one's existence within the culture. To give an example, I've repeatedly heard teachers say, "nobody has been in to observe my teaching for years" (translated as "nobody cares what I am doing"). The customary visit by an administrator is interpreted as "at least someone up there will see what I am doing." The administrator may consider this act as "show and tell" by the teacher and not worthy of his/her time, or may be deluded into thinking that it improves the teacher's instruction. This is a form of ritualistic behavior in supervision. When it works, it reaffirms the teacher's worth. When it doesn't work, it is a futile exercise.

The primary setting for supervisory ritual is the conference. The preceding passage by Goffman points out the implicit surface

---

[23] Goffman, p. 11.

[24] Arthur Blumberg, *Supervisors and Teachers: A Private Cold War* (Berkeley, Calif.: McCutchan, 1974).

agreements in the conference environment. Consider: both parties know there is limited time to cover the multitude of possibilities (or sins, as the case may be). The supervisor's credentials are often in question (What does he/she really know about effective teaching?). The supervisor will open with, "How do you feel about the lesson?" or "Let's consider first your strengths and then your weaknesses."

Over the years I have listened to hundreds of conferences with script themes of striking similarity. At one point I began to pick up recurring patterns analogous to the religious confessional:

— Supervisor officiates
— Teacher confesses his/her transgressions
— Supervisor suggests ways to repent
— Teacher agrees to recant
— Supervisor assists in penance
— Teacher makes Act of Contrition
— Supervisor gives absolution
— Both go away feeling better.

The clinical supervisor recognizes the powerful undercurrent of ritualistic conferences and can change the ceremonial aspects into educational alliances — those encounters during which participants learn something about their professional actions.

Involvements with Genuine Participation

When people deal with one another honestly, transcending the ritualistic tendencies to "maintain face" or give "temporary lip service," educational alliances can be established. As Goffman points out in the previous passage, the working acceptance is not "a 'real' one since it tends to be based not on agreement of candidly expressed, heartfelt evaluations . . . ." The emphasis here is agreement, the act of making explicit statements about the shared events so that the participants have a common language and accept each others' perception of the events from a similar frame of reference. For the clinical supervisor the imperative is language development, not only as it refers to communication, but also as it regards the capacity to mediate alternative modes of reality.[25]

One basic principle of the meaning of language development in supervision might be: *To know the real name of something is to have power over it.*[26] Early in the clinical practice, the supervisor develops a keen ear for precise vocabulary and, in a sense, becomes bilingual. He/she acquires one language which speaks about the inner world of personal feelings and attitudes and another for describing, interpreting, and judging the

[25] Lawrance LeShan, *Alternate Realities* (New York: Ballantine, 1976).
[26] LeShan, p. 85.

outer world of professional acts and consequences. Concept formation, mentioned earlier, is a primary skill, since intelligent communication is the basis on which our profession rests. Initial responsibility for collaboration is placed on the supervisor who is expected to have the appropriate language to make explicit what the nature of educational agreements means to the participants.

In addition to communication, language development in supervision is concerned with the need for all members involved in educational alliances to have basically the same experience; that is, they construe reality from a shared frame of reference.[27] (Concept formation, to a great extent, is a way for us to *invent* modes of reality as much as it is for us to discover them.) The four colleagial "frames of mind" and the four "types of collaborative involvement" that I present in this chapter are actually representations of alternate modes of reality. The realness of each depends on the reader's ability or willingness to identify each mode as "real." To mediate alternate modes of reality, therefore, the supervisor can deliberately act within a given mode while recognizing his/her ability to move from one mode to another in a reconciling way; a way that does not negate the existence or importance of the other modes. The skilled supervisor is also able to recognize the mode (or modes) of reality within which other participants are acting and, if need be, to resolve serious discrepancies if collaboration is in jeopardy.

Educational alliances, then, are educational involvements based on working agreements during which the participants understand the conditions of the agreement and willingly work within them. In another sense, the group that forms an educational alliance becomes culture-like, using Cassirer's definition of culture, which is "minds acting in cooperation through a similar definition of reality."[28] As I suggested earlier, ritualistic activity may be viewed as marginal aspects of educational alliances, in that much of what we do during our professional encounters gives the appearance of "minds acting in cooperation." It may well be that when our acts are made explicit through appropriate language, we find we are actually not in agreement. In any case, when we work toward mutually explicit agreements we have the opportunity to experience a different type of collaboration — one of genuine participation.

When we imagine the concept of collaboration, there is at least one assumption that bears close scrutiny. It is often assumed that if participants are acting with honesty and trust, eventually they will generate a degree of genuine participation. This may be a naive point of view. There are basic differences among honest, trusting people that can deter

---

[27] This subject is reflected in the works of Ernst Cassirer, especially *Language and Myth* (New York: Dover, 1953) and *The Philosophy of Symbolic Forms* (New Haven, Conn.: Yale University, 1955).

[28] Cassirer, *Language and Myth*.

the collaborative effort.[29] For example, we can examine one area of difference and speculate concerning the supervisory implications.

People tend to negotiate agreements based on their own proclivities related to internal and external structure.[30] In addition, the nature of the explicit agreements themselves reflects two basically different structures, referred to as open and closed agreements. The closed agreement assumes that the events within the involvement are reasonably predictable, therefore the negotiators are able to focus the terms of the agreement on the particular conditions and expected outcomes. The agreement is, by design, restrictive. The open agreement, by contrast, implies that events will emerge and may not be predictable enough to direct the terms of the agreement toward the probable outcomes. This agreement is basically non-restrictive. In the closed agreement, people generally agree to the explicit objectives and outcomes; the salient features are determined a priori. In the open agreement, people agree to the process of involvement with the significant meanings to be determined after the events occur.

The negotiating aspects of collaborative agreements are most clearly delineated in the Cogan method by the preobservation conference. Acheson and Gall[31] and Reavis[32] appropriately describe the essential reasons for a moderately restrictive type of conference by suggesting that this is a way to deal from the teacher's point of view with the teacher's concerns. (It is also a way to help a new supervisor focus on specific aspects of teaching while he/she is still in the early stages of developing the supervisory skills of data analysis and a language of teaching.) Anderson and Krajewski[33] imagine the ''contractual'' aspects in a broader sense and allow for short term and long term agreements in their preobservation conference including the possibility of facing the ritualistic enactments of supervision.

As supervisors, we need to look carefully at the reasons we negotiate for either an open or a closed agreement. Reavis, for instance, states, ''It is very important that the teacher suggest observation objectives'' and he gives recommendations for getting the teacher to do this. Some teachers prefer the open approach and find the restrictions

[29] I find the notion of differences in the learning modes of adults an important one in supervision. The growing field of interest known as learning styles is useful for background. See: Student Learning Styles: Diagnosing and Prescribing Programs (Reston, Va.: National Association of Secondary School Principals, 1979).

[30] See Julian Rotter, ''Generalized Expectancies for Internal Versus External Control of Reinforcement,'' Psychology Monographs: General and Applied 80, 1 (1966); also, ''External Control and Internal Control,'' Psychology Today, June 1971.

[31] Keith A. Acheson and Meredith Damien Gall, Techniques in the Clinical Supervision of Teachers (New York: Longman, 1980). The authors present a detailed description of specific techniques in a useful format for new supervisors.

[32] Charles A. Reavis, Teacher Improvement Through Clinical Supervision (Bloomington, Ind.: Phi Delta Kappa, 1978), p. 12.

[33] Robert H. Anderson and Robert Krajewski, Clinical Supervision, Special Methods for the Supervisor of Teachers (New York: Holt, Rinehart and Winston, 1980), p. 35.

untenable. In some cases, the supervisor may be meeting his/her own preferred style of agreement and not necessarily that of the teachers. I am convinced that effective clinical practice depends on our ability to articulate and thereby manage this diversity.

As we begin to think of clinical supervision beyond the Cogan method, we can alter our image of the conventional scenario with the two person cast. We can imagine a clinical supervisor who acts in different configurations with diverse groups of educators in face-to-face activities (such as planning, fact-finding, working on materials) exploring new realms together. It is especially important for the supervisor to develop a repertoire of ways to describe basic individual differences among the members of larger groups. Collaboration in this way may depend on the ability of each group member to understand some of the differences in order to be able to transcend the subconscious fear of them. Furthermore, to encapsule the richness of the diversity is to create the potential for dynamic tension inherent in the involvements manifesting organic reciprocity.

Involvements with Organic Reciprocity

When a group of educators comes together in an educational alliance there is opportunity for the unit to become involved in a rich encounter with a heightened sense of reciprocity. The term synchronicity is often used to describe this condition. It is when the participants work harmoniously toward achieving their own goals and the goals of the group. In many instances the goals are similar. I have observed two recurring characteristics of organic groups which relate to the nature of reciprocity. First, at some point members are able to accept each other's "realness" with a degree of compassion, respect, and eventually with genuine affection. Second, the group begins to function with an optimum level of dynamic tension. The extreme anxieties due to individual differences have been reduced: the level of dissonance and discord has been dissipated. Yet the individuals in the group remain interesting enough to one another that they offer stimulation and challenge as well as a sense of commitment. Part of the dynamic tension is generated by each individual's own fascinating inner world. They find themselves learning from each other in very different ways. The other aspect of dynamic tension comes from the excitement that spawns a collective spirit as a result of the recognition that the aims and action of the group are toward worthy goals. Members are said to be "in sync" with one another, thereby regenerating the collective spirit and then revitalizing themselves from it as they work together.

Within the past few years the organic team has become a visible force in formal and informal school endeavors. Some are initiated by the administrators of the school, some begin as grassroots groups with common interests. I find I'm devoting more of my clinical practice to these efforts and other clinicians have reported similar activities as well.

The Reynolds Model was a team sabbatical for six teachers who were given one year's release time from their classroom assignments in order to function as a learning team. They were responsible for directing their own activities, choosing to do so without a designated leader. In their Interim Report to the school board they summarized their important work as follows:

a.   Established collegial relationships through growing trust of one another and a strong faith that something meaningful was possible, that we could make it happen

b.   Set goals and tasks to accomplish the goals

c.   Internalized the goals as a guiding force and identified new materials necessary to complete the tasks

d.   Learned appropriate behaviors (at first through trial and error) for accomplishing specific goals

e.   Learned how to identify and use resources to develop concrete products

f.   Reassessed original goals and revised the plans for tasks and products

g.   Developed strategies for introspection — "Learning *what* we were learning and *how* we were learning." (Organic learning as related to model building.)[34]

I spent twenty days with the team during the year. In the report they described my role:

Her function, as a team member, has been as a facilitator with an organic sense. Among her roles she has (1) guided the direction of an organic model, (2) guided the direction of our learning experiences by giving us a language to use, (3) acted as a resource person in the learning team.

I think what I really did was help them gain a sense of courage and faith in themselves.

This kind of group approach is a logical extension of the conventional clinical mode where the teacher and supervisor work in a diadic relationship. Comparison might be made to similar changes in the counseling practice of the clinical psychologist. Group counseling has become a common function within the traditional client/counselor domain. Many clinical psychologists now work with clients in different configurations. In both professional fields it is assumed that the clinician offers a skilled service to those who want the involvement.

Skilled Service

The clinical supervisor is able to claim that he/she can offer a service to teachers in the educational community as a result of prolonged and specialized intellectual training and practice. The nature of the service is made explicit to the teacher who becomes client-colleague during the supervisory alliance. The professional practice of clinical supervision is derived from the assumptions that the supervisor understands

[34] Noreen B. Garman, "The Team Sabbatical: An Extraordinary Field-Based Experience," Unpublished manuscript, University of Pittsburgh, March 1978.

the nature of educational encounters and has the inquiry skills to make sense out of the events under consideration.

Educational Encounters: The school is a unique place, a teaching-learning community where educators can shape the involvements; where events have special meanings; where actions are significant because they are part of a larger action. Schooling implies that all participants "encounter" learning in contrived ways. The clinical supervisor is at home in this environment. He/she knows that tradition as well as technique guide the action: that nonrational forces such as faith and caring are as important as appropriate intervention methods and materials for the success of encounters. Together, the supervisor and teacher can come to know the significant acts.

Inquiry Skills: At the heart of the Cogan method are the stages of observation and analysis, the basis for the empirical approach that Cogan used in his own practice. Observation refers to the supervisory function of recording actual events of educational encounters in order to collect stable data accepted by both the teacher and supervisor as reliable and useful. Analysis is the process of systematically making sense out of the data. If the process is interpreted narrowly it can cause frustration. Data collecting and analysis are cumbersome, often too ambiguous and awkward for itinerate supervisors to manage in the daily school routine. They generally advocate a checklist approach instead of the empirical approach for classroom visitations. The competence of the clinical supervisor, however, depends upon the various skills of inquiry used in clinical practice.

A four year study,[35] recently completed at the University of Pittsburgh, examined the actions and attitudes of 300 supervisors during clinical observation and analysis. The research helped me to conceptualize the nature of supervisory inquiry. Results from the study revealed at least five different modes of inquiry necessary for supervisory practice: *discovery, verification, explanation, interpretation,* and *evaluation.* The concept *modes of inquiry* is derived from essentially different "ways of knowing" about the events of a classroom encounter; a different paradigm exists for each mode. It is important to recognize that each paradigm presents a different way of looking at the world under examination with a particular set of insights or hunches. Each paradigm represents different assumptions and methods for data collection and treatment. Each has a different, yet vital, purpose in a comprehensive plan for supervision. The following brief description of the modes of inquiry can merely suggest some distinctive features:

Discovery has as a goal the inductive search for well-articulated phenomena and appropriate questions inherent in the classroom scenario. Both qualitative and quantitative data are appropriate here.

[35] Noreen B. Garman, "The Mousetrap Study: A Three Paradigm Research Effort on Practice in Clinical Supervision." Summary published in the *1980/81 Proceedings of the Council of Professors of Instructional Supervision Annual Conference* by the University of Georgia.

The analysis often begins by identifying the teacher's stated intent of the lesson and the signs of consistency or inconsistency as a result of subsequent actions. In his article "Toward a Theory of Clinical Supervision," Sergiovanni[36] describes "the concept of surfacing dilemmas," as one focus for productive results. The primary emphasis, however, is toward an eclectic approach free from a predetermined system. The supervisor continues to look for a fresh perspective in familiar situations through discovery.

Verification is a deductive mode that provides for a degree of objectivity (which suggests that others using the same method with the same data can arrive at similar conclusions). When the salient features of the lesson have been discovered, it is imperative that the supervisor verify, usually with quantitative methodology, the extent to which the discovery was justified. Objectivity is also regarded as a general frame of mind that helps the supervisor assume a detached and neutral posture. Hypothesis testing is a feature of the verification mode.

Explanation is both inductive and deductive. Its purpose is to explain the verified phenomena through inference derived from the content analysis of stable data. The supervisor and teacher bring their subjective "best estimates" of what is happening from their own reality base. Concept formation is a vital part of the process since this becomes the means for the two to share their construed realities from both worlds. Understanding through language is the basis for explanation.

Interpretation is the search for meaning in the events under study. The interpretive mode often provides a way to get to what really matters, to derive mature interpretations from that which has been verified and explained. Through appropriate methodology one has the sanction to go beyond the literal, encouraged to look for deeper meanings than the inferences derived through explanation. The supervisor understands internally by intuitively referring to his/her experience and externally by searching for symbolic acts which reveal insights about the myths and predispositions of those involved. Through the interpretive mode the supervisor and teacher are able to seek deeper significance beneath the surface content that may appear trivial.

Evaluation is a normative mode which addresses values and judgments about the events under consideration. Evaluative methods are used to determine the effectiveness of a particular action or the worthiness of the meaning. They help the teacher answer such questions as, "How well have I performed?" or "Am I doing what I should be doing?" By valuing, the supervisor and teacher come to know the internal and external criteria for setting priorities and making judgments in the evaluation mode.

The clinical supervisor understands the distinctive features of in-

[36] Thomas Sergiovanni, "Toward a Theory of Clinical Supervision," *Journal of Research and Development in Education* 9, 2 (1972): 20-29.

quiry inherent in each of the modes. He/she can determine when a decision represents a mature or a premature discovery, verification, explanation, interpretation, or evaluation. Because the inquiry modes present different purposes, methods, and results, they are ways to come to know the significance of educational encounters. This is the skilled service offered through clinical supervision.

Ethical Conduct

Ethical conduct generally implies that we subscribe to a belief in the constant exercise of discretion and judgment in supervisory action through standards of behavior so that those involved can be confident in knowing that a professional attitude will maintain trust and protection. Ethical conduct is different from a code of ethics which is a series of statements developed by professionals. In clinical supervision one doesn't have ethics, one does ethics. The manner in which we choose to respond to people and situations will continually challenge the ethical spirit. Conflicts and dilemmas are everpresent. At each turn we can make judgments based on self-interest, expediency, or pragmatism. We can also choose that which is fair, good, and wise. We may not always know the difference. Yet, on the basis of ethical conduct, we are obliged to make the conscious choice.

When Are We Really Clinical Supervisors?

Throughout the narration of this chapter I have attempted to develop a reliable and useful way to describe the people and events in clinical supervision so that we can understand why we perform as we do in regard to various skills. The question remains: when is one considered a clinical supervisor and not an itinerant? I would presumptuously suggest the following:

A person becomes a clinical supervisor when he/she begins to think and act as if the "cycle of supervision" were a metaphor as well as a method; when observation and analysis are not only procedural phases for actions in classrooms, but also represent the empirical approach inherent in a skilled service; when the notion of conference not only means two people meeting before and after classroom visits, but also suggests dynamic forms of collaboration in educational alliances; when the image of "cycle" not only guarantees repeated performance, but also refers to high levels of involvement and commitment that press participants toward the "connectedness" of colleagiality; when the teacher-supervisor relationship stands for ethical conduct as it is lived out in important choices. The specificity of the method can inform us about the unbounding qualities of the metaphor.

Ultimately a person becomes a clinical supervisor when he/she can use the method, act through the metaphor, and thereby sort out the nontrivial from the trivial in order to bring meaning to educational endeavors.

Chapter 4.
An Artistic Approach to Supervision

Elliot W. Eisner

ONE OF THE IRONIES OF CONTEMPORARY EDUCATION is that although teaching is often regarded as an art or a craft, it is most often studied as if it were, or aspired to be, a science. Almost any teacher will tell you that teaching is far from scientific. Yet the study of teaching and the conduct of supervision has, in general, been undertaken using scientific — some would say scientistic — assumptions and methods.

What do we mean when we say that something is a science or that it is studied scientifically? Examinations of the vernacular use of the terms science and art will be useful, not because they provide sophisticated theoretical explications, but because their connotations are revealing.

In vernacular discourse we often hear people say, ''He's got it down to a science,'' meaning that the individual has so mastered a set of procedures that he or she can repeat those procedures to secure the desired results time after time. To have it down to a science means having a predictable routine, being able to hit the target every time. The baking of bread is ''down to a science,'' I am sure, at the factories that produce Wonderbread and Silvercup. No surprises for them. They seek standardization, control, and predictability.

Consider what it means when someone says of a practice within a field that it is ''the state of the art.'' This statement, sometimes heard at social science research conferences, implies that the practice, and by implication the field, is not yet a science, but *only* an art, and that with time a science of the practice will emerge. An art in this context is considered less dependable and not fully understood, something that chugs along at less than full steam.

These vernacular uses of the terms science and art are in no way adequate characterizations of either science or art. But they are indicative of the ways people think about science and art in the context of education and educational research. The implications of such connotations are significant for they reveal the tacit aspiration to move teaching and by association the supervision of teaching from a practice that is ar-

Elliot W. Eisner is Professor of Education and Art at Stanford University, Palo Alto, California.

tistically grounded to one that is grounded in science. The usual analogies for justifying this aspiration for teaching and supervision are to medicine and engineering, two fields that differ fundamentally from education but whose differences are often overlooked.

I raise the question of the relationship of science and art to education at the outset because I believe it is important for the reader to have a context for considering what an artistic approach to supervision would require. Furthermore, I'm not that happy with the term supervision. It has connotations that seem at least somewhat incongruous with educational practice — at least as I regard it. Consider for a moment what the term supervision implies. In the first place a supervisor is supposed to have super vision. The relationship between the supervisor and the teacher is hierachical and while hierarchy will never be absent from human relationships, in the context of supervisor/supervisee relationships it suggests that the former has the right to prescribe to the latter how the job is to be done. A sense of dialogue or interchange between two professionals trying to improve the educational experience of the young tends to get lost.

In the second place the term supervisor (like the term superintendent) is most often used within an industrial context. Factories and offices have supervisors whose job it is to see that other employees perform their jobs as prescribed. Indeed, one of the basic tenets of scientific management as formulated by Frederick Taylor around the turn of the century was that efficiency could be greatly increased in industrial settings if the behavior of the worker could be scientifically managed.[1] Time and motion study was the means to scientific supervision. Much supervision still tacitly draws from that tradition. This is not to say that all supervisors in education embrace the view that Taylor advocated. It is to say that the term supervisor has an industrial ring and that prescriptive, evaluative, and hierarchical connotations are related to it.

To drive the point home, simply reflect on the connotative differences between the terms supervisor and consultant. A consultant is someone invited in, someone one talks to, someone who provides views to consider. The initiative is with the individual who invites the consultant. The term supervisor has quite another set of connotations. It is someone on the managerial side of the ledger that the workers on the line must heed.

The Fallacies of "Scientific" Supervision

I believe several problems have been created by treating teaching as if it could be scientifically executed and by implication conceiving of supervision as the scientific management of teaching. I list some of these problems here.

[1] See Raymond Callahan, *Education and the Cult of Efficiency* (Chicago: University of Chicago Press, 1962).

The first problem might be called the *fallacy of additivity* which is committed by attempting to study or supervise teaching using a procedure that implies or assumes that the incidence of particular teaching behaviors — structuring, giving examples, positive and negative reinforcement, and so forth — all have equal pedagogical weight and can be added together to secure an index of the quality of teaching.

For example, more student initiated questioning is considered better than more teacher initiated questioning; indirect discourse is better than direct discourse. What is utterly neglected is the quality of the content of the interaction. Discussions are not necessarily better than lectures. Discussions having a high frequency of student participation can be inane and lectures can be brilliant. The reverse, of course, can also be true. Simply recording incidents and adding scores are an inadequate and, even worse, misleading way to appreciate what has gone on in a classroom.

I mention the fallacy of additivity because state departments of education and school districts send brigades of supervisors into classrooms armed with checkoff sheets listing dozens of teaching behaviors. Ticks in boxes are then summed and averaged to create a profile on a grid. The absense of these behaviors, however, may not indicate weak teaching, or their presence excellent teaching.

Second, associated with the fallacy of additivity is the *fallacy of composition*, that the whole is equal to the sum of its parts. This is committed when the quality of teaching is determined by counting the incidence of teacher behaviors in a variable or category and then adding to this sum the scores produced in other variables. This method assesses the quality of teaching based on the presence of discrete characteristics. Thus, one state teacher observation schedule contains 14 teacher characteristic variables.[2] Each variable contains from four to seven subvariables. Three observers rate the teacher on all subvariables using a seven point scale. The scores from each subvariable are then added for each variable and a total score emerges for each of the seven major variables. Excellence in teaching is supposed to be indicated by having high scores on all seven major variables.

But what if a teacher is superb in three of the variables and weak in the other four? Might not the excellence of the three far outweigh the limitations in the four? In our daily lives, do we have for friends only those sterling individuals who are faultless on all major variables? I think not. Among friends (and even close relatives!) there are trade-offs. God never made anything without a crack in it. One cannot simply add the parts to get the sum. The whole is more — it is sometimes less — than the sum of its parts.

Third among the fallacies in both the study of teaching and in supervision is the *fallacy of concreteness*. This fallacy is the offshoot of

[2] *Teacher Observation Rating Scale*, Georgia State Department of Education, 1979.

behaviorism which holds that the exclusive referent for observation is the manifest behavior of the student. Now it is clear that few people who study teaching or who supervise are bona fide, card-carrying mind readers. Behavior *is* a primary referent for observation, but it is not the only referent or the most important one. When we observe pupils or teachers we do not merely look at the behavior they display, but also at its meaning and the quality of their experience. Even the term behavior is misleading since it suggests that an individual's actions are bodily movements rather than activities that are motivated, purposeful, instrumental to aspiration, and reflecting a great deal more than the blink of an eyelid. Indeed, even a blink requires interpretation to distinguish between an autonomic response and, say, flirtation.[3]

To focus exclusively on behavior and to neglect meaning or experience because it requires inference and imaginative forms of empathetic participation in the life of another can be to misinterpret what one looks at. Again, in our daily lives we seldom regard manifest behavior as the primary referent of our interpretive eye. If at a cocktail party we receive the compliment, "You never looked better," we usually respond in kind, understanding this cultural gambit is not to be taken literally. When someone asks "How are you doing?" the person does not expect a description of our physical condition or the size of our bank account.

Manifest behavior is, in general, a cue from which we imaginatively construct meaning. Construing what we encounter entails a great deal more than recording its incidence. Thus, the fallacy of concreteness leads us to neglect what we cannot see. In the pursuit of an illusive "objectivity" we disregard the character of experience and the psychological significance of what is taking place.

A fourth problem that emerges in the use of scientific approaches to the study of teaching and the conduct of supervision might be called the *fallacy of the act*, although it is gradually being rectified. This is the tendency to neglect the process of educational life as it unfolds in classrooms and schools. For years the paradigm for social science inquiry into educational practices was the classical experiment. What was sought was the *isolation* of variables that made a significant difference in student outcomes. To locate these variables and to determine their contribution to teaching and learning the experiment rather than the correlational study was regarded as the most robust and rigorous method. To control for confounding effects, experimental treatments had to be brief and, as a result, artificial. The conclusions drawn from such studies all too often have been either so qualified (that is, the results applied to male subjects in the fifth grade who lived in urban areas when taught by a female teacher with less than three years of teaching ex-

---

[3] Clifford Geertz makes this point in his book, *The Interpretation of Cultures* (New York: Basic Books, 1973), see p. 6.

perience, provided the range of ability in the class in the subject taught did not exceed two years) as to make them impossible to use. Or, the so-called treatment was so vaguely described that there was no way of knowing how to replicate it.[4]

This penchant for precision led to a neglect of the messy processes that are part of any non-regimented classroom. The aspiration to be rigorous — which I regard as a virtue — became a device that made the study of teaching, and the recommendations about how to improve it, naive.

Related to the problem of neglecting the process is the more general tendency to neglect those aspects of teaching that are immune to the criteria and instruments that the researcher employs. This may be regarded as the *fallacy of method*. When certain criteria are regarded as sacrosanct, methods of inquiry that do not meet those criteria are rejected. For example, if it is assumed that a valid judgment about the classroom requires the independent concensus of more than one judge, observations on which there is little overlap are likely to be dismissed. In the process some of the most interesting information may be discarded. We do not necessarily seek unanimity among critics who write about plays or books; each might have something different and interesting to say. In the social sciences this model won't do, the conditions needed for reliability prohibit it. Hence, to secure interjudge agreement we often choose to describe those aspects of teaching that are most easily described and to neglect the rest. Ironically, what often emerges is a radically biased view.

The problem of *any* approach to the world blocking out certain aspects of that world is not limited to scientific inquiry. But, because the scientific tradition has held such a commanding position in the study of educational practice, its impact both negatively as well as positively deserves special attention.

Still another problem or limitation of scientific approaches to the study of teaching and their meaning for supervision is the forms through which they represent to the world what they have revealed. Throughout history human beings have devised a variety of forms through which they share and make public what they know. These forms of representation[5] each convey unique kinds of knowledge and make particular kinds of understanding possible. Thus, poetry is a form of representation that makes meanings possible that are inexpressible in prose. Visual images make meanings possible that text cannot convey. Number conveys meanings with a precision that poetry and music cannot achieve. Each form of representation is a vehicle through which differing conceptions find their public expression; each form houses its

---

[4] The amount of text describing treatment conditions in the research reported in the *American Educational Research Journal* is about two inches.

[5] Elliot W. Eisner, *Cognition and Representation: A Basis for Deciding What to Teach* (New York: Longman, Green, forthcoming).

own potential for meanings that cannot be replicated in other forms. The history of culture shows that a diversity of forms, many common to all cultures, are used to convey or represent what humans have learned or imagined and that each form sets its own constraints on what can be expressed.

In applying this concept of the utilities of forms of representation to the study of teaching and the conduct of supervision, we find that only a few of the forms that have been invented have been used. In social science research the forms of representation that are used are propositional language and number. Researchers report what they have learned in language that aspires toward the literal, while using number to provide evidence to support their propositions.

Propositional language and number are useful. They make certain kinds of precision possible that are not possible, say, in poetic statement. But neither literal proposition nor number carried to the fourth decimal exhausts all that can and needs to be said about classrooms or teaching. Some things — perhaps some of the most important things cannot be expressed in this way.

This characteristic of scientific inquiry, of using propositional forms of representation as carriers of meaning, is both its greatest asset and its greatest weakness. While the logic of its methodology is rationally persuasive, and at times even beautiful, it cannot reveal more than what its carriers can contain. What is not contained is left out of the entire realm of what meaning means. Indeed, the view that scientific discourse has a monopoly on meaning is held by many in the academic world. Nonpropositional expressions are regarded as utterances or as forms of emotive discharge, but not as meaningful statements. The consequences of this view are extremely important since the tone it establishes for the conduct for supervision and research on supervision restricts validity to what can be put into literal language.

Another aspect of the scientific orientation to the study of teaching and the conduct of supervision is the aspiration to maximize control and prediction in classroom practice. As I indicated earlier, to have something "down to a science" in the vernacular refers to the ability to repeat routines that lead to predictable consequences. By analogy, the effective teacher is regarded as one who can control student behavior so that prediction is maximized.

It is true that some of what goes on in classrooms should indeed be predictable. Neither random behavior nor chaos are educational virtues. Yet it is a mistake from an educational point of view to regard teaching as primarily the ability to produce known student behavior relevant to known ends. While prediction is a virtue in arithmetic and spelling (no one seeks creative spellers), novelty and surprise in the classroom are also desirable as are exploratory conditions that lead to unforeseen outcomes.

The model that works so well in producing refrigerators is not an adquate model for educational practice. Yet a great deal of research that has sought "the best method" for teaching X, Y, or Z has assumed that scientific research would eventually provide such control and that true excellence in teaching consisted of knowing how to predict outcomes.[6] The tacit image of the teacher was that of the competent technician.

This orientation to teaching also neglects the satisfactions that teachers need in order to work happily in the classroom. If the research-er's or supervisor's major focus is the production of certain student behaviors, the tendency is to prescribe to teachers what they need to do in order to achieve these outcomes. The concept of teacher-proof cur-riculum materials is related to this line of thought. What occurs is a failure to appreciate the fact that teachers need a sense of pride and satisfaction in the classroom and that highly prescriptive methods reduce the scope of their own ingenuity and diminish their sense of pride and satisfaction. When considering an innovation in education, we seldom ask, "What's in it for the teacher?" If there is nothing in it for the teacher, the likelihood of its effective and sustained use is small.

An Artistic Approach to Supervision

In the previous section of this paper I have described a context within which an artistic approach to supervision can be placed. I have done this because contrast is necessary for seeing contours. It is difficult to appreciate the qualities of the new without understanding how it departs from the old. Supervision as a field and as a form of educational practice has, I have suggested, developed within a scientific tradition. The aspiration to produce a science of educational practice has gone hand in hand with the treatment of supervision as a scientifically based technology. Many of the efforts that have been made have misconstrued the nature of educational practice and have had some unfortunate ef-fects on teachers, pupils, and on life in schools. Let us now turn to the question of what an artistic approach to supervision might look like.

There are two basic ways to grasp the meaning of "artistic" super-vision. One is through definition, the other by observing what those who engage in artistic modes of supervision do.

Numerous definitions of art exist; I claim here only to be arbitrary. By artistic I mean using an approach to supervision that relies on the sensitivity, perceptivity, and knowledge of the supervisor as a way of appreciating the significant subtleties occurring in the classroom, and that exploits the expressive, poetic, and often metaphorical potential of language to convey to teachers or to others whose decisions affect what goes on in schools, what has been observed. In such an approach to

[6] Lee Cronbach, "Beyond the Two Disciplines of Scientific Psychology," *The American Psychologist* 30, 2 (February 1975).

supervision, the human is the instrument that makes sense of what has gone on. The major aim is to improve the quality of educational life in school.

If we use the second way to determine what is artistic (observing people who engage in artistic supervision) perhaps some of the most vivid examples are found among music coaches, critics of the arts, and social and group case workers. Consider the work of Jacqueline DuPré coaching students playing the cello or Jascha Heifetz's master classes in violin at UCLA. There are, of course, important differences between an individual listening to a single performer playing an instrument and a supervisor in the schools observing a single teacher working with 32 nine-year-olds. Yet, there are illuminating similarities as well. First of all, both DePré and Heifetz have developed an acute ability to hear what is being played. Now this might seem to some a simple and straightforward task. It is not. To hear the subtleties of complex musical passages, the various possibilities of vibrato or pizzicato, the expressive contours of a slow, mordent tremolo requires what I have referred to in the literature as connoisseurship.[7] Both DuPré and Heifetz are able to hear, not merely listen to, music. This accomplishment is as critical to the supervisor as it is to the music coach. The forms of awareness that the connoisseur achieves provide the basis for subsequent action. What he or she hears makes it possible to comment, to offer advice, to reflect back to the performer what has been performed.

The achievement of *hearing* the music, like the achievement of *seeing* the teaching, takes two forms. The first of these deals with grasping what has unfolded over time: the character of the passage played, the words spoken, the pace and timing of the moves, and in the case of the classroom, the quality of the responses received by the teacher from the pupils and how, in turn, the teacher responds. The mode of perception here is primarily aimed at appreciating the character and quality of the performance as a whole and the various "parts" that compose it.

But there is more. Every performer may be said to have a characteristic mode of expression and the first-rate supervisor or music coach is able to recognize this mode and help the performer move in the direction he or she is "by nature" inclined. Glenn Gould's crisp and methodical handling of the piano is fundamentally different from the romanticism displayed by Artur Rubinstein. It would, I think, be a disservice to try to move Gould in Rubinstein's direction, or Rubinstein to Gould's.

What is the analogy to teaching? Simply this: teachers, too, are differentiated by their style and by their particular strengths. Artistically-oriented supervision would recognize this style and try to help the teacher exploit it by strengthening the positive directions already taken.

---

[7] See Elliot W. Eisner, "The Use of Qualitative Forms of Evaluation for Improving Educational Practice," *Educational Evaluation and Policy Analysis* 1, 6 (November - December 1979).

Some teachers may never really shine at leading small group discussions, but might be first-rate lecturers. Some are magical in their sense of timing and in the relationships they establish with individual children, while others provide a sense of clarity and rigor that is remarkable. The connoisseur of teaching, like the connoisseur of the violin or cello, would appreciate these characteristic traits of the performer in addition to the general overall quality of the performance. In other words, both the general level of teaching competence and the unique characteristics of the performance would be perceived and appraised.

The ability to appreciate such qualities requires access to the process. In the context of music, both DuPré and Heifetz sit with the performer and comment on what they hear. Furthermore, they hear the performer repeatedly over a period of several months. Thus they can compare what they are hearing to what they have heard. This is no small advantage since the performances of the past do much to establish the reasonable parameters for present criticism. How far and how fast one can move depends on where one starts and what the prior rate has been.

I believe that such considerations are relevant to the supervision of teaching. The one-shot, 40-minute visit severely constrains what a supervisor is able to do, if for no other reason than the problem of establishing rapport. Furthermore, the aspects of teaching that need modification might be due to habits and needs that simple feedback is unlikely to alter. Our most ingrained habits, the things we do because of the kinds of needs we have, are not likely to be changed by a brief conversation or a paragraph or two of recommendations prepared by a supervisor. Such change requires substantial attention and support. On the appreciative side, an artistic approach to supervision would aim at the dual modes of perceiving performance; it would seek to appreciate the overall quality of the performance, including the quality of the "parts" that constitute it, and it would seek to appreciate the distinctive character of the performance. It would ask, "What does *this* teacher do that is unique or distinctive?"; "What are the particular characteristics of this teaching that give it special value?"; and, ultimately, "How can I as a supervisor strengthen those values that are consonant with quality education?"

Content of Perceptions

The content of what is perceived also warrants special emphasis. I have already mentioned that behaviorism is limited by its preoccupation with manifest behavior, with the movements the organism makes. These are, of course, easy to observe. One can calculate the percentage of words uttered by the teacher compared with those uttered by pupils. One can count the number of incomplete sentences or determine the amount of time pupils speak. An artistic approach to supervision would attend to the expressive character of what teachers and students are doing, the meta messages contained in the explicit actions they engage in. It would attempt to understand the kind of experience that pupils and teachers have, and not simply describe or count the behaviors they display. What the situation *means* to the people who are in it and how the actions within the situation convey or create such meaning are the phenomena of interest in an artistic approach to supervision. But more dramatically, the supervisor must artistically construct the situation. This requires far more than the ticking off of variables on a five point scale.

The appreciative side of supervision, what I refer to as educational connoisseurship is but half of the equation. Appreciation can be done in private; it need not be shared in order to occur. But private pleasures and pains, though of significance to those who have them, need to be made public in order to be useful to others. This side of the equation is called educational criticism. By the term criticism I mean rendering in artistic language what one has experienced so that it is helpful to the teacher or to others whose views have a bearing on the schools. I do not mean by criticism the negative appraisal of something. I use the term as a kind of analogue to art criticism, film criticism, music criticism, drama criticism. Perhaps one can do no better than to quote Dewey on the function of criticism. In *Art as Experience* he said, "the end of criticism is the reeducation of the perception of the work of art."[8] Critics write or speak about works so as to function as a midwife to perception. The critic's function — and I would argue one of the major functions of the supervisor — is to help others appreciate what has transpired. Supervisors can do this by first having developed a high level of educational connoisseurship since it is this process that provides the content for criticism and, second, by being able to convey to others, often through expressive or artistic use of language, what has taken place.

Examples of such criticism are found in the arts and also in the work that my students at Stanford have been doing over the past ten years. Let's consider first an example from the area of music. What follows is a rendering of one of Zubin Mehta's first rehearsals after he was appointed Director of the New York Philharmonic. It provides a revealing sense of the character of the situation and Mehta's role in creating it.

"Let's get started." He gave a brisk downbeat for Ravel's "La Valse," which begins with a deep murmur of string basses, a whisper of cellos, and a bassoon solo. After a few bars, he stopped, and looked around at the orchestra. "I would like the first four basses to play pizzicato," he said, "Also, basses, the second and third part of the two trills should be softer." A few minutes later, when the basses were accompanying the violas, Mr. Mehta stopped them again and said, "Sometimes I've done this with one

[8] John Dewey, *Art as Experience* (New York: Minton, Balch, 1934), p. 324.

bass, because if you use too many you get a blur. How many are doing it?'' Four bass players raised their hands, and Mr. Mehta looked skeptical. ''Why don't you change the bow on the F,'' he said, ''so the accent can make the passage clearer. And then, if you could *all* play also piano. . . .'' The musicians began again, and Mr. Mehta gradually swept them up into the complex patterns of Ravel's mordant apotheosis of the Viennese waltz, pausing from time to time to adjust a transition, correct a dynamic, or redefine an entrance. (''Cellos and basses, that pizzicato chord two bars before thirty-four sounds forced. Maybe we can taper down . . . . Brass, how staccato can you play those triplets? . . . Basses, don't lose the downbeat after thirty-four; it's the only impulse that is carried right through the piece. . . . Bassoon, more legato after sixty-one; it helps the strings.'') As ''La Valse'' reached its turbulent climax, Mr. Mehta seemed to become intoxicated by the collective sound of the orchestra. He leaned over the violins, smiling ferociously, his knees bent, his right foot stamping out the rhythm on the podium; whirled in a semi-crouch to encourage the cellos with his mouth open in a silent scream; and flung his body back in an arch, both arms outstretched above his head, to punctuate each shattering crescendo. During these gymnastics, he was also balancing the orchestral voices with great care, giving precise instrumental cues to produce crisp attacks, and maintaining a clear, rapid beat with the baton clenched in his right hand. As we watched and listened, an invisible current seemed suddenly to flow between musicians and conductor. When the orchestra took a break at the end of the piece, most of the tension in the hall had vanished.[9]

Reading this material makes it possible with little difficulty to envision what has taken place. We can see Mehta's crouch and feel the relationship that he has to the orchestra. We can experience the crescendo of the music by the momentum of the language the critic has used. Through the words we are helped to see.

Such description is a far cry from what most studies of teaching provide. The average number of soliciting behaviors, the quantitative relationship of teacher talk to student talk, the number of responding to reacting moves simply are not adequate for achieving a conception of how the teacher and the students engage each other. When the characteristics of classroom life are formalized, as they are when check-off observation schedules are used, the quality of that life and its meaning for those who are in the situation is radically reduced.

There are two things that we can learn from the criticism of Mehta's rehearsal. First, we can learn something about Mehta's style as a conductor and his relationship to the musicians, the kinds of cues he gives them, the fact that he not only directs and selects, but explains *why* a certain beat has to be sustained. We also learn something about the character of the music. We learn something of the general environment that Mehta was able to generate. The criticism allows us to appreciate the qualities of the situation. Such forms of awareness are not irrelevant to the understanding and improvement of classroom life.

The second thing we can learn is what the critic did to make this possible. Notice how the critic first creates the setting and provides a context for what is to follow. Notice how the language used almost replicates the growing tension in the music, the musicians, and the con-

---

[9] ''Talk of the Town,'' *The New Yorker,* September 4, 1978, pp. 22-23.

ductor. Notice the use of metaphor, the willingness and the ability to exploit the potential of language to communicate character and mood. And finally, notice how in the last lines, the relief in the music is paralleled by the relief in the critic's language. The language used becomes an expressive analogue to the developing situation. Its movement over time seems to keep pace with the music being played.

What about educational criticism, material written not about symphony rehearsals but about classrooms? Consider the following section of an educational criticism about a second-grade classroom in an upper-middle class suburban school. The section describes the physical characteristics, and by implication the psychological characteristics of the room.

The room invites me in. It is a large, extended room drawn at the waist: it was once two single rooms that have come together to talk. Surely I could spend a whole childhood here. A wealth of learning materials engulfs me, each piece beckoning me to pick it up. The patchwork rug that hides the floor is soft and fluffy and warm. Some desks have gathered together for serious business. Chairs converse across semicircular tables. At the bookshelf, dozens and dozens of books slouch around, barely in rows, leaning on each other's shoulders. Children's drawings line the walls. What are those masses of shiny objects growing from the ceiling like silver stalactites in the secret corners of the room? I focus in on thousands of tiny . . . beer can pull-tabs . . . crunched together, straining to pull the roof in.

A massive wooden beehive called The Honeycomb, with geodesic cubicles in which to hide yourself. A towering ten-foot dinosaur made of wire and papier-mâché, splotched with paint . . . blue and red colors crawling up its body. The monster is smiling helplessly — is he not? — because a convoy of tiny people have just been tickling him with their paintbrushes.

In another corner, there are several plants growing in small cups. An incubator with eggs. Over there a phonograph and some records. A map on the chalkboard locates the hills I just drove through — the ones presided over by those houses. Next to the map there are frozen smiles on faces captured within tiny squares of paper. Strings connect the smiles with places on the map. This smile lives *there*; that one *here*. But all of the smiles, I have come to learn, live inside this room.

Mostly in this room there are letters and words. Lined up on the walls: Aa Bb Cc Dd Ee Ff. In combinations which have meaning — at least for me: leave, would, said. Blue next to a dab of blue paint. The words appear on the faces of the books and gather together in great multitudes on their insides. On the map. On the material that covers the couch. Soon in my eyes, even when I shut them. And later they pop out of the smiles of the children and hang in the air. Caressing each other in a low murmur, the omnipresent words pervade the room.

Soon I am not alone. The other children are pouring through the door, infusing the room with life, brimming with energy hankering for release. Mostly fair-skinned, light-haired, blue-eyed, and all fresh and ebullient, these are yesterday's Gerber babies. Lots of Erics and Chrises and Heathers and Lisas. Each seems to be drawn to his own corner of the room, his energy pulling him toward a special task. One moves to the bookshelf and snatches up a book. Several take themselves to the math table. Three crawl in the Honeycomb. One tickles the dinosaur with a paintbrush. Others string pull-tabs or watch a film.[10]

---

[10] Tom Barone, "Of Scott and Lisa and Other Friends," in Elliot W. Eisner, *The Educational Imagination* (New York: Macmillan, 1979), pp. 240-245.

As from the description of Mehta before it, the reader is able to secure from the writing a vivid image of what the situation is like and to infer some of the educational values that it reflects. Later in the criticism the writer gives greater detail about the character of the relationships between the teacher and the children, as well as the character of the tasks (in this case, the extensive use of contracts which students complete).

But also in this bit of descriptive narrative, the writer uses language carefully. The writer is not afraid to use metaphor or to exploit the poetics and tempo of language to communicate a tone appropriate for that particular classroom. Far from a "scientific" description, the writer has relied on both a perceptive eye and a disposition and ability to communicate in an artistic mode to help readers acquire a picture of this classroom, one that is probably like a host of other upper-middle class classrooms in suburban settings.

The ability to see a situation is crucial for supervision. One of the roles of the supervisor is to enable people to grasp aspects of the situation that they are often too close to appreciate. Habit and familiarity that make automatic responses possible and that contribute to efficient action are, at the same time, likely to blind one to important characteristics. How many of us who have been teaching for ten or twenty years know what we do not see in our own classrooms? Equally important as the ability to describe is the ability to interpret what has been seen and appraise its educational value.[11]

Interpretation is the process of making theoretical sense out of what one has seen and described. While the descriptive aspect of educational criticism makes the situation vivid, the interpretative phase of criticism explicates the relationships that have emerged. It explains by using whatever theories, models, generalizations, and concepts are appropriate. Interpretation goes beyond the surface and attempts to explain how the classroom functions as it does.

The appraisal or evaluative aspect of educational criticism seeks to address the educational import of what has been described and interpreted. What is educationally significant in educational practice cannot be determined through statistical tests of significance; such tests deal only with questions related to probability. By themselves, they have nothing to do with questions of value. The educational critic and the supervisor who use an artistically-oriented approach to supervision are obligated to judge the worth of what has been seen by applying to it educational, not simply statistical, criteria. To do this competently the critic needs to be aware of the variety of ways in which educational virtues can be displayed so that appraisals are not parochial and ineq-

---

[11] Those wishing to pursue this area further should consult the works cited in the footnotes. See Elliot W. Eisner, *The Educational Imagination* (New York: Macmillan, 1979), especially Chapters 10, 11, and 12.

uitable. One needs to be able to recognize the unique qualities of teaching and the special ways in which *this* classroom affects the educational development of students.

What can be said therefore about the characteristics of an artistic approach to supervision? What are its most important features? Eight such features appear to me to be especially important.

1. Artistic approaches to supervision require attention to the muted or expressive character of events, not simply to their incidence or literal meaning.

2. Artistic approaches to supervision require high levels of educational connoisseurship, the ability to see what is significant yet subtle.

3. Artistic approaches to supervision appreciate the unique contributions of the teacher to the educational development of the young, as well as those contributions a teacher may have in common with others.

4. Artistic approaches to supervision demand that attention be paid to the process of classroom life and that this process be observed over extended periods of time so that the significance of events can be placed in a temporal context.

5. Artistic approaches to supervision require that rapport be established between supervisor and those supervised so that dialog and a sense of trust can be established between the two.

6. Artistic approaches to supervision require an ability to use language in a way that exploits its potential to make public the expressive character of what has been seen.

7. Artistic approaches to supervision require the ability to interpret the meaning of the events occurring to those who experience them and to be able to appreciate their educational import.

8. Artistic approaches to supervision accept the fact that the individual supervisor with his or her strengths, sensitivities, and experience is the major "instrument" through which the educational situation is perceived and its meaning construed.

Chapter 5.

Toward a Theory of Supervisory Practice: Integrating Scientific, Clinical, and Artistic Views

Thomas J. Sergiovanni

ONE SELECTS A TITLE THAT INCLUDES THE WORD "THEORY" with some risk when writing for large numbers of professionals in need of hands-on insights and suggestions for improving practice. Key to the title, however, is the word practice. In this essay I wish to speak not to theory per se but to a theory of supervisory practice sensitive to the needs of professional action. Such a theory would serve to inform the intuition of supervisors and teachers alike and would emphasize both explanation and understanding in the analysis of teaching. Its purpose would be to provide a helpful framework to supervisors and teachers in an effort to improve teaching. It is not likely that we will be able to develop a theory of supervisory practice unless we turn the tide on the science-art debate in our field from that of a zero-sum game in which teaching is considered a science or an art, to that which considers the science *and* art of teaching as two interdependent dimensions requiring integration in an effective supervisory program.

Facts and Values in Evaluation

One distinguishing feature of a theory of practice is its normative emphasis. Theories of practice are designed to improve things, to bring about higher standards, to strive for a better life. Traditional theoretical science, on the other hand, is concerned with the discovery of truth, the establishment of fact, and the accurate recording of the world as it is. The principles of traditional theoretical science are typically articulated separate from a normative emphasis. Indeed one of the canons of traditional theoretical science is the separation of fact and value with the conviction that the former is to be prized and the latter to be considered a nuisance that should be controlled. In a theory of practice, however, both fact and value are considered important.

Accepting the importance of facts about the real world of teaching and values about what ought to be does not resolve the science-art dispute in supervison. Indeed this dichotomy of key evaluation dimen-

---

Thomas J. Sergiovanni is Professor and Chairperson, Educational Administration and Supervision at the University of Illinois, Urbana-Champaign.

sions plays into the hands of scholars and practitioners in both camps. Advocates of science, for example, claim the importance of intents, goals, and objectives and consider these normative statements as key to the process of evaluation. Since such goal statements are often empirically-based (teacher effectiveness research and studies of student productivity, for example) the normative standards used often appear to have more "truth density" than those found in other views of teaching and evaluation. The charge is now simple. Using the most advanced techniques, establish the level and quality of teaching actually present and hold this up against the standard. In essence, establish the facts of teaching and hold these up against empirically-derived values. Though both "is" and "ought" dimensions are recognized, they are pursued as *separate* entities and essential ingredients in a discrepancy analysis.

Scholars and practicing professionals in the artistic camp are more likely to consider facts and values to be inseparable and thus the process of supervision is viewed more subjectively. They would dispute, as well, the scientific supervisors' pursuit of the facts, complaining that the methods used yield only "thin" descriptions of the real world of teaching. Preferring "thick" descriptions and believing that facts and values cannot be pursued separately, they seek a richer and more in depth view of teaching and are willing to sacrifice the rigor, objectivity, and unambiguity typically associated with scientific approaches to supervision.

In Search of Meaning

Facts and values remain important in a theory of practice but attention is given as well to the pursuit of meaning. A theory of practice in the supervision and evaluation of teaching would be concerned initially with three questions. What *is* going on in this classroom? What *ought* to be going on? And, what do these events, activities, and aspirations *mean*? Meaning is the added dimension. Establishing what is requires the development of accurate descriptions and explanations of the real world of teaching. Establishing what ought to be requires that one give attention to stated values and attempt to discover those more implicit in teacher and teaching. Establishing what events mean requires a closer study of classroom life and its events in pursuit of understanding. Establishing meaning requires that supervisors cultivate the art of interpretation.

The scientific approach to supervision, so masterfully articulated and evaluated by John McNeil in Chapter 2, can help to establish what is going on in the evaluation of teaching and can contribute as well to identifying empirically based aspects of what ought to be. Establishing meaning, however, requires that we tackle the problem with a depth and sensitivity not possible by employing *only* scientific methods.

Elliot Eisner's eloquent essay articulating the artistic view, which appears as Chapter 4, points the way toward shifting the emphasis in supervision from what is to what it means. His emphasis on developing thick descriptions of classroom life is more than an alternative way to establish what is. The essence of criticism is the art of interpretation, and one learns of classroom life less from the development of detailed descriptions than from interpreting what these descriptions mean to supervisor, teacher, and others. But the values of science are necessary nonetheless and the tools and techniques of scientific supervision cannot be lightly dismissed. Interpretation and meaning cannot occur separate from description any more than it is possible to pursue standards without benchmarks. Despite the tendency of scientific approaches to sacrifice analysis and detail in exchange for breadth and scope of coverage, the descriptive power of scientific methods in accounting for an array of issues is too important to be ignored.

As an example, a carefully constructed record of the number and types of questions asked, linked to a classification of type of student responses evoked, can mask such important issues as the quality of questioning, the quality of student response, and the substantive worth of question content. One good question and one meaningful student response observed in a particular classroom may be more significant than "higher scores" observed in another class for question and response, frequency or type. On the other hand, though the quantitative and categorical array of question and answer responses is not sufficient to understanding teaching, it is helpful and may well be necessary if a more complete picture of events and meanings is sought.

Clinical supervision is a process, a way of life, a cultural structure within which one works with teachers in the evaluation of teaching and classroom life. Some see clinical supervision as more a technique that mechanically specifies a series of steps through which supervisor and teacher must travel. Noreen Garman's sensitive rendering of clinical supervision in Chapter 3, as a cultural structure within which the supervision and evaluation of teaching takes place, raises the concept to new heights. With care, she portrays the struggles that must be endured as supervisor and teacher strive to discover what is, what ought to be, and what events mean. Within its rubric both scientific and artistic aspects of supervision can be brought together. A theory of supervisory practice within the concept of clinical supervision will require, however, that scientific and artistic approaches not exist side by side but integrated into a comprehensive design.

The case for integrating scientific and artistic approaches to supervision is built upon a belief that the perspectives of each contribute to a theory of supervisory practice that emphasizes interpretation and meaning.[1] Classroom meanings, however, cannot exist separate from

---

[1] This analysis is based in part on T. J. Sergiovanni, "Interpretation and Meaning in the Evaluation of Teaching," Joint National Council for Measurement in Education and American Educational Research Association Conference, Los Angeles, April 1981.

classroom facts. Admittedly, the facts revealed by scientific and artistic inquiry often differ but if both are considered perhaps one's vision of reality will be enhanced. Interpretation and meaning are not now evidenced by scientific supervisory strategies. They are, at present, more compatible with artistic views but sometimes artistic supervisory strategies neglect them in favor of presenting alternative descriptions and alternative renderings of the facts.

Perhaps the case for emphasizing interpretation and meaning in supervision can be made by paraphrasing an allegory attributed to Gustav Ichheiser[2]: Suppose there is a windowless classroom with three doors A, B, C; next to each door is a switch; the switch by door A turns on a green light, the switch by door B a red light, the switch by door C a blue light. Suppose that students, teacher, and supervisor enter the room often, each always using the same door, but never the door of the other. Students use door A, teachers uses door B, and supervisor door C. Each of the parties will firmly believe, and have evidence that substantiates his or her belief, that the room is a specific color. Is it the task of the supervisor in this case to establish the facts as he or she sees them? What is truth and what facts exist in this instance? No matter how carefully the supervisor builds a case, truth and fact cannot be separate from the meanings and realities of each of the participants involved in this allegory and such is the case as well in the real world of supervision.

There are at least two dimensions in describing a classroom event or action; a configuration dimension and a meaning dimension. In its configuration sense, the emphasis in evaluation is on describing an element's features and factual basis. In the jargon of social science, this emphasis has been referred to as establishing "social facts." What are the social facts of teaching and its observed or otherwise documented effects in a given classroom? Carefully delineated, objective, criterion-referenced test questions and student response data; an accurate record of teacher "moves" on a classroom map; a chart depicting how students spend time; a transcript of the teacher's lecture designed to assess uses of advanced organizers; and a recording of student winks, smiles, nods, and frequency of hand waving are examples of social facts. Evaluation that seeks to determine social facts relies heavily on what might be referred to as "brute data."[3]

In its meaning sense the emphasis in evaluation is on establishing the meanings of an element to an individual or a group. In the jargon of social science this emphasis has been referred to as establishing "social meanings." What are the meanings of a particular classroom element or of several in combination to an individual or group? The extent to

[2] The Ichheiser allegory is described by Zygmunt Bauman, *Hermeneutics and Social Science* (New York: Columbia University Press, 1978), p. 106.

[3] Charles Taylor, "Interpretation and the Science of Man," *The Review of Metaphysics* 25, 1 (1971).

which behavior modification techniques of classroom management are being used and their subsequent effect on student attention spans can be accurately recorded in a brute data sense, but the meanings to students and teachers that result from using this technique can escape undetected.[4]

In contrast to emphasizing exclusively brute data, the evaluator should be interested in "sense data" as well.[5] Social facts, as determined by brute data, are typically the starting point in an evaluation, but brute data cannot stand alone and still have sense in a particular context any more than a word can stand separate from its context or a color from its field. The word *spirit,* for example, defies understanding separate from its use in context (is it whiskey, ghost, elan, or soul?). And even a word as basic as *eat* takes on different meanings in use and different meanings in different cultural contexts. As a further example, yellow is a color quite different against a field of white than black. And so it is with brute data recorded from classroom activity. Observation A, when combined with B, may have quite different meanings and significance than when combined with C.

At a simple level, supervision and evaluation of teaching emphasize meaning when seeking to determine teacher intents or to understand the intended outcomes of a particular curriculum format and related teaching sequence. But classroom meanings can be understood at three levels: intended, common, and intersubjective.[6] Common meanings, for example, are the shared sentiments and beliefs of those having a common social identity. Though symbolic interactionists might view my definition as too simple,[7] for our purposes common meanings might be thought of as the shared meanings derived from membership in or identity with a particular school culture such as teacher, student, or supervisor.

Within these cultures, identities may be further broken down into such subcultures as academic teacher, shop teacher, basics teacher, open education teacher, or, in the case of students, college bound, aggie, grit, and so on. Intersubjective meanings are those derived individually from interaction with or from experiencing a particular classroom element or event. Basic to intersubjective meanings is that the same element or event has different meanings for different people and takes on different meanings when combined with other elements.

---

[4] The standard behavior modification practice of "ignoring undesirable behavior," for example, raises a number of ethical and psychological issues relating to manipulation, arbitrary authority, coercion, rejection, and due process that may seem unimportant given the specifically desired behavior and the time frame in question, but could have long lasting consequence to all parties involved as subsequent behavior, learned attitudes, and longer time frames are considered.

[5] Taylor, "Interpretation and Science."

[6] Taylor, "Interpretation and Science."

[7] See for example, Herbert Blumer, "Society as Symbolic Interaction," in *Human Behavior and Social Processes,* ed. A. M. Rose (Boston: Houghton Mifflin, 1962).

The Domains of Inquiry

Classrooms are social systems and, like other social systems, can be viewed as possessing three interdependent components: a theory, a structure, and a technology.[8] Theory refers to the rules, beliefs, and standards that help define and promote understanding of reality; structure refers to the set of roles and relationships that exist among system members; and technology refers to the actual procedures and practices by which things get done. With respect to classrooms, the interdependent components might be thought of as educational platforms, social structures, and educational activities.

In seeking the domains of inquiry in teacher evaluation one can look to the social system components on the one hand, and the actions and activities that take place and their multiple meanings, on the other. The domains as depicted in Figure 1 suggest that the task of teacher evaluation is more complex than normally assumed and that a variety of techniques might be appropriate given the particular domain of interest at the moment.

Brute data collection strategies, therefore, have a role to play along with sense data strategies if a complete picture is sought. Further, since the social system features of classroom life are interdependent, evaluation needs to be viewed as dynamic. A change in classroom practices or in the organization of instruction, for example, influences the existing social structure and the shape and texture of the educational program. As these social system dimensions change, so do the meanings to be inferred from the brute facts of what is.

In the remaining sections of this essay, I wish to emphasize the interpretive aspects of the pursuit of meaning in supervision. This emphasis is taken with full recognition that the pursuit of meaning is an exercise of little value without having established as well what is, and what ought to be. I conclude the essay by suggesting a model that presents some necessary dimensions to be developed if a theory of practice in supervision and evaluation of teaching is to emerge.

Three major avenues of inquiry are suggested as being important in a theory of supervisory practice. Interpretation is an art that is enhanced by multiple perspectives on reality and meanings are sufficiently idiosyncratic to require that avenues of inquiry be pursued in partnership by teachers and supervisors. Though I am sure of the roles of students and parents in the process, they too would likely be involved. The avenues of inquiry are suggested by the three questions already raised.

1. *What is going on in this classroom?* How does it work? Can it be explained and predicted? What laws and rules govern behavior in this

[8] Donald A. Schön, *Beyond the Stable State* (New York: Random House, 1971).

	Intended Meanings	Observed Events	Common Meanings	Intersubjective Meanings
Educational Platform	stated intents	intents observed	culturally interpreted intents	subjectively interpreted intents
Social Structure	relationships desired	actual relationships	cultually interpreted relationships	subjectively interpreted relationships
Educational Activity	developed plans	activity observed	culturally interpreted activity	subjectively interpreted activity

What ought to be? (espoused theories)	What is? (brute data)	What do "is" and "ought" mean? (Sense data)

Figure 1. The Domains of Inquiry in the Supervision and Evaluation of Teaching

context? How can I accurately and vividly describe classroom events?

Thin descriptions of reality are important in presenting an overall map of classroom events. Such a map gives a general orientation to the classroom's breadth and scope much like a road map provides for a particular region. Thick descriptions of reality are important in identifying and recording aspects of the hidden curriculum, estimates of quality, and indicators of cultural imperatives that provide a more vivid portrayal of classroom life. The maps in a travel atlas, for example, present a general descriptive orientation of a particular region but the accompanying text and photos describe the mind and pulse of this region. Each is useful to the traveler.

2. *What ought to be going on in this classroom?* What cultural imperatives should determine action? What values should be expressed? What qualities of life should be in evidence? What standards should be pursued?

"Ought" dimensions of classroom life can be obtained and verified from empirically established standards (for example, teacher effectiveness research) on the one hand and from cultural preferences, values, and beliefs (for example, conservative or humanistic ideology) on the other. Admittedly, the two sources are more easily separated in word than action. Symbolic interactionists, for example, would suggest that values are products of interaction among people and are qualities of mind that arise both through such interaction and through symbolic meanings.

Establishing that a particular level of student achievement can be obtained if teachers follow closely a given set of teaching procedures suggests a standard of fact. Such relationships ought to be rigorously pursued and empirically established as *teaching facts*. Deciding that the particular level of student achievement that might be obtained is valuable, and that the trade offs of what is lost to students and others by obtaining this gain in achievement or by adopting this method of teaching are acceptable, however, does not necessarily follow from teaching facts. Making decisions among alternatives is the establishment of *teaching values*. Strong teaching facts scientifically determined are important prerequisites for establishing teaching values but are not substitutes for these values. The establishment of teaching facts and teaching values are both important in the development of the theory of supervisory practice.

3.   *What do events and activities that comprise the "is" and "ought" dimension of classroom life mean to teachers, students, supervisors, and significant others?* What is the cultural content of the classroom? What implicit educational platforms exist? What values are suggested by actual behavior and events? What are the meanings implicit in discrepancies between the espoused and in use theories?

The discovery of meaning and the creation of meaning in teaching await the further development of the art of interpretation. The work of Eisner is an important step in this direction. Perspectives of both science and art will be key to this effort. Social meanings are derived from social facts and neither scientific images nor artistic images have a monopoly on establishing social facts.

It may be helpful in illustrating the importance of social facts and social meanings in the evaluation of teaching to distinguish between "picturing" and "disclosure."[9] Picturing models of evaluation try to be as much like the teaching activity and classroom life under study as possible. Disclosure models, on the other hand, contain key characteristics of the teaching activity and classroom life under study but move beyond picturing per se to interpreting meaning by raising issues and testing propositions about the phenomenon. Picturing and disclosing are constrasted below. In examining the disclosure side of the ledger, notice the emphasis given to going beyond the data in the strictest sense to telling a story represented by the data. The data are enriched in disclosure as a means of communicating more vividly and fully. But disclosure is not invention and the story developed is based on the social facts present in teaching. Meaningful disclosure requires accurate picturing.

[9] See for example, Ian Ramsey, *Models and Mystery* (London: Oxford University Press, 1964).

Picturing	Disclosure

Intents

To describe the teaching phenomenon under study as exactly as possible. To develop a replica, photo image, or a carbon copy of reality. Agendas and issues are intents embedded in the data.	To interpret the teaching phenomenon under study. To illuminate issues, disclose meanings, and raise hypotheses and issues are intents that emerge from the data.

Analogies

Legal transcript, videotape, photo-replica, interaction-analysis, electronic portrait, music or dance score, play script, historical chronology.	Impressionistic painting, collage, book review, interpretative photo, music, dance or play performance, story.

Key Questions

What exactly happened in this classroom? How can I describe events objectively?	What issues emerge from the study of this class? How can I represent or illuminate these issues in a meaningful way?

Validity Check

Are events described accurately?	What actual events are observed? Do they reasonably lead to the inferences and interpretations?

I have suggested that the problems of supervision and evaluation of teaching need to be addressed in a fashion that emphasizes interpretation and meaning. Developing accurate and objective records of the real world of teaching as defined by the canons of objectivity would be only part of the process. Of no less importance would be the subjective world of teaching. The phenomenological life of the classroom, teaching as expressions of cultural, and hermeneutical inquiry are the areas that should now receive our attention. Looking to hermeneutics as a method of analysis, supervision and evaluation of teaching would require that one give attention to both normative and descriptive knowledge and both theoretical and practical perspectives.[10]

[10] Hermeneutics is a "science" of interpretation. Interpretation is an attempt to clarify, to make sense of an object or event under study. The "hermeneutical circle" is language used by scholars to suggest the alternating attention given to an array of factors in pursuit of meaning. As each of the parts of the puzzle is viewed in relationship to others, they become more intelligible. The circle is theoretically endless, with interpretation and meaning enhanced as the whole becomes clearer from continuing and further analysis of interrelated parts. See for example, Charles Taylor, "Interpretation and Science," and Jurgen Habermas and Jeremy J. Shapiro, *Knowledge and Human Interests* (Boston: Beacon Press, 1971).

Of interest in using a hermeneutical frame of reference would be the accurate recording of concrete facts that describe in practice classroom events. Important is sensitivity as well to what the best of educational research says are the predictable relationships between and among these classroom events. For example, what does educational research say about the relationship between the academic engaged time of students and subsequent results on mathematics achievement tests? And, to what extent are youngsters in a particular classroom academically engaged?

Also of interest would be the teacher's stated and unstated intents, stated and unstated assumptions, and stated and unstated beliefs that compose an educational platform. Important would be sensitivity as well to the broader social and cultural imperatives that delineate and define a value system from which standards of quality and excellence are born. For example, what does this teacher say are his or her intents and what intents can be inferred from the teacher's actual behavior and from other factors found in the classroom? These dimensions are illustrated in Figure 2. The quadrants compare descriptive and normative knowledge with practical and theoretical perspectives. One quadrant, for example, is concerned with descriptive knowledge of a practical nature, a second with descriptive knowledge of a theoretical nature, a third with normative knowledge of a practical nature, and a fourth with normative knowledge of a theoretical nature.

The quadrants of Figure 2 depict the avenues of inquiry that should be considered in a practical theory of supervision and evaluation of teaching. The task is more complex than rating teachers' effectiveness against a standard of validated teacher competencies or in conducting a discrepancy analysis between stated intents and actual student achievement. Hermeneutical inquiry for example, would require that one move from quadrant to quadrant repeatedly in the analysis of classroom events in search of meaning. Of interest are not only teacher behavior and other descriptions of what is, but the quality of life that exists in the classroom and the cultural imperatives that define that quality. Meaning, it is assumed, is the vehicle for increasing one's vision about classroom happenings and for informing one's intuition. These in turn are keys to understanding and improving teaching.

Toward a Theory of Practice

Though I speak of a theory of practice, I have in mind the development of a number of such theories each emphasizing different dimensions and each able to illuminate different problems and issues in supervision and evaluation. They would share, nevertheless, some common

The Pursuit of Descriptive Knowledge

1. Practical - Descriptive	2. Theoretical - Descriptive
Supervisor and teacher seek to record the facts that exist in a particular classroom. Scientific strategies yield "thin" descriptions on an array of concerns and artistic strategies yield "thick" descriptions on selected concerns. The intent is to establish "what is."	Supervisor and teacher review social science and educational research as well as the humanities disciplines (culture, ethics, values) in an effort to determine "what is" good practice. Scientific perspectives favor researching the wisdom of empirical research and theoretically establishing facts and artistic, the humanistic disciplines. Both provide insights into "what ought to be" but as established facts rather than individual preferences.
The supervisor seeks to understand and help the teacher understand his or her stated and implied goals and objectives. Scientific strategies favor the analysis of stated goals and objectives and artistic, the implied. The "ought" dimension is of concern in both manifest and latent forms. Ought refers to stated and implied individual preferences of the teacher.	The supervisor seeks to understand the teacher's stated and implied educational platform and the stated and implied cultural value system that determine classroom life. The emphasis is on interpretation and meaning which in turn fuels further inquiry into the other three quadrants. Artistic strategies are better able to provide interpretation and meaning.
3. Practical - Normative	4. Theoretical - Normative

The Pursuit of Normative Knowledge

Figure 2. Avenues of Inquiry in the Supervision and Evaluation of Teaching

characteristics and rest on similar epistemological assumptions.[11] As has been suggested, *a theory of practice would be integrative.* It would recognize the value of both normative and descriptive views and would seek to bring them together as alternate and integrative ways of knowing. Further, *a theory of practice would be concerned with meanings of events.* Such a theory would seek to turn the facts of what is and what ought to be into meanings that are important and useful to those involved in the process of supervision and evaluation. Brute data would become sense data and it is sense data that would influence teacher practices. As Blumer suggests, "We can and, I think, must look upon human group life as chiefly a vast interpretive process in which people, singly and collectively, guide themselves by defining the objects, events, and situations which they encounter."[12]

To what end is such a theory proposed? Is the purpose of inquiry as described in this chapter to advance the science and art of evaluation? Are the prime beneficiaries, theorists and analysts? I think not. *A theory of measurement and evaluation is not being proposed here but a theory of practice is.* Of concern is improving the practice of teachers and the quality of classroom life. Thus a key fourth question must be considered. Given what is (descriptive science), what ought to be (normative science), and what events mean (interpretive science), what should supervisors and teachers "do" (practice)? Theories of practice are ultimately concerned with action taken to improve a present situation and in our case the beneficiaries would be teachers and students.

The development of a theory of practice in the supervision and evaluation of teaching is a task well beyond the scope of this chapter. My purpose is to provide some indication of directions such a pursuit might take. Progress in developing such a theory will require a fuller integration of a variety of points of view. Scientific views and artistic views of supervision as articulated by McNeil and Eisner can each contribute importantly. If Noreen Garman's rendering of clinical supervision is taken to heart, then perhaps this process can provide the cultural system and way of life within which teacher and supervisor can work together with honor and dignity in pursuit of both social facts and social meanings on the path to improved teaching.

---

[11] T. J. Sergiovanni, "Theory of Practice in Educational Policy and Administration: An Hermeneutics Perspective." American Educational Research Association Annual Conference, Los Angeles, April 1981.

[12] Herbert Blumer, "Sociological Analysis and the 'Variable.'" *American Sociological Review* 21 (1956): 386.

Part III.
The Human Factor in Supervision

APPLIED FIELDS SUCH AS EDUCATIONAL SUPERVISION differ from the more academic disciplines in the nature of knowledge that is of most importance. Applied fields are interested in theoretical knowledge but they are also interested in practical knowledge. Philosophers of science differentiate between proof reasoning and practical reasoning. Proof reasoning is more universalistic, objective, and rational. Practical reasoning is more particularistic and subject to the unique meanings given knowledge by the people involved and goals pursued. Supervisors are interested in improving teaching and the quality of classroom life. They want to "do" something about educational matters with the intent that tomorrow will be better than today. These actions and intents characteristic of educational supervision lend themselves to practical reasoning as the dominant mode of inquiry.

When one considers the practical nature of our field along with the fact that supervisory activity in education involves intense human interaction it is easy to appreciate how important the human factor in supervision is. Scientific knowledge about supervision simply cannot be considered separate from the human factors involved in converting this knowledge to actions. Knowing which particular textbook is "best" in a proof sense, for example, cannot be converted into action separate from the practical issue of which textbook will teachers accept and use with enthusiasm. Facing up to the fact that doing in educational supervision involves working closely with teachers and that successful doing involves teachers being committed to and freely accepting ideas, suggestions, and practices suggests the importance of human factors in supervision.

Among the many topics and issues that belong under the heading "Human Factors," only four are considered in this Yearbook. Leonard Valverde discusses the relationship between the growth and development of supervisors as persons and professionals and similar growth aspirations for teachers in his chapter "The Self-Evolving Supervisor." He argues that the two are linked. In his view, growth and development of supervisors is key to building a set of norms and a way of life in schools conducive to teacher growth and development.

Robert Alfonso and Lee Goldsberry explore possibilities for bringing teachers into the process of supervision in their chapter

"Colleagueship in Supervision." They assume that supervision and evaluation is not something one does to a teacher but is a process designed to improve teaching; and, that this process is facilitated by teachers becoming fuller partners to the enterprise.

Human resources supervision as a theoretical framework for providing supervisory leadership to teachers, and issues of organizational climate conducive to teacher growth and development are explored in Chapter 7, "The Context for Supervision." Part III concludes with Ethel Greene's chapter themed to "Issues of Race and Sex in Supervision." She provides a historical overview of racism and sexism in education and discusses how contemporary interpretations of this problem affect the supervisory process. Critical to her is whether any of the humanistic aspirations espoused in other papers in this section can be fulfilled under the shroud of prejudice. She points out that though historically certain groups have been more victimized than others, prejudice affects all groups.

Chapter 6.
The Self-Evolving Supervisor

Leonard A. Valverde

AN EXAMINATION OF THE LITERATURE ON INSTRUCTIONAL SUPERVISION and scrutiny of supervision as a practice reveal the dominant focus has been on what supervisors can do with and for teachers. Neglected is what supervisors can do for themselves. Surprisingly little thought has been given to the inservice professional growth of the instructional supervisor.

Since the supervisor's major concern and focus of effort is to help teachers so that teachers in turn can increase their chances of helping children, it would seem natural that much attention be devoted to developing the supervisor's professional growth. This chapter explores an alternative by which professional educators can continue to learn. The alternative is neither novel nor new, but it is certainly different from the commonly used approach. In brief, my position is that a supervisor should depend on *self* for learning rather than depend on others to provide instruction. A supervisor who adopts the concept and practice of self-learning for professional growth becomes, as I use the term, a self-evolving supervisor.

Before advancing the alternative approach, it is advisable to outline the prevailing views educators have about their professional learning, their behavior, and the practices used to deliver professional growth experiences.

Staff Development: Inappropriate Assumptions and Dysfunctional Practices

In order for the reader to determine the feasibility of the proposed self-development alternative, it is necessary to present my interpretation (biases) about how teachers, supervisors, administrators, and other educators receive instruction while in service. The other reason for describing the general state of staff development, as I perceive it, is to justify the alternative approach I advocate. The following discussion of the supervisor's role may appear to stray from the topic; its relation to

Leonard A. Valverde is Associate Professor of Educational Administration and Director of the Instructional Supervision Program, The University of Texas, Austin.

self-learning, however, will become evident.

There are many definitions of what the supervisor's role ought to be—possibly as many as there are authors. The concept of supervision was perhaps best captured by Kimball Wiles when he stated, "The supervisor's role has become supporting, assisting, and sharing rather than directing."[1] Wiles assumes that the supervisor should be a *helper* of teachers or a *teacher* of teachers. However, when teachers need or desire assistance, they normally turn to another teacher. Hence, just as students depend on a teacher for their learning, so teachers depend on another person who can help in their professional development. Theoretically, teacher growth should depend on another professional: a person who is knowledgeable by way of formal training, on-the-job experience, and organizational position. However, this in only what *should be* the supervisor's role and not what the supervisor's role is in practice. For many reasons, elaborated by Sergiovanni in Chapter 8 of this Yearbook, the supervisor's role of being supportive, helpful, and cooperative is perceived quite differently by teachers. School districts and schools have many bureaucratic characteristics. The climate and structure that result from these characteristics are such that most supervisors display more controlling behavior than collegial behavior. In theory, the supervisor's relationship with teachers is based on expert knowledge but, in practice, the relationship is based on reward and coercive power—power associated with a traditional bureaucratic organization. Hence, in practice, teacher development is hindered because supervisors are restricted by bureaucratic characteristics from helping teachers. Teachers, in turn, are reluctant to ask for assistance since most requests are likely to be interpreted as evidence that the teacher is having trouble.

It is necessary to comment on one important supervisory function directly related to the construct of learning: planning, conducting, and evaluating inservice programs for the purpose of promoting teacher development. The term *program* is usually a misnomer, since typically inservice training is in the format of a one-time session or workshop. Rarely do inservice programs have theoretical constructs, sequential and logical organization of curriculum, or multiple meeting sessions spaced over an extended period of time. District-offered staff development is often characterized by inservice topics chosen on the basis of high interest and the extent to which they appear to address district problems. Topics arise from deficiencies participants have in common, or difficulties they seem to be experiencing. Instruction is provided by someone recognized as an expert, or by a supervisor who is asked to study the problem and to instruct others about overcoming the perceived deficiency or difficulty. Ideas are presented and suggestions offered, using such typical instructional techniques as lecture, demonstrations,

---

[1] K. Wiles, *Supervision for Better Schools*. 3rd ed. (Englewood Cliffs, N.J.: Prentice Hall, 1967), p.10.

and hands-on experiences. In essence, the inservice training format closely resembles the classroom model in which the teacher, as expert, typically determines student deficiencies and difficulties and organizes information to present to students as a group, demonstrates lessons, and assigns exercises and other work for them. Philip W. Jackson refers to this type of inservice approach as defective:

Permeating this view is the notion that someone knows more about how the teacher should behave in his classroom than he does himself. In many ways the defect position partakes of one of the most enduring of all conceptions of the educational process. It is the one in which the student is seen as essentially helpless and the teacher as omniscient; only in this case the teacher himself is in the role of the student and his all-knowing guide is the designer of the inservice program.[2]

This discussion underscores two points about the present state of inservice education: 1. Learning is single directional; it is received from the instruction of an expert. Instruction comes from someone other than self. In short, learning is perceived to occur when two individuals interact and when one person knows what the other person needs. 2. The continuing education of teachers as well as other educators, including supervisors, is conceptually related to and patterned after the teaching/learning model designed for students. However, assumptions applied to children are inappropriate for adults. For example, young children lack fundamental knowledge, lack basic skills and processes for self-learning; therefore, they are at least initially dependent on others and require learning activities that place them in relatively passive roles as learners. Surely adults who have advanced preparation for roles as professional educators are qualitatively different from young children. Because we have not formulated other assumptions about learning applicable to professionals, supervisors and other instructional leaders organize and direct staff development sessions in the image of classrooms for elementary and secondary students.

Inservice training programs that suffer from these characteristics have some benefits when properly planned and expertly implemented. Such programs can produce satisfied teachers and supervisors who carry away usable instructional materials, who can replicate a lesson in a classroom, and who can restate useful suggestions to others. But such inservice sessions do not aid or guide educators to be imaginative, to be analytic of situations, to formulate strategies for instruction applicable to their special environment, to rely on their own resources, or to be active, independent learners.

Professional Growth: Alternative Assumptions

Inservice programs often fail to incorporate some accepted ideas that expand our vision about learning. For example, most educators

[2] P.W. Jackson, "Old Dogs and New Tricks: Observations on the Continuing Education of Teachers," in *Improving Inservice Education*, ed. Louis J. Rubin (Boston: Allyn and Bacon, 1973), p. 25.

know and agree that personal learning styles and learning rates vary among all persons—not just among children.[3] We have come to recognize that there is no universal model of teaching suitable for all.[4] Further, increased student populations, larger professional staffs, and the multiplicity of services rendered in addition to instruction have diminished material resources and time for group learning. Moreover, efforts to superimpose cultural values, organizational procedures, and professional philosophies for the purpose of homogeneity and uniformity are being challenged. In addition, curriculums that build on the strength of diversity, plurality of values, and flexibility are being promoted as a democratic ideal. Thus, just as teachers are slowly beginning to introduce individualized instruction and prescriptive teaching, so educators will need to include these assumptions and others in their own learning and development.

Such concepts as life-long learning, continuing education, and staff evaluation for professional growth are gaining a permanent place in public education and, more important, such concepts represent a maturing mind-set within education. For these reasons it is time for new assumptions to be adopted and implemented. Other than those expressed above, what are some of these new assumptions? The first and the major assumption is borrowed from the medical profession: "Supervisor, teach thyself." As medical doctors are responsible for staying abreast of the latest developments in medicine, so should educational supervisors accept such responsibility. In order for the supervisor to grow professionally, a new viewpoint, centered internally, is necessary. The supervisor should realize that he or she is a self-resource to draw from and build upon; that is, instructional leaders possess basic and advanced knowledge developed through formal training, observation, and behavioral skills sharpened by years of experience. Furthermore, supervisors have access to resources by virtue of their position, such as command of their time, contact with numerous individuals both within and outside the school district, and opportunities to travel (at least locally). But in order for a supervisor to capitalize on these human and organizational resources for continued learning, the supervisor should internalize responsibility for professional growth. Supervisors should diagnose their own strengths and weaknesses, identify available and accessible human and material resources, determine activities to pursue, and determine the amount of time to spend on learning. Professional growth, like personal fulfillment, is best "purchased" and "owned" by the individual. Supervisors must no longer consider themselves merchants selling staff development to teachers. Rather,

---

[3] R. Dunn and K. Dunn, *Teaching Students Through Their Individual Learning Styles: A Practical Approach* (Reston, Va.: Reston Publishing, 1978).

[4] T. Good and J. Brophy, *Looking in Classrooms*, 2nd ed. (New York: Harper and Row, 1978).

supervisors must expand the seller role to include the investor role—that is, take advantage of their own expertness in order to enhance their own capabilities.

Complementing this key assumption, Bunker[5] posits five other assumptions that facilitate self-learning by teachers but which are also suitable for other educators. They are clearly stated and thus are offered without modification:

1.   People are their own instruments for growth.

2.   People learn to do what they do.

3.   Readiness for growth is built by focusing on people's strengths.

4.   Learning occurs when people receive new ideas and have an opportunity to interact with them.

5.   People are more effective helpers when they feel good about themselves.

The first assumption has been covered and the second will be treated in a following section. Bunker's third assumption asks us to be concerned with people's strengths. Regarding the third assumption, though, educators hold fast to two principles that are erroneous and harmful to learners, be they students or adults. James Lewis discusses this in the context of teacher performance appraisal:

First, the traditional performance appraisal program is based on a poor theory of human motivation, that telling an educator where he is doing a poor job will provide the necessary effective motivation to get him to improve his performance. Research has proven that this is not always the case. . . . Second, the traditional performance appraisal program is based on the false assumption that the roles of the administrator and the teacher are compatible and that criticism in itself will bring on the necessary improvement in performance. The administrator, in evaluating the teacher, implies that the staff member needs to improve his performance in the direction of the objectives and standards of the administrator. Failure to achieve according to this expectation often leads to criticism, threat, anxiety, and a poor working relationship between the administrator and the teacher.[6]

Bunker's fourth assumption addresses the construct of learning as an interactive process. But unlike the common interpretation used for children, where interaction is between two persons, one knowledgeable and the other ignorant, Bunker's assumption permits individuals to interact with thoughts and ideas on an individual basis. Dependence on others is no longer a requirement nor a restriction. Assumption five, concerned with the affective domain, will be discussed in the next section.

---

[5] R.M. Bunker, "Beyond In-Service: Toward Staff Renewal," *Journal of Teacher Education* 28, 2 (March/April 1977): 31-34.

[6] J. Lewis, *Appraising Teacher Performance* (West Nyack, N.Y.: Parker, 1973), p. 12.

All these assumptions argue for a teaching and learning model for educators that is different from the student model, and that is characterized as heuristic by Bush[7] and others. The term *heuristic* emphasizes the development of self-initiated and self-directed learning; it stresses discovering rather than absorbing knowledge; it places the learner in the role of inquirer; it represents more than one teaching and learning activity; and it treats the learner as a person who can produce knowledge and understanding.

Self-Learning: How?

A case has been presented for moving people away from inappropriate assumptions about adult learning and the corresponding classroom model of inservice training. The question now arises: how can alternative assumptions be put in practice? Or what model can the self-evolving supervisor practice for continued learning? The supervisor devoted to self-growth can undergo four learning activities, preferably in the sequence offered here but not necessarily so. Each learning activity is independent, meeting a particular intent.

One learning activity is *reflection*. The supervisor must examine his or her situation, behavior, practices, effectiveness, and accomplishments. Reflection means asking questions of oneself. The basic and comprehensive question asked during reflection is, "What am I doing and why?" Reflection is a form of slightly distorted self-evaluation—distorted in the sense that judgment is emphasized rather than data collection. The individual asks value-laden questions and responds on stored, selected data (memory), and then concludes whether he or she is satisfied or dissatisfied. Reflection, then, is an individual's needs assessment and continued self-monitoring of satisfaction with effectiveness. As with any type of evaluation, reflection should be formative, that is, periodic, constructive, and deliberate. Putting reflection into practice can be as simple as every three months setting aside two hours to write down perceptions.

Another self-learning activity is *exploration*. Exploration is a means of collecting information through reading, observing, and listening. Exploration as a learning activity includes identifying, locating, gathering, selecting, and marshaling resources. Exploration, if used following reflection, is a means of searching for answers. It is a way of augmenting existing knowledge, to validate or dispel faulty self-perceptions. Supervisors can engage in exploration by browsing through a professional library, reading current journals, or visiting with experts.

A third means of independent learning is *stimulation*. Stimulation is an activity performed to revitalize interests in one's job or to remotivate performance. Stimulation, since it relates to the affective domain, is best accomplished by seeing and hearing. As in the arts, supervisors can be energized to recommit themselves to doing more or doing better by seeing another supervisor perform gracefully or by hearing an instructional leader eloquently speak about his or her experiences. Compared with reflection and exploration, stimulation requires less action, but it is nonetheless effective in promoting learning. The more pleasure associated with an experience, the more likelihood of remembrance, rethinking to identify useful elements, and attempting to incorporate such elements in one's own behavior. (For a discussion of learning by way of the arts, see Chapter 4 in this Yearbook.) An example of stimulation is an art supervisor viewing an art exhibit of student work or a math supervisor visiting a computer center of a large business.

The fourth self-learning activity is referred to as *experience*. Application of thought or abstract learning is acquired by doing. Putting thought to practice, structuring one's behavior to conform to collected and organized knowledge is experience. While experience can be accumulated random behavior, as in trial and error, if associated with one or all of the three activities mentioned experience becomes guided behavior. Experience places the learner in an active role and places him or her in control of the activity. Learning by performing the job, attacking the task in new ways, produces *experienced* growth.

The following scenario illustrates experience: a science supervisor, after reading about a particular teaching strategy in a professional journal, decides to practice the method in a science teacher's fourth period. The science supervisor does not view this practice as the end of learning but rather as a phase in learning. He or she may need to rethink (reflection), to read more (exploration), to observe or talk more (stimulation), and plan more (experience), before gaining command of the teaching technique.

Accommodating Self-Development: Requisite Organizational Changes

As with any model, the four self-directed learning activities of reflection, exploration, stimulation, and experience have drawbacks. Two of major concern are time and autonomy, though neither is an inherent disadvantage. The two drawbacks arise because the educational structure does not provide instructional staff with sufficient independent time and adequate individual authority. Therefore, organizational changes will have to be made in order to permit supervisors and others to practice self-development. Time must be created for supervisors to educate themselves. This can be accomplished by cutting out unnecessary, but time consuming, tasks supervisors are called on to do as part of their daily work (committee attendance, making out reports, delivering instructional materials, attending ceremonies).

Most supervisors would agree that many of their present activities are relatively unimportant. If school boards and superintendents believe that supervisors should not be released from some of their present activities, then they should consider employing additional supervisors to assume some duties from existing supervisors. More free time will then be available for self-instruction. If the employment of a small number of additional supervisors is economically prohibitive, then another possibility is for the school board to designate certain days each academic year as learning days for supervisors. Many states, like Texas, have legislated that each school district have a certain number of pupil-free days for teacher inservice training. Supervisors should also have time relieved from all normal supervisory duties to spend on learning. Still another option would be supervisors covering for each other to release them for personal learning.

But along with the time to learn, supervisors must also have the autonomy to determine how, with whom, when, and where this learning will occur. Without the freedom of self-determination, the time earmarked for learning will be of little value. Consequently, the second organizational change needed is the altering of decision-making authority. Decision rights that superiors possess about the inservice training of supervisors should be transferred to or shared with supervisors. If educational leaders are to be serious about staff development, and if they are to make a deliberate effort to improve staff capability, then supervisors will have to be viewed as having greater value and worth and concomitantly, given more authority to determine their own improvement.

Given the additional time and autonomy to learn, supervisors will not only be able to conceive of new learning approaches, but also to practice self-learning. They will be able to learn alone or with others on an *ad hoc* or team basis, in different settings such as classrooms, demonstration centers, or university campuses. They will be able, as well, to identify and have access to resources they need for self-learning. However, if time and autonomy are not forthcoming, and if supervisors are not allowed to be professional about improvement, then we should resign ourselves to expect young teachers to continue leaving teaching because they do not receive appropriate and adequate help. We can continue to expect creative teachers to leave the classroom because they were not supported or challenged. We can continue to expect supervisors of instruction to perform their responsibilities mindlessly, and to expect administrators to approach their tasks routinely. Further, we should not be surprised when surveys indicate a malaise among educators, a "business" attitude among administrators (productivity, accountability, efficiency), an "overworked and underrespected" attitude among supervisors, and a lack of appreciation toward learning among students. The model or anti-model of a supervisor as an independent learner permeates the entire educational community.

In Conclusion

The way instructional supervisors come to learn and regenerate themselves has meaning that reaches out and touches teachers, students, and administrators. Teachers learn through formal means such as inservice training and informal means such as role models. For this reason, supervisors must become more self-evolving if they are to improve the teaching and learning process in public schools. If educators are going to develop a genuine interest in learning and to value continued growth, then the individual, regardless of designated title or position, will have to be honored. The concept of value and the abstract quality of honor are translated into concrete action by not just saying to people that they are competent to learn on their own, but by advocating, writing, and adopting policy that permits them to make and carry out their own decisions about learning. Supervisors will not permit teachers to be independent learners if they themselves are denied that practice. In turn, teachers will not give to students what they themselves do not have—the belief of self-worth, internal motivation to continue to learn, and the time and autonomy to be self-directed learners.

Finally, it is important to understand that I am not advocating that every supervisor or educator be forced to be a self-learner. I have argued for self-learning only to emphasize the need for and the viability of such a learning alternative. What I am positing for serious consideration is nothing more than an alternative way of learning for professional educators, a way of learning that is effective for some, under certain conditions and circumstances. This learning model should be an option for supervisors.

The growing complexity of education and the increasingly difficult role of the instructional supervisor require alternative models for professional growth. If educators expect to stay equal to the challenge of an ever developing endeavor like education, then educators will have to be self-fulfilling and self-evolving.

The link between teacher growth and development and that of their supervisor is direct and strong. For this reason the concept of the self-evolving supervisor needs to be brought to the forefront of staff development training.

Chapter 7.
Colleagueship in Supervision

Robert J. Alfonso and Lee Goldsberry

IN RECENT YEARS, interest in helping teachers assume greater responsibility for improving their own instruction and the instruction of their colleagues has grown. Because both literature and practice in the area of peer supervision are still so underdeveloped, it is not always clear what is referred to by the terms "peer supervision" or "colleagueship in supervision." These terms might describe a loose arrangement of teacher interaction and influence, the involvement of teachers on instructional and improvement teams under the direction of an administrator or supervisor, teachers taking more responsibility for developing instructional improvement programs, or the evaluation of nontenured teachers by colleagues. Sometimes the terms imply a nearly total teacher responsibility for the improvement of instruction; such responsibility is, of course, characteristic of the highest level of professionalism—members of a profession monitoring, disciplining, and seeking to improve themselves and their colleagues. Few professions obtain such a level, and those that do seldom work in bureaucratic structures as large and complex as school systems.

In general, proponents of peer or colleague supervision define such supervision in rather narrow terms. Most typically, proponents ask for the involvement of teachers in particular kinds of supervisory acts: planning inservice efforts, evaluation of nontenured teachers, classroom visitation and feedback, or observation of a colleague's instruction while using an interaction inventory system. Conceivably, enough teachers in the system, involved in enough different supervisory acts, and sufficiently trained in them, could represent a very broad range of typical supervisory behavior. Without coordination, however, these behaviors would lack direction and substance and would be merely random and unsystematic. It is unlikely that such acts could be very helpful over a long period of time, nor could they, in a technical sense, be viewed as supervision unless they were tied to and part of an on-going, comprehensive plan of instructional improvement.

Robert J. Alfonso is Associate Vice President and Dean of Faculties at Kent State University, Kent, Ohio. Lee Goldsberry is Assistant Professor of Supervision at Pennsylvania State University, University Park, Pennsylvania.

Perhaps one explanation for the current interest in colleagues providing supervision is that too little formal supervision is available for teachers. The professional teacher has a strong desire for help, for involvement with other professionals, for feedback on instructional processes and outcomes, and for new ideas. While much is made of the importance of instructional supervision, the typical teacher sees little of it and what is available is frequently of limited use. When supervisory time is in short supply and when the interests and abilities of the supervisor are unrelated to the needs of the classroom teacher, it is not surprising that teachers turn elsewhere for help. One place they can turn is to colleagues, persons who can frequently provide immediate help, practical suggestions, and support in times of difficulty and uncertainty. Furthermore, if supervisors are not technically competent—that is, skilled in the performance of those tasks most directly related to the teachers' work and to the improvement of it—then self-directed teachers are forced to seek help elsewhere. Colleagues have the value of proximity, immediacy, and a first-hand understanding of the other's "workspace." Frequently, teachers who need help or seek observation or opinion have no one to whom to turn, no one to whom to say, "How am I doing, how do you think it went today?"

In many school systems, formal feedback on teaching performance may come no more than once a year and then in a quite perfunctory way. One of the tragedies of American education is that teachers work in isolation. Their immediate superiors often have only a rather generalized perception of their teaching performance. Teaching is still largely a solo act, observed, appreciated, and evaluated primarily by students. There is little contact among colleagues, classroom doors are seldom opened to each other, and teachers who are members of the same staff in the same school, even in the same grade or discipline, maintain a collusive and almost deliberate ignorance of the work of their peers. It is essential that such barriers be broken down and that teachers feel responsible for improving their instruction and for assisting their colleagues in their own self-improvement; this concept characterizes other professions. Although there is little contact and mutual responsibility among teachers, studies still show that teachers report other colleagues to be their first source of professional help, even when supervisory assistance is available.[1]

Another possible explanation for the growing interest in colleagueship in supervision is the uncertain authority of instructional supervisors. Supervisors have frequently been admonished to operate

---

[1] Dan C. Lortie, *School Teacher: A Sociological Study* (Chicago: University of Chicago Press, 1975); Mary Lou Holly, "A Conceptual Framework for Personal-Professional Growth Implications for Inservice Education" Ph.D. dissertation, Michigan State University, 1977); Gilbert De Landsheere, "The Causes of the Resistance of Teachers to Innovation," in *The Teacher and Educational Change: A New Role*, vol. I (Paris: Organization for Economic Cooperation and Development, 1974).

from the authority of competence rather than the authority of position.[2] As a result, they are tempted to play down if not reject their formal organizational authority and behave in a clearly "helping" relationship, if not a collegial one. At the same time, teachers and teacher organizations, with a heightened sense of professionalism and a growing desire for control of their work, have also resisted the imposition of formal authority. Further, when either a helping relationship or one based on position power is not backed by technical competence, the rejection of authority becomes more complete. In addition, teacher negotiators attempt to gain collective bargaining contracts giving teachers as much control as possible over their work, the processes of instructional improvement, decision making on assignment, additional responsibilities, and, of course, employment and tenure.

In rejecting their legitimate authority, supervisors contribute to the problems of instructional improvement. While the authority of position is useless if not backed by technical skill and good human relations, a supervisor's competence is made more powerful when it is supported by the authority of position. Position authority will do little to strengthen an otherwise weak instructional supervisor, but an intelligent and competent supervisor can be even more effective when seen as having formal authority. When neither formal authority nor competence is present, instructional supervision is a hollow exercise, fully meriting the disdain and disregard with which many teachers view it. Under such circumstances, it is not surprising that intelligent and committed teachers turn to others for help in improving their instruction.

This chapter will explore the concept of colleagueship in supervision through discussion of the definition and purposes of instructional supervision, will describe the potential of colleagues and teacher collaboration as a professional development resource, and will conclude with a discussion of some of the organizational barriers to colleagueship in supervision.

Colleagueship and Formal Supervision

Supervision is a function found in all formal organizations; no organization can exist without it, yet the nature of the organization, its work system, and its purpose determine the form supervision takes. In most organizations, supervision occurs in close proximity to the work setting. In fact, it is from that proximity that supervision, in a generic sense, acquires its definition. In the strictest sense it means constant presence, overseeing or directing others, and monitoring their work in order to ensure effectiveness and efficiency. Supervision exists so that an organization's goals can be understood, procedures followed,

[2] Thomas J. Sergiovanni and Robert J. Starratt, *Supervision: Human Perspectives,* 2nd ed. (New York: McGraw-Hill, 1979), pp. 37-50; Arthur Blumberg, *Supervisors and Teachers: A Private Cold War,* 2nd ed. (Berkeley: McCutchan, 1980).

schedules met, and adjustments made when goals are not reached. Supervision is related to and responsible for the productive life of an organization. The purpose of supervision, then, is the same in all types of organizations: "To provide the conditions and promote the behavior necessary for the achievement of organizational goals."[3] The classic definition of supervision is to support and enhance an organization's work system and to ensure productivity, quality, and achievement of organizational goals. In all organizations, supervision is the critical link between organizational goals and production. Typically, the supervisor provides constant direction and help. Betts describes a supervisor as a person "who is given authority and responsibility for planning and controlling the work of the group by close contact. . . . Broadly speaking, this definition means that a supervisor may be delegated the authority to engage, transfer, suspend, reprimand, or dismiss an employee under his control."[4]

In the precise meaning of the term, there are probably very few supervisors in education. While many have the title, analysis of their behavior indicates a rather sharp divergence between what they do and the classic definition of supervision. But, as noted, the nature of an organization defines supervisory processes; one would not expect the supervisory structure in schools staffed by highly trained professionals to be the same as the supervisory structure on an assembly line in a large industrial plant. The greater the autonomy and right to make individual decisions in relation to one's work, the less "close-in" the supervision. Teachers seek and need control over their work and see themselves as professionals and independent decision makers. Therefore, supervision in schools is expected to be less frequent and more informal. While the classic definition of supervision also applies to supervision in schools, it must be recognized that the unique characteristics of schools and of teachers shape the form that supervision takes.

In schools, supervision is both a function and a role. Supervision is carried out by many persons; some carry the title of "supervisor," others do not. Those who carry the formal designation of supervisor seldom behave as supervisors 100 percent of the time; they frequently engage in managerial or administrative responsibilities only remotely related to the task of instructional improvement. On the other hand, there are those in school systems who carry administrative titles who occasionally engage in supervisory behavior. The function of supervision is generally widespread in schools, and there are times when teachers themselves engage in behaviors that could be described as supervisory.

If supervision is a function—not merely a role—to which many persons in a school contribute, then teachers can also be viewed as on

[3] Robert J. Alfonso, Gerald R. Firth, and Richard F. Neville, *Instructional Supervision: A Behavior System*, 2nd ed. (Boston: Allyn & Bacon, 1981), p. 6.

[4] Peter Betts, *Supervisory Studies* (London: MacDonald and Evans, 1968), pp. 6-7.

occasion contributing to the purposes of supervision. *Contributing* to supervision and carrying out *formal* responsibilities for supervision are two different things. In the technical sense of formally-conferred organizational authority, a teacher cannot be a supervisor; when such organizational authority is granted, the teacher then leaves an instructional role—ceasing to be a teacher—and enters a supervisory one. Given the classic definition of supervision (control, direction, assignment, evaluation) teachers cannot also be supervisors. Supervision is a formal organizational act; moreover, supervision always implies a superordinate-subordinate relationship. The terms "peer supervision" and "colleague supervision" may be contradictions, for one cannot be both a peer/colleague and a supervisor at the same time. Clearly, teachers can and should help each other in a variety of ways, but a supervisor is vested with organizational authority for decision making about others.

The profession at large and the Association for Supervision and Curriculum Development have long had difficulty accepting a concept that is so generally accepted in other organizations and professions. We have long struggled to make a supervisor a colleague of teachers rather than an authority figure, thus reducing the potential effectiveness and power of supervision.[5] Now the concept of "teacher as supervisor" is being explored. Such discussions blur the purpose and importance of supervision in organizations and mislead both supervisors and teachers about their respective roles.

A clear distinction needs to be made between the contributions of teachers to the improvement of instruction and the act of supervision as a formal, organizational expectation. For organizational purists, the concept of "teacher as supervisor" is impossible to accept. How one defines supervision, of course, has much to do with whether such a concept can be accepted. Given the blurred definitions of instructional supervision and the continued arguments about the extent of authority in such roles, the concept of peer or colleague supervision is an attractive one to many people. Without a clear understanding of formal supervision and of the possibilities and limitations of colleagueship, the continued discussion and promotion of greater roles for teachers in supervision may only further weaken the effectiveness of instructional supervision.

But formal supervision in schools is in short supply, and teachers, in helping, supporting, and assisting each other, can provide a valuable addition to formal supervision. Moreover, in work systems with a high

---

[5] Richard L. Foster, "Educational Supervision: Dead or Alive?" in *Changing Supervision for Changing Times* (Alexandria, Va.: Association for Supervision and Curriculum Development, 1969), p. 31; John C. Lovell. "A Perspective for Viewing Instructional Supervisory Behavior," in *Supervision: Perspectives and Proposition,* ed. William Lucio, (Alexandria, Va.: Association for Supervision and Curriculum Development, 1969), p. 18; Louise M. Berman and Mary Lou Usery, *Personalized Supervision.* (Alexandria, Va.: Association for Supervision and Curriculum Development, 1966), p. 49.

percentage of professionally trained personnel, colleagues commonly share knowledge in order to improve each other's practice.

Because it is so fragmented, instructional supervision is difficult to identify and describe; it is the responsibility of many persons, not just a few who hold the title of supervisor. While such a fragmented system of influence has some inherent weaknesses—lack of focus, inefficiency, mixed signals, and a certain haphazardness—it also has some strengths. Making persons at several levels responsible for the improvement of instruction can create links and, if effectively coordinated, requires dialog and cooperation among many persons. The nature of schools and the nature of the supervisory process within them not only make possible but require the active collaboration of teachers in the process of instructional improvement; they are a very important part of the process and an invaluable growth source for colleagues. Although teachers cannot be supervisors, their rich potential as a source for the growth of their colleagues has never been adequately tapped. A good supervisory program would fully utilize such a rich resource.

Colleagues as a Professional Development Resource

Does "colleagueship in supervision" refer to teams of supervisors working together to improve the effectiveness of schools and simultaneously to refine their own professional skills? Does it suggest that supervisors and teachers should pursue these ends in partnership? Or does it suggest that teachers should collaborate with one another for the same reasons? To all three questions, the answer is yes.

As used in this chapter, "colleagueship" refers to a relationship characterized by collaborative efforts to accomplish common goals. Collaboration implies both mutual involvement in identifying and selecting specific objectives and mutual responsibility for designing, implementing, and evaluating strategies to achieve these objectives. Common ownership of both the "targets" and the processes used to "hit them" is achieved through shared authority. Too often schools adopt a participative approach in the pursuit of predetermined objectives regardless of the appropriateness or importance of these targets *as perceived by the teachers*. The result is a flimsy facade of collaboration in which the only latitude given the individual teacher is how to comply. Such teacher participation is *not* an example of colleagueship since only nominal collaboration is used. Further, instead of producing common commitment to the task at hand, this artificial involvement of teachers in the decision making process is more apt to produce staff alienation.[6]

A goal common to both teachers and supervisors is instructional improvement. When a supervisor and a teacher (or group of teachers) cooperatively interact to identify and implement changes that will

---

[6] Sydney Thompson, "Motivation of Teachers." ERIC document, ED 78 009, 1979.

positively influence student educational growth, and when these decisions are made jointly, irrespective of formal authority, they are operating in colleagueship. Sergiovanni and Starratt state that "Neither the teacher's autonomy as a professional nor the supervisor's responsibilities as a professional are compromised in the process since the relationship is based not on authority but on a commitment to professional improvement."[7]

Advantages of Colleagueship

Three advantages of developing colleagueship in supervision are noteworthy. First, the human resources of the school are mobilized in a joint effort to improve instruction. Second, the long overdue recognition that classroom teachers have much to contribute to the quest for instructional improvement, coupled with increased responsibility for the design and implementation of improvement strategies, can produce a sense of personal achievement as well as a better functioning school. Recognition, responsibility, and achievement are termed "motivators" by Herzberg and are associated with job satisfaction.[8] Therefore, successful colleagueship may well contribute to increased job satisfaction for classroom teachers. In an era when teacher turnover is low and when "burn-out" is a growing problem, increasing the intrinsic rewards of teaching might be the single greatest contribution of colleagueship.

Third, the successful introduction of instructional innovations is more likely in schools having active colleagueship. Berman and McLaughlin report that the quality of working relationships among classroom teachers has a powerful effect on the effective implementation and continuation of projects involving educational change.[9] A history of collaboration among teachers and supervisors would likely contribute greatly to good working relationships. Further, successful collaborative efforts may well enhance teachers' perceptions of their own professional competence by reinforcing their belief that they can positively influence the achievement of their students. This sense of efficacy also has a powerful positive effect on the success of innovations in schools.[10]

Recognizing the potential contributions to instructional improvement through teacher collaboration, instructional supervisors must assume responsibility for fostering such interaction. Merely providing structured opportunities for teachers to share and to reflect upon their accumulation of "ordinary knowledge" (discussed by McNeil in Chapter 2 of this volume) would be a fruitful first step in harnessing and

---

[7] Sergiovanni and Starratt, *Supervision,* p. 298.

[8] Frederick Herzberg, as cited in Sergiovanni and Starratt, p. 164.

[9] Paul Berman and Milbrey Wallin McLaughlin, *Federal Programs Supporting Educational Change, Vol. VIII: Implementing and Sustaining Innovations* (Santa Monica, Calif.: Rand Corporation, 1978).

[10] *Ibid.*

coordinating the vast human resources available in schools. The onus for providing the leadership and coordination necessary to develop a climate conducive to and the impetus for such collaboration belongs to instructional supervisors. It will not be an easy task. Because channels of communication among teachers are typically so poorly developed, concerted effort is necessary to develop active collaboration.[11]

Leadership in the Development of Colleagueship

While colleagueship among administrators within a school district, and even among representatives of several school districts, is desirable in order to coordinate common activities, the focus in this chapter is on developing colleagueship within a *single* school. Not only does the proximity of educators in a single building enhance the opportunity for regular collaboration, but "there is increasing evidence that shows the largest unit of successful change in education is the individual school."[12]

Given the poorly-developed channels of communication in schools, the development of colleagueship where it has long been absent is a substantial change for most schools. Introducing and developing active collaboration within a school is, therefore, an ambitious, innovative project. Berman and McLaughlin comment that "The importance of the principal to both the short- and long-run outcomes of innovative projects can hardly be overstated."[13] The necessity for active support from the building principal in developing a working colleagueship in supervision seems obvious. The development of the shared leadership characteristic of colleagueship demands committed effort from the school's formal leadership.[14] According to Blumberg, "The higher the value the principal places on, *and behaves in,* an openly communicative and collaborative style, the more teachers will be inclined to risk being open and collaborative [Emphasis added]."[15] By openly espousing and modeling collegial interaction, the building principal provides needed support for the development of colleagueship—necessary, but not sufficient, impetus for change. In addition to the visible commitment of the school leadership, structured opportunities for meaningful, collaborative interaction are also needed.

The formation of staff groups to address ad hoc concerns, as discussed by Sergiovanni in Chapter 8 of this volume, suggests one

[11] Robert S. Fox and Ronald Lippitt, "The Innovation of Classroom Mental Health Practices," in *Innovation in Education,* ed. Matthew B. Miles (New York: Bureau of Publications, Teachers College, Columbia University, 1964).

[12] Fred H. Wood and Steven R. Thompson, "Guidelines for Better Staff Development," *Educational Leadership* 37, 5 (February 1980): 375.

[13] Berman and McLaughlin, *Federal Programs.*

[14] David Weingast, "Shared Leadership—'The Damn Thing Works,' " *Educational Leadership* 37 (March 1980): 502-506.

[15] Blumberg, *Supervisors and Teachers,* p. 211.

forum in which collegial interaction can be modeled and developed. Whether the group is addressing classroom management, the language arts curriculum, or inquiry learning, the experiential base for collaborative effort is present. The role of the supervisor in such a group is to facilitate the collaborative process by drawing ideas and opinions from all participants and by contributing his or her own expertise as an active member of the group. Ideally, groups of this sort will generate, implement, *and then evaluate* innovative approaches. Through participation in this informal approach to action research, a teacher becomes an active partner both in designing potential instructional improvements and in assessing their impact. By sharing benefits or difficulties of implementation unique to their own classrooms, teachers assume a functional leadership role conducive to and characteristic of colleagueship. As the functional leadership of the group develops, the supervisor's role within the group shifts from primary initiator to one of more equal footing with the rest of the group. Frequently, teachers need individual help in translating innovative ideas into classroom practice and, in such cases, clinical supervision may prove invaluable.

Clinical supervision emphasizes and works to develop collegial relations between supervisors and teachers.[16] (Clinical supervision is discussed by Garman in Chapter 3.) Oversimplified, clinical supervision is a structured approach to classroom observation and conferral intended to help teachers evaluate and improve instructional performance. Jackson says:

As everyone who has been in charge of a classroom knows, it is very difficult to teach and to think about teaching at the same time. What is needed, therefore, is both the time and the tools for the teacher to conceptualize his experience, to imbue it with personal meaning in a way that alters his way of looking at his world and acting.[17]

Through the careful collection of classroom data and through collegial conferences in which the "personal meanings" of the teacher are emphasized, competent clinical supervison exemplifies colleagueship in supervision. Yet, properly done, clinical supervision requires expertise and time not currently available in most schools. While most schools could feasibly offer clinical supervision to a few teachers so that the technique is modeled and colleagueship demonstrated, staffing plans preclude delivering clinical supervision to all teachers who could profit from it. How then can teachers get the support necessary to analyze their classroom performance and to identify and implement needed improvements?

---

[16] Robert Goldhammer, *Clinical Supervision: Special Methods for the Supervision of Teachers* (New York: Holt, Rinehart and Winston, 1969); Morris Cogan, *Clinical Supervision* (Boston: Houghton Mifflin, 1973).

[17] Philip W. Jackson, "Old Dogs and New Tricks," in *Improving Inservice Education: Proposals and Procedures for Change,* ed. Louis J. Rubin (Boston: Allyn and Bacon, 1971).

Colleagueship Among Teachers

I would like one day to see schools in which teachers can function as professional colleagues, where a part of their professional role was to visit the classrooms of their colleagues, and to observe and share with them in a supportive, informed, and useful way what they have seen.[18]

The notion of practitioners collaborating with colleagues is certainly not new. In many occupations, interaction between co-workers directed toward improved peformance is expected and common, for example, among partners in a law firm, physicians in practice together, carpenters on a job site, or actors in a play. Interaction between and among teaching colleagues is not, per se, supervision, but when teachers exchange ideas regarding promising practices, when they seek out one another for counsel on an instructional problem, or when they simply provide encouragement after a particularly tough day, the major function of instructional supervision, to improve instruction, is being served. Unfortunately, these peer linkages among classroom teachers are usually ignored by the formal supervision system—leaving teachers on their own to develop these potentially helpful relationships. When teachers are unable to develop collaborative links with their colleagues, they are deprived of a powerful resource for professional growth and support. It is not surprising that words like lonely and isolated have described the job of teaching.[19]

The structure of schools, generally characterized by the bureaucratic features of formalization and stratification, further insulates the classroom teacher. Not only are teachers at work almost always separated from their colleagues but traditional bureaucratic structures generally provide minimal, if any, opportunities for meaningful dialog among teachers regarding the aims and means of the educational effort. Hage indicates that bureaucratically-oriented structures inhibit the adaptiveness and job satisfaction of workers.[20] In schools, where the structural characteristics of bureaucratic organizations are compounded by the physical isolation of teachers at work, the resultant dearth of professional interaction among teachers not only deprives them of a valuable tool for self-improvement, but also *deprives the school organization of a rich pool of human talent for organizational improvement efforts.* By developing collaborative networks among teachers and by providing structured opportunities for peer review, schools can enrich the organizational climate while providing classroom teachers a potentially powerful vehicle for instructional improvement:

[18] Elliot W. Eisner, "The Impoverished Mind," *Educational Leadership* 35 (May 1978): 622.

[19] Louis Kaplan, *Education and Mental Health* (New York: Harper and Row, 1971); Marc Robert, *Loneliness in the Schools (What to do About It)* (Niles, Ill.: Argus, 1973); Lortie, *School Teacher;* Blumberg, *Supervisors and Teachers;* Betty Dillon-Peterson and Bruce Joyce, "Staff Development/Organization Development—1981," in *Staff Development/Organization Development* (Alexandria, Va.: Association for Supervision and Curriculum Development, 1981).

The collegial relationships between and among teachers have been minimized and undersold as a means of growth. Given time and opportunity, teachers cannot only learn from each other, but also serve as confidantes for feedback on teaching approaches and as respondents to teaching philosophy and style. . . Without this opportunity, it is easy to retreat into a shell of secrecy and become defensive about teaching practice.[21]

In spite of the dearth of formal mechanisms for developing collegial support, teachers still report that their best sources for innovative ideas regarding their teaching are other teachers.[22] Recognition by supervisors that teachers turn to their teaching colleagues with problems and for new ideas is long overdue; it is time for supervisors to maximize the value of this collegial approach to professional growth by organizing and coordinating these collaborative efforts. A structured system of intervisitation is one way to start.

The value of observing the teaching methods, techniques, and styles of other teachers (intervisitation) has long been recommended as a professional development tool for teachers.[23] When combined with post-observation conferences, intervisitation offers a potentially powerful avenue for teacher collaboration directly pertaining to classroom practice. Evans attributed to intervisitation among teachers in British infant schools the successful development of self-analysis and continued improvement.[24] Roper, Deal, and Dornbush explored a system of intervisitation and peer evaluation among elementary teachers and reported that "teachers can and will help each other perform better on their jobs."[25]

The attractions of intervisitation as a vehicle for colleagueship to improve performance are: first, actual classroom performance is the basis for improvement; second, the observing teacher is in a position to note details that may elude the teacher who is absorbed with teaching; and, third, the observing teacher may improve his or her own teaching as a result of the intervisitation. However, teachers' skills in observing teaching and in conferring to analyze classroom events may not be adequately developed. Further, teachers who are unfamiliar with observation and conferral techniques may be reluctant to serve as observers, may resist broaching sensitive topics, or may do so in a manner that provokes alienation or defensiveness rather than collaboration.

[21] Charles Galloway and Edward Mulhern, "Professional Development and Self Renewal," in *A School for Tomorrow*, ed. Jack R. Frymier (Berkeley, Calif.: McCutchan, 1973).

[22] Gilbert DeLandsheere, "The Causes of the Resistance of Teachers to Innovation," in *The Teacher and Educational Change: A New Role*, Volume I. Paris: Organization for Economic Cooperation and Development, 1974; Sergiovanni and Starratt, *Supervision;* Blumberg, *Supervisors and Teachers.*

[23] Arvil S. Barr and William H. Burton, *The Supervision of Instruction* (New York: Appleton, 1926); Kimball Wiles, *Supervision for Better Schools* (Englewood Cliffs, N.J.: Prentice-Hall, 1955).

[24] Ellis D. Evans, *Contemporary Influences in Early Childhood Education* (New York: Holt, Rinehart, and Winston, 1975).

[25] Susan Roper, Terrence Deal, and Stanford Dornbush, "Collegial Evaluation of Classroom Teaching: Does It Work?" *Educational Research Quarterly* 1 (Spring 1976): 66.

Some writers recommend peer-delivered clinical supervision as a collaborative device to improve instruction.[26] Harris disagrees: "Those who argue that sensitive, competent teachers with limited training can guide the clinical supervision processes are engaging in wishful thinking."[27] Perhaps the controversy is one of semantics; it may well be inappropriate to refer to a system of peer review and conferral as clinical supervision. First, it is *not* supervision. As discussed earlier, supervision involves a superordinate-subordinate relationship. This is clearly not the case in peer review. (In fact, in our opinion, "peer supervision" is a contradiction in terms much like "democratic dictatorship.") Further, the originator of the term "clinical supervision," Morris Cogan, clearly establishes that the competencies needed by clinical supervisors are complex and difficult to master, requiring extended preparation and a "critically examined induction into practice."[28] Yet, Cogan makes equally clear that a central objective of clinical supervision is to develop within teachers the abilities to be analytical of teaching performance, to interact openly with others about teaching, and to be self-directing. Given teachers with these capabilities and realizing that clinical supervision can currently be offered to only a small number of teachers, is it wishful thinking to suggest that teachers who have benefited from clinical supervision could observe and confer with other teachers to mutual advantage? Goldhammer answers this question explicity: "The supervision we envision is intended to increase teachers' incentives and skills for self-supervision and for supervising professional colleagues."[29]

The limited research into systems of peer review based on the clinical supervision model is encouraging, although inconclusive. Simon briefly oriented teachers in an elementary school to clinical supervision in preparation for intervisitation.[30] Each teacher both observed and was observed by a fellow teacher, and Simon reported that teachers valued this approach.

In a study by Goldsberry, 15 elementary teachers from four schools in a single school district voluntarily participated in a semester-long course on colleague consultation, a form of peer-delivered clinical supervision.[31] During this training, each teacher was observed teaching for three cycles of consultation, served as an observer-consultant for

[26] John Withall and Fred H. Wood, "Taking the Threat Out of Classroom Observation and Feedback," *Journal of Teacher Education* 30 (January-February 1979): 55-58.

[27] Ben M. Harris. *Improving Staff Performance Through Inservice Education* (Boston: Allyn and Bacon, 1980).

[28] Cogan, *Clinical Supervision*, p. 10.

[29] Goldhammer, *Clinical Supervision*, p. 55.

[30] Alan E. Simon, "Peer Supervision: An Alternative," paper presented at the Annual Conference, Association for Supervision and Curriculum Development, Detroit, March 3, 1979.

[31] Lee F. Goldsberry, "Colleague Consultation: Teacher Collaboration Using a Clinical Supervision Model" (Ed. D. dissertation, University of Illinois, Urbana-Champaign, 1980); Lee F. Goldsberry, "Colleague Consultation: Instructional Supervisor Augmented," in *Critical Policy Issues in Contemporary Education: An Administrator's Overview,* ed. Louis J. Rubin (Boston: Allyn and Bacon, 1980).

three cycles, and monitored three cycles of consultation. During the semester following the training, 13 of the 15 teachers trained as colleague consultants paired with teachers in their schools who had not participated in the training and delivered six cycles of colleague consultation. All 13 teachers who received the colleague consultation reported it to be helpful. Twelve of these teachers specified some change in their approach as a result of the experience: nine specified changes in actual teaching practice; three reported altered classroom structures or increased awareness of aspects of their teaching. Three of the 13 teachers who served as colleague consultants reported the experience did not affect their own teaching; five reported the experience had a positive effect on their attitude toward teaching or being observed; the remaining five reported performance improvements made as a result of the experience. Teachers involved in this study specifically mentioned increased colleagueship as a benefit of their participation.

When teachers collaborate with one another, the role of the supervisor is altered but not at all diminished. Initially, the supervisor is the catalyst for organizing colleagueship among teachers. The supervisor must provide training in observation and conferral techniques, must model both the techniques and colleagueship, and must arrange time for training and for peer review and conferral. As peer review is implemented, the supervisor serves both as a resource for process improvement and as the initiator and model for evaluation of the process. The leadership demanded of a supervisor in a school with active colleagueship is greater than that required in the traditional bureaucratic school because the complexity of coordinating the involved professionals in an adaptive situation cannot be done through generating formal rules, or even standardized procedures. Ample time, zealous effort, and a tolerance for frustration are necessary to develop and maintain colleagueship in supervision. The payoff is active involvement in a collaborative effort to improve instruction — to think that meaningful improvement can occur without such an investment is truly wishful thinking.

Organizational Barriers to Colleagueship

This chapter, thus far, has explored the concept of colleagueship in supervision, the distinction between colleague contributions and formal supervision, and colleagues as a resource for professional development. While colleagues are, without doubt, a valuable resource and can make important contributions to the processes of instructional improvement, there are obstacles to the development of colleagueship. Chapter 11 of this book details the numerous ways school bureaucracy inhibits the development and implementation of supervision. While the discussion of bureaucratic structures deals primarily with their impact on formal processes of supervision, school organization structure also poses problems for the development of colleagueship in supervision. The typical workday of a teacher, the inadequate time for interaction with colleagues, the cellular organization, and the physical structure of most school buildings—compartmentalizing each teacher in a room almost impervious to the influence or observation of colleagues—all work against the concept of colleagueship in supervision as discussed in this chapter.

If one were to design a physical structure and a workday that would virtually guarantee isolation from one's colleagues, one could hardly find a better model than a typical school building and the typical workday of a teacher. If teachers are to be resources in a program of instructional supervision, barriers of time and distance and the tradition of privacy will have to be overcome. With some exceptions, schools are not characterized by a high level of professional interaction among staff. The use of colleagues as a resource for professional development requires a modification in school organization as well as school climate. Historically, many attempts to involve teachers in curriculum planning and instructional improvement have failed because of time constraints; teachers have been asked to add new responsibilities to an already full schedule or squeeze work sessions into an inadequate time span. In order for colleagueship in supervision to be truly effective, a more professional model of teaching and an improved teaching environment must emerge. While time and work load are certainly barriers, another obstacle to colleagueship is the kind of expectations a school system has for teachers. If teachers are not viewed and treated as professionals, they cannot be expected to be effective in assisting colleagues in instructional improvement. A high level of professional behavior first requires a parallel level of professional respect and treatment.

The prevailing milieu of the school is also a barrier to colleagueship. When hired, teachers seldom see themselves as joining a teaching team, since other teachers are rarely involved in the interview and selection process. Neither does the faculty see the new person as joining a team, and they feel little or no responsibility for helping to ensure the success of a new teacher. As a result, experienced teachers seldom share effective practices with new colleagues. A new teacher quickly seeks to establish an identity, built on a grade assignment, a teaching discipline, and a classroom—a domain that becomes a private enclave and a retreat from the outside world as well as, in some cases, a retreat from the world within the school. A call for colleagueship in supervision is also a call, then, for new organizational forms and patterns of interaction in schools.

In some cases, there is not only a lack of communication and interaction among teachers, but a deliberate effort to avoid sharing good ideas. Administrative and supervisory staff are in large measure responsible for the kind of climate that exists in a school. If a climate exists in which teachers feel they are in competition, they will seek advantage over others by holding on to good ideas. Research indicates that in competitive professions and businesses, ideas are seldom shared.[32] Doctors, for example, may share new ideas on medical practice but restaurant owners do not share recipes. Leadership behavior creates similar behavior patterns among followers, and administrators and supervisors are responsible for creating the kind of climate in schools that contributes to or inhibits colleagueship. The absence of colleagueship and sharing of practices is an unhappy commentary on a group of people who, in fact, all serve the same client or clients.

In school systems operating under collective bargaining agreements, there may be additional barriers to teacher collaboration for instructional improvement. While collective bargaining agreements could be written in ways that recognize and support such efforts, an analysis of agreements indicates they generally restrict rather than support such work.[33] Agreements typically specify the number of hours a year during which teachers can be asked to engage in instructional improvement and the amount of advance notification needed, the maximum length of any one meeting, how observations shall be reported, the number of classroom observations allowed per year, and who should be involved in an evaluation conference. While these are only a few examples of provisions in contracts, the kind of prescription and rigidity that charcterizes most negotiated contracts works against the climate and openness necessary to develop colleagueship. Teachers and supervisory personnel will have to find ways of working within the constraints of collective bargaining agreements and, if a supervisor is to be a contributing partner in colleagueship in supervision, then certain kinds of supervisory involvement may need to be viewed as falling outside the terms of the contract and, therefore, not in conflict. In cases where collective bargaining or other issues create sharp divisions and a "we-they" attitude between teachers and administrators, rigid adherence to the terms of a contract will make colleagueship far more difficult. Supervisors need to create formal communication systems that are unaffected by contract provisions, and the promise of colleagueship is that teachers, themselves, can help create such systems and initiate involvement with their colleagues—involvement which, if promoted formally by supervisors, might be seen as violating contract provisions.

The secondary school poses special problems for those interested in colleagueship in supervison. Long a bastion of privacy and independence, a feifdom presided over by the strong figure of the principal, the high school has always been difficult terrain for the instructional supervisor to navigate. The majority of research and development in supervision has taken place in elementary schools, and writers

[32] Herbert F. Lionberger, "Diffusion of Innovations in Agricultural Research and in Schools," in *Strategy For Curriculum Change* (Alexandria, Va.: Association for Supervision and Curriculum Development, 1965), p. 45.

[33] Alfonso, Firth, and Neville, *Instructional Supervision,* pp. 441-452.

in the field of supervison continue to neglect the high school.

The high school and its faculty are fragmented by both departmental structure and by the orientation of the faculty to their teaching field. Such departmentalization works against communication, against the open-door classroom, and against schoolwide efforts of instructional improvement. In contrast with elementary teachers, secondary teachers are less interested in inservice programs and maintain a far more private world of teaching.

Yet, despite these constraints to instructional improvement and supervision, high schools offer unique opportunities not found in elementary schools. The failure of the profession has been its lack of recognition of the unique characteristics of secondary schools and the dynamics of life within them. Effective supervision in secondary schools and effective colleagueship in supervision require that attention be directed to those issues that are of most concern to high school faculty. They must be met on their own "turf," and for them this is the discipline they studied and have been hired to teach. While there may be other concerns that supervisors and administrators believe to be of critical concern, the entre must almost always be through the teaching field.

It is the teaching field that provides commonality and colleagueship among high school teachers, and the compartmentalization of the disciplines in the high school that so frequently makes instructional supervision difficult, can work as a valuable aid in developing a program of colleagueship as a resource. The high school department, for example, can become the initial unit for colleagueship in supervision, and the department chairperson can play a critical role in developing the climate and process to bring it about. The field of instructional supervision has rather badly neglected the department chairperson; yet, the chairperson is in a unique position to provide the kind of "close in" supervision that resembles the classic definition of supervision. Moreover, the chairperson has the unique ability to make a major contribution to the development of colleagueship as a resource for professional development, as a chairperson is one of the few individuals in the school system who is seen both as a colleague and a supervisor. The chairperson is daily involved in the teaching act, yet also has daily responsibility for providing leadership for a faculty group.

The secondary school, generally viewed as unresponsive to instructional improvement efforts, might in fact—when properly understood—be a very fertile ground for the development of the concept of colleagueship in supervision.

Summary and Conclusion

"Colleagueship" has been defined in this chapter as a relationship characterized by collaborative efforts to accomplish the common goal of instructional improvement. "Supervision" denotes a function characterized by a superordinate working through and in close proximity with subordinates to accomplish organizational goals. For instructional improvement—the primary mission of supervision in education—to be successful, the active cooperation of teachers is essential. The development of colleagueship between teachers and supervisors and among teachers seems to offer three major benefits: 1. mobilization of the human resources of the school for the formidable task of instructional improvement; 2. increased intrinsic rewards to and hence job satisfaction for teachers; and 3. increased likelihood of successful implementation of instructional innovations.

The individual school is recommended as the largest administrative unit in which to initiate efforts to develop colleagueship, although in some high schools the department may well be the place to begin. Active support from the building principal is crucial for successful development of colleagueship. Instructional supervisors must assume responsibility for initiating collaborative, collegial interaction. Ad hoc groups and clinical supervision are two vehicles for developing and employing colleagueship in a supervisor-teacher relationship.

As a complement to formal supervision, structured opportunities for teachers to collaborate with other teachers offer great potential for professional development and instructional improvement. Colleagueship among teachers is typically ignored, and often inhibited, by the school's formal organization; consequently, teachers are frequently isolated from their colleagues. This isolation, combined with the dearth of supervisory support, drastically impedes the professional development of even the most conscientious and dedicated teachers. Despite a paucity of research, evidence indicates that systems of intervisitation or colleague consultation seem promising and are valued by teachers.

Developing colleagueship in schools where it has been long absent will not be an easy task. The long accumulated inertia in schools characterized by secluded classrooms that are the private domains of individual teachers, by busy schedules and the time-consuming preparation required for effective teaching, and by organizations emphasizing formalization and stratification will require time and concerted effort to overcome. The counterproductive, adversarial competition between administration and teacher organizations, and among some teachers themselves, poses difficult obstacles to the development of active colleagueship in supervision. Organizational change requiring committed and patient leadership is needed to alter existing interaction patterns in schools. Colleagueship in supervision will necessarily lead to an altered, yet crucial role for instructional supervisors.

It is clear that if supervision is to be improved its base must be broadened. It is simply not possible for those who carry the formal title of supervisor to have any direct impact on large numbers of teachers. Over the years, despite best efforts, instructional supervision has remained a fragmented activity. It is often a response to a crisis or, in other cases, a routine of occasional visits to classrooms. On other occasions a major school or systemwide effort at instructional improvement is undertaken, only to terminate when the impetus or funding of the effort ceases.

The critical need for instructional supervision and the corresponding lack of formal supervision (some school systems report supervisor-teacher ratios of 1 to 200 or more) suggest a new role for supervisors. They might become "orchestrators" of instructional supervision, persons who serve a broker role in the school system, identifying needs and then selecting and recruiting from throughout the school or school system those persons who can contribute to specific tasks of instructional improvement. In so doing, formal supervision does not lose its tie with organizational goals, nor does it set aside its own authority base. On the contrary, it uses the authority of position as well as knowledge to identify teachers and others who possess experience and expertise uniquely appropriate to a particular task. Such persons may temporarily become members of instructional supervision teams, organized for the completion of a particular task, or may contribute a special ability over an extended period of time.

Such a concept recognizes the rich resources available among experienced teachers and helps create the kind of colleagueship that characterizes professions. We strongly endorse the use of colleagues as resources for professional development, but also recognize that the characteristics of schools make such colleagueship difficult. It is necessary that someone in the school system create a process for developing colleagueship, give it organizational approval, and ensure that it is directed both to the immediate, personal needs of teachers as well as to the long range goals of the organization. This is a uniquely appropriate role for the instructional supervisor.

This role may call for new skills, for it requires supervisors to work well not only with individual teachers but with groups of teachers and instructional supervisory teams. In becoming an orchestrator of instructional improvement resources, a supervisor does not give up authority, but rather makes more effective use of it. Formal resources are inadequate for the task at hand, while at the same time rich resources throughout the school system and in the broader school community remain untapped. In identifying and organizing such resources, the process of instructional supervision is made more powerful. In addition, the use of the rich talents of others in a school system—especially teachers—contributes to colleagueship and a heightened sense of cooperation and professionalism.

Chapter 8.
The Context for Supervision

Thomas J. Sergiovanni

OUR ASPIRATIONS IN ASCD ARE MORAL AND SOUND, our goals are firm, and our convictions are strong. Highly motivated, hard working, and growing teachers are key ingredients in effective teaching and schooling. These ideals are implicit in the Yearbook chapters by Valverde, Garman, and Alfonso and Goldsberry as they discuss the self-evolving supervisor, clinical supervision, and the concept of colleagueship in supervision. This chapter deals with the ideals of teacher growth and effective schooling by examining some important contextual issues. As supervisors, we need to show a broader concern for the human condition in the schools, one that reaches beyond immediate strategies for working effectively with teachers to the richer context of organizational life.

How can we provide a context for supervision that best supports teacher growth and development on the one hand and that releases the energy and talents of teachers to the fullest on the other? This is the question that will be addressed. In mind is a commitment from teachers broader than achieving mere self-satisfaction and aggrandizement. Individual indulgence and personal self-fulfillment are neither sufficient or key. Needed is satisfaction and fulfillment that stem from a common ideal and a common commitment to quality schooling and a delight in having achieved something substantial on behalf of the school and its students. To this effort, fulfillment of a personal nature is secondary to that of fulfilling student and school needs, and personal growth comes to be linked closer with professional growth.[1]

Two aspects of the context for supervision will be discussed: climate and structure. Though other contextual aspects exist (the political environment and governance arrangements, for example) climate and structure can be readily influenced by supervisors and others directly responsible for instructional programs. The context we need will result from: school climates that evolve from an emphasis on

[1] See, for example, Christopher Lasch, *The Culture Narcissism: American Life in an Age of Diminishing Expectations* (New York: Norton, 1978).

Thomas J. Sergiovanni is Professor and Chairperson, Department of Educational Administration and Supervision at the University of Illinois, Urbana-Champaign.

human relations to human resources; structures that evolve from an emphasis on the school as a professional bureaucracy to a professional ad hocracy.

The contextual aspects of supervision will be discussed unevenly. I have written before of the need for school climates to evolve from human relations based principles to those of human resources.[2] Views on these matters will, therefore, be only summarized. Greater attention will be given to the role of structure as it relates to supervisory effectiveness. To now the professional bureaucracy has been advocated as a viable and necessary alternative to more traditional and delimiting bureaucratic structures. It is time to move beyond this form of thinking about school organization and structure. To this end the professional ad hocracy will be examined as a possible viable alternative to organizing schools.

From Human Relations to Human Resources

Perhaps no professional organization deserves more credit than ASCD for championing the human dimension in educational administration, supervision, curriculum, and instruction. This is a proud heritage which has questioned and challenged the traditional bureaucratic school structure with its emphasis on management and control. The original vehicle for this challenge was the ideology of human relations. Unlike traditional management control practices that viewed teachers as appendages of management hired to carry out prescribed duties in accordance with the wishes and directions of management, human relations suggested that teachers be viewed as whole persons in their own right. Human relations supervisors, for example, work to create a feeling of satisfaction among teachers by showing an interest in them as people. It is believed that a satisfied staff works harder and is easier to work with, to lead, and to control. Providing for high morale, good group relationships, and a friendly atmosphere are considered important. Shared decision-making is practiced as a means to let teachers feel that they are appreciated and involved. Speaking to the role of supervisor Kimball Wiles, perhaps the best known advocate of human relations practices in supervision, noted "they are, above all, concerned with helping people to accept each other, because they know that when individuals value each other, they will grow through their interaction together and will provide a better emotional climate for pupil growth. Supervisor's role has become *supporting*, *assisting*, and *sharing* rather than directing."[3]

---

[2] Thomas J. Sergiovanni, "Human Resource Supervision" in *Professional Supervision for Professional Teachers*, ed. Thomas J. Sergiovanni (Alexandria, Va.: Association for Supervision and Curriculum Development, 1975), pp. 9-13.

[3] Kimball Wiles, *Supervision for Better Schools*, 3rd edition (Englewood Cliffs, N.J.: Prentice Hall, 1967).

Human relations views, still popular among many within the ASCD community, represent a definite improvement over more traditional management control views.[4] But human relations is limited by its inability to provide teachers with maximum opportunity for professional growth and to fully unleash the talents and interests of teachers. Human relations focuses primarily on humankinds' lower order needs. Interpersonal climate and social needs of teachers are paramount. Achievement, challenge, responsibility, and feedback from accomplishment do not receive sufficient attention, though recent evidence indicates that these have the greatest potential for providing lasting and meaningful satisfaction to teachers as well as providing important benefits to the school.

Human resources views, by contrast, seek to better integrate the needs of individuals with the work of the school. The assumptions underlying human resources practices can be summarized as follows:

1.   Teachers desire to contribute effectively and creatively to the accomplishments of worthwhile objectives.

2.   The majority of teachers are capable of exercising more initiative, responsibility, and creativity than their present jobs or circumstances allow.

3.   Supervisors should work to help teachers contribute their full range of talents to the accomplishment of school goals.

4.   Supervisors should encourage teachers to participate in important as well as routine decisions. Indeed the more important the decision the greater should be the supervisor's efforts to tap faculty resources.

5.   The quality of decisions made will improve as supervisors and teachers make full use of the range of insight, experience, and creative ability that exists in their school.

6.   Teachers will exercise responsible self-direction and self-control in the accomplishment of worthwhile objectives that they understand and have helped create.[5]

A convergence of research from a variety of fields lends support to the relationship between enhanced teacher roles and performance increases of teachers and students. The human capital research of the Nobel prize-winning economist Theodore Schultz is an example. In lamenting the apparent shift from professional to job orientation of

---

[4] In many quarters we can find renewed interest in traditional management control views. Extremely rigid and heavily prescribed curriculum systems, highly segmented direct instructional systems, accountability designs, and blueprint-like evaluation systems are examples. These are proven methods for achieving low level objectives but widespread use limits critical rationality and other forms of intellectual activity and robs discretion from teachers, thus lessening the intrinsic interest of teaching.

[5] Adapted from Raymond E. Miles, "Human Relations or Human Resources," *Harvard Business Review* 43, 4(1965):153.

teachers in many school districts he notes, "Most of these manifestations of school teachers should have been anticipated in view of the way schools are organized and administered. The curriculum is not for them to decide; nor is the content of the courses to be taught and the plans to be followed. These decisions require the specialized talents of professional educators . . . . in assessing performance of teachers, it is a dictum of economics that incentives matter. School teachers are responding to the much circumscribed opportunities open to them as should be expected."[6] Upgrade the job, Schultz seems to suggest, and teacher performance will increase, which will contribute greatly to the improved quality of schooling.

The research of organizational analysts Litwin and Stringer is suggestive as well.[7] They contrasted the climates of traditional bureaucratic, human relations,and human resources organizations, noting that traditional bureaucratic leadership was associated with closed climates; human relations leadership with warm, supportive, and friendly climates; and human resources leadership with supportive, goal-oriented climates. These results are summarized in Figure 1. Note that satisfaction is very high where human relations is emphasized, but performance is low. The human resources climate seemed most associated with high performance and innovation and provided a good deal of satisfaction to individuals as well.

Perhaps the most convincing support for human resources views comes from job enrichment research. The work of Hackman and Oldham is an example.[8] The job enrichment model they propose is shown in Figure 2. Their research suggests that personal and work outcomes such as intrinsic motivation, high quality work performance, high satisfaction with work, and low absenteeism are a function of the presence in individuals of three psychological states: *Experienced meaningfulness of the work, experienced responsibility for work outcomes, and knowledge of results.* Further, five job characteristics that evoke these psychological states are identified. Three of the characteristics — skill variety, task identity, and task significance — combine additively to determine meaningfulness. Autonomy, a fourth job characteristic, is associated with feelings of responsibility. Feedback, a final job characteristic proposed by these researchers, is associated with knowledge of results.

The job enrichment model suggests that in teaching, jobs that re-

[6] Theodore W. Schultz, "Human Capital Approaches in Organizing and Paying for Education," paper presented at the "Efficiency and Equity in Educational Finance National Symposium," University of Illinois, Urbana-Champaign, May 3-5, 1979.

[7] George H. Litwin and Robert A. Stringer, Jr., *Motivation and Organizational Climate* (Boston: Harvard University, Division of Research, Graduate School of Business, 1968).

[8] J.R. Hackman and Grey Oldham, "Motivation Through the Design of Work: Test of a Theory," *Organizational Behavior and Human Performance* 16, 2(1976):250-279. See also "Job Enrichment as a Motivational Strategy," Chapter 7 in T.J. Sergiovanni and Fred D. Carver, *The New School Executive, 2nd edition,* (New York: Harper and Row, 1980) pp. 123-134.

Figure 1. Leadership, Climate, and Effectiveness: Litwin and Stringer

Leadership	Climate	Effectiveness
Bureaucratic leadership	Closed	Performance low Satisfaction low
Human relations leadership	Warm Supportive Friendly	Performance low Satisfaction very high Innovation high
Human resources Leadership ·	Supportive Goal-oriented	Performance very high Satisfaction high Innovation very high

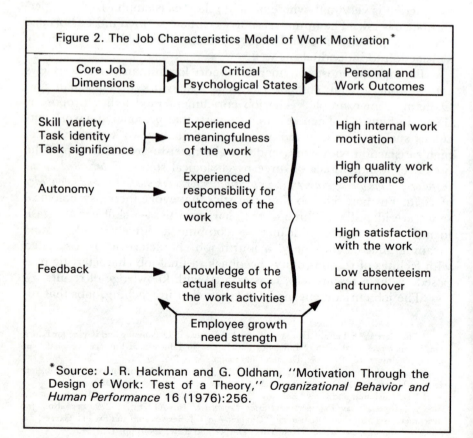

Figure 2. The Job Characteristics Model of Work Motivation*

*Source: J. R. Hackman and G. Oldham, "Motivation Through the Design of Work: Test of a Theory," *Organizational Behavior and Human Performance* 16 (1976):256.

quire different activities in carrying out the work and the use of a variety of teacher talents and skills (skill variety); require that teachers engage in holistic or complete and identifiable tasks (task identity); are viewed by teachers as having a substantial and significant impact on the lives or work of other people (task significance); provide substantial freedom, independence, and direction to individual teachers in scheduling work and in deciding classroom organizational and instructional procedures (autonomy); and provide teachers with direct and clear information about the effects of their performance (feedback), are likely to evoke the psychological states of meaningfulness, responsibility, and knowledge of results. These in turn, the research of Hackman and Oldham suggests, will result in high work motivation, high quality performance, high job satisfaction, and low absenteeism among teachers.

Beyond the Professional Bureaucracy

Schools are professional bureaucuracies. Unlike the traditional bureaucracy where management control is direct and worker behavior is orchestrated by a system of close supervision, the professional bureaucracy is characterized by a great deal of decentralization and supervision is general at best.[9] In schools teachers are considered to be expert specialists who, because of their professional training and certification, should be provided with discretion in their work. Teachers work individually and without supervision. They work independently of other teachers and support staff but closely with students. As Bidwell observes, "Teacher autonomy is reflected in the structure of school systems, resulting in what may be called their structural looseness. The teacher works alone within the classroom, relatively hidden from colleagues and supervisors, so that he has a broad discretionary jurisdiction within the boundaries of the classroom."[10] Professional bureaucracy shares with other organizational designs certain universal characteristics necessary to survival. The work of all organizations, for example, must be coordinated in order for tasks to be accomplished and organizational goals realized. Mintzberg[11] suggests that organizations can choose from among five coordinating mechanisms as follows:

Direct supervision whereby one person takes responsibility for the work of others. This is the traditional superordinate-subordinate relationship possible only in the simplest organizations.

---

[9] Clearly a range of organizational types can be found among schools with some being quite mechanistic or machine-like in their bureaucratic form but, by and large, schools as a group can be considered professional bureaucracies.

[10] Charles E. Bidwell, "The School as a Formal Organization," in *The Handbook of Organization*, ed. James G. March (New York: Rand McNally, 1965), pp. 975-976.

[11] Henry Mintzberg, *The Structuring of Organization* (Englewood Cliffs, N.J.: Prentice Hall, Inc.), pp. 1-16.

Standardization of work processes whereby the contents of work are specified and arranged programatically as in the case of highly programed and "teacher proof" curriculum formats and in many forms of "direct" instruction.

Standardization of work outputs whereby results, objectives, and other products of work are clearly specified and teachers are held accountable for meeting these specifications.

Standardization of skills whereby professionals and other workers are provided with common training and education and/or common socialization to ensure reliability in their response to organizational problems. (Medical doctors, for example, are trained in such a fashion that several will respond reliably in their diagnosis of a similar case.)

Mutual adjustment whereby coordination of work is accomplished by the process of informal communications among groups of workers involved interdependently in the actual work of the organization.

Given the discretion accorded to teachers in the professional bureaucracy and the fact that work is typically accomplished by individuals separate and invisible from others, direct supervision is not a viable coordinating mechanism. Standardizing the socialization and the skills of teachers through universal and systematic pre- and inservice education is seen as a highly desirable coordinating mechanism by many. But a universally-acknowledged view of teaching does not exist and ideological debates suggest that we characterize teaching as a low level technology at best. Certainly, when compared to the sciences of medicine and engineering or the arts of drama and painting, common socialization and standardization of skill in eduation, seem less developed.

The school as a professional bureaucracy relies heavily on the standardization of work processes and the standardization of outputs as coordinating mechanisms. These, in turn, delimit the one virtue offered by the professional bureaucracy as an organizational design for schools — teacher discretion or teacher autonomy. When coupled with discretion, standardization of work processes and outputs leaves us with the unhappy picture of teachers being free to do as they please in the classroom *providing* they follow the same curriculum, keep to the same schedule, and accomplish the same outcomes. What differs from class to class is not substance, but style. Chair arrangements, classroom rules, the small range of teaching styles permitted by the standard curriculum, combined with certain personality characteristics that individual teachers bring to their classroom and variance in teacher competence account for differences. The differences that do exist as one moves from classroom to classroom are very important, but insufficient. Indeed what results in many cases from relying primarily on the standardization of teaching work processes and teaching output in order to achieve coordination is less enriched jobs for teachers with probable negative effects on student learning. A sense of ownership among teachers is lost. Teaching becomes a routine activity. Teachers become followers of directions rather than diagnosticians and become implementors rather than creators. As suggested earlier in reference to the work of the economist Schultz, we are only now beginning to understand the effects on student achievement of such developments for teachers.

Other problems associated with the concept of professional bureaucracy as a design for schools result from the discretion that teachers have independent from other professionals and from working in isolation from other professionals. Feedback is a common dimension in most job enrichment models and is extremely difficult to obtain in a natural way and in a continuous fashion under these conditions. Certainly indirect supervision exists as part of a system of standardizing work processes and outputs. But this is a controlling and restrictive form of supervision that seeks reliability in teacher behavior rather than teacher growth. To this indirect system of supervision is added a system of direct supervision characterized by formal classroom observation often of a summative nature. But this formal system seems out of place in a supposedly collegial organization characterized by a great deal of teacher discretion.

In sum, discretion combined with the coordinating mechanisms of work standardization and standardization of teaching outputs presents a paradox. Appearances to the contrary, true teacher discretion may well be wanting in the school organized as a professional bureaucracy. Teacher discretion is itself an issue separate from linkages with coordinating mechanisms. Typically, teachers work independently of other professionals. What one teacher does day-by-day seems not to be dependent upon what other professionals are doing. Further, classrooms are private places and, typically, the work of a teacher is not visible to other professionals. Thus feedback and other job enrichment characteristics are difficult to obtain and supervision is difficult to implement. Affording wide discretion to professionals low in the organization is its chief virtue. But in occupations such as teaching, where neither the art or science of technique or the undergirding values are fully developed or widely accepted, schools cannot rely primarily on common socialization or common professional skill as a coordinating mechanism.

Coordinating the work of individuals toward some overall purpose is a universal requirement of all organizations. Thus, to obtain coordination, the school provides for standardizing the work of teachers and for detailing specifically the outcomes of teaching. Paradoxically, these forms of coordination constrain the discretional prerogatives of teachers. They are free to do as they please providing that they stick to the schedule, follow the prescribed curriculum, and achieve standard outcomes. We can do better for both teacher and student. An important step in this direction is to move beyond the professional bureaucracy to more satisfying and more effective organizational designs for schools.

Toward a Professional Ad Hocracy

How can we provide a context for supervision that best supports teacher growth and development on the one hand, and that releases the energy and talents of teachers to the fullest on the other? The professional bureacracy has contributed a great deal to this quest, but the benefits of this design have leveled in such a fashion that it appears as though dysfunctions are now dominant. The logical evolution of the professional bureaucratic design, I believe, is to move closer to the professional ad hocracy.[12] The fully developed ad hocracy has a number of features that distinguish it from other organizational designs:

1.   The ad hocracy is a temporary system designed with a specific life to solve a particular set of problems.

2.   Solving new problems is more important than perfecting ways of accomplishing standard routines and ends.

3.   Professionals are drawn from a variety of disciplines or specializations and placed into ad hoc teams.

4.   Coordination is achieved by a process of *mutual adjustment* and is based on felt-needs of people working together. An assumption basic to mutual adjustment is that experts bring diverse talents and specialities to work; that they are interdependent and thus must cooperate to be successful.

Let's examine these characteristics seeking implications suitable for adaption to schools. Keep in mind that I propose not to replace the professional bureaucracy but to modify it in the direction of an ad hocracy.

First some educational program considerations. We now organize the curriculum primarily into subject matter modules according to the logic of the disciplines and, indeed, this strategy makes sense. But the problems we face today are increasingly interdisciplinary. The curriculum of the future will of necessity be more integrative, combining the disciplines in the study of complex problems. As this occurs, a matrix type design or other *ad hoc* arrangements will become increasingly popular in schools. This design permits the incorporation of features of ad hocracy as part of the professional bureaucracy. Teachers in a high school could be grouped into teams, each assigned a group of students. Teams would be responsible for planning, implementing, and evaluating an educational program for students that utilizes the

---

[12] See, for example, Warren G. Bennis, "Post-Bureaucratic Leadership," *Transaction*, July-August 1969; Alvin Toffler, *Future Shock* (New York: Bantam Books, 1970); and Mintzberg, *The Structuring of Organization*, pp. 431-468.

cooperative talents of team members. Teams could be formed in accordance with a variety of themes. Some could provide a particular academic or vocational emphasis but with members whose specialties vary. Some teams could have members with matched skills who simply operate as schools within schools. One need not fear for loss of traditional instruction by disciplines. Teachers could be organized, as well, into traditional administrative and disciplinary homes (English or math departments, for example). The school could offer traditional instruction by department for part of the time, and interdisciplinary or other theme instruction by teams for part of the time (alternate days, half days). Some faculty members could work primarily under department arrangements and others in ad hoc teams. We are not breaking new ground here. Teaching teams and other grouping patterns have been proposed before[13] and though noticeable, are not widespread in schools. These plans need to be examined anew and further developed in the direction of ad hocracy. Viable educational programs of the future will require such designs. Higher education will not be immune from pressures to integrate the disciplines. Consider the following excerpt from the recent and prestigious Club of Rome policy study on learning:

Some reorganization of academic and administrative structures should be reconsidered to combine university departments according to issues rather than only and always according to disciplines. These newly constituted groupings could be considered as task forces, to be dissolved once their original objective is attained and to be recombined when new objectives are sought. Teaching, as well as research work, could then be organized around broad themes, . . . reducing the present segmentation and sectorialization of the curricula. Such a focus would bring the university closer to the basic concerns of society. It would . . . introduce some vital issues currently underemphasized on the university agenda — such as rural development, malnutrition, unemployment, illiteracy, housing, and juvenile dilinquency. These are but a few of the areas which require research and practical action and where the university population of students and teachers alike could be of great significance.[14]

The curricular implications of adopting features of an ad hocracy are rich and interesting but space does not permit further elaboration. The emphasis here is on supervisory and staff development implications, and this is the theme of the next section.

Supervision in the Professional Bureaucracy-Ad Hocracy

The key feature of ad hocracy that is attractive to supervision is mutual adjustment as a coordinating mechanism for operational teams. It is assumed, of course, that team members are well trained but that

[13] Team Teaching, IGE groups, middle school clusters, and schools within a school are all examples with features of ad hocracy.

[14] James W. Botkin, Mahdi Elmandjra, and Mircea Malitza, *No Limits to Learning: Bridging the Human Gap* (London: Pergaman Press, 1979) as quoted in Judith Barnet, "Learning: In Crisis the World Over," *Phi Delta Kappan* 61, 2(1979):113.

skills need not be standard. Further, little reliance is placed on standardizing or specifying detailed standard outputs. Since specialists on a team bring different skill emphases and since they need to cooperate with one another, they are forced into a system of mutual adjustment through communicating informally as they plan, teach, and evaluate together. Being interdependent often requires that individual autonomy be sacrificed. Wide discretion is given to the team as a whole, not the individual teacher. But this is discretion with substance. Teachers as a group make the significant decisions about objectives, curriculum, scheduling, and so on. They accept real responsibility for what goes on, how, and why. Discretion is not only limited to the stylistic responsibility that goes with implementing someone else's decisions as is normally the case in teaching. Teaching is upgraded, the job is enriched, responsibility is real, and achievement belongs to the professionals involved. Indeed, the virtues of human resources so difficult to implement in the professional bureaucracy become natural characteristics of the professional bureaucratic-ad hocracy.

Teachers will typically work in view of each other, often side-by-side as partners. Feedback is continuous. The reward system for good ideas and excellence in teaching emerges from adult peers as well as students. What we have is an informal and natural system of supervision that emerges from the normal course of events in a continuous fashion. The role of teacher-leader is important. But unlike the supervisor in the professional bureaucracy who supervises by appointment, the process of supervision is informal, integral to the work, and collegial. The team leader is involved in the daily work of the team as together they plan, teach, and evaluate.

In recent years a number of tools and techniques for illuminating, mapping, understanding, analyzing, and otherwise evaluating teaching and classroom life have been developed. Despite what we know, the implementation gap remains large. One reason is that the human context for supervision is not sufficiently advanced to accommodate this developed array of supervisory artistry and technology. Human resources supervision can help enrich the supervisory context. But this is not enough. We need to examine critically the professional bureaucracy as an organizational design for schools, appreciate its strengths but deal as well with its weaknesses. A viable system of supervision is not possible under the organizational constraints found in the school as a professional bureaucracy. Modifying this design in the direction of ad hocracy is a hopeful alternative.

Chapter 9.
Issues of Race and Sex in Supervision

Ethel Greene

• She is a young black woman who is charming, graceful, well-groomed, and holds a doctorate in education. She has functioned superbly in the position of vice president at a fairly large university for more than one year and now has the opportunity to apply for the position of president.

• He is a black man who has functioned as second in command in a large urban school system for the past ten years. He is now in charge of the system and is doing a fine job. The system is open for a permanent superintendent.

• She is Latino and an ex-nun. She has the responsibility of planning and developing a bilingual center for a small midwestern university. She has made a good start in that direction.

• He is a black man and has functioned as second in command to the mayor of a large industrial city. On many occasions, he successfully ran the city in the mayor's absence. Now, he has the opportunity to take over as interim mayor of the city.

The individuals mentioned here were capable, well-qualified, and experienced. In addition to being minorities, what else did they have in common? The answer is, in each instance when they applied for the position, they were passed over in favor of a white male. This happened despite the fact the all had the qualifications to function in a top level supervisory position.

In recent years, much has been done by the federal government, as well as the private sector, to combat bias against minorities and women. Affirmative action in the areas of education and employment has become an accepted way of life. Women, both white and minority, are more vocal for women's rights than at any time in history. The civil rights movement for racial equality and assurance of rights for minorities to share equally in the wealth of this country has never been greater. Nevertheless, despite the widespread movement for racial equality and women's liberation, the above incidents are still too com-

Ethel Greene is Professor and Co-Director, Race Desegregation Training Institute, Northeastern Illinois University, Chicago and Rockford Illinois.

monplace in our society. Can it be assumed that women and minorities have fair representation of earning power and fair representation in supervisory positions when incidents such as those described remain commonplace? With the many affirmative action programs, women's organizations, and the millions of dollars that are appropriated each year for their administration, why is so little progress being made in providing equality for women and racial minorities in the obtaining of supervisory positions?

Who Should Supervise?

How did our society arrive at the concept that white males should lead, supervise, or be in charge of most activities of importance? Are they endowed with some special ability at birth? Do white males actively seek leadership and supervisory roles to the exclusion of minorities and women? The author is of the opinion that women and racial minorities are as capable of functioning in high level positions as white men. The crucial difference is in the opportunities offered and the attitudes and ideas embedded in our society. For the most part, male members of the white race are afforded both the opportunity and the societal concepts necessary for leadership. They have positive role models with whom to identify and the availability of various types of experiences, hence, proper job connections for upward mobility.

Similarly the white female is fortunate to be exposed to the same role models and opportunities as the white male. All of the ingredients necessary to supervise are present in the white female, with the exception of one. The missing ingredient, possibly the most important one, is the attitude of society. Much of this societal attitude came about through conditioning that the woman's place is in the home. Further, it is the feeling and attitude of many members of society that if women do indeed work outside the home, their labor is less valuable than that of men. This concept is even sanctioned in the Bible. Leviticus (27:3-4) states that the adult female's labor worth in Biblical times was 30 shekels of silver or 60 percent of the worth of a male.

Minorities, by contrast, have had very few leadership role models and few opportunities for leadership jobs. They, like the white female, fail to have the sanction of society that indicates they can function as leaders and supervisors. For years, much of society considered black minorities as property and, consequently, gave little or no attention to them as human beings, not to mention supervisors or leaders.

The decision as to who should supervise or lead comes from society. Years of conditioning has caused society to lean toward the white male for leadership and supervision. Even with affirmative action programs and the women's liberation movement, there is little change in societal attitudes. As a result, it has been found that for the same job or for jobs with similar skills and education requirements, minorities and women often have to demonstrate greater skills and more education than white males.[1]

Where Does It All Start?

Children, regardless of race or ethnic origin, are born more or less equal in terms of self-concept. However, minority children tend to fall behind white children on this dimension at a very early age. Children learn most things through experience and by identification with role models. Role models are usually the people who are close to them. Consequently, much of their development is based on what they see, hear, and experience in their everyday lives. If children are surrounded by people who have a poor self-concept, they will start to think and feel badly about themselves. This is especially true for minorities. Because of their color, language differences, religion, and ethnic origin, minority children are often treated differently from white children. Black children, for example, are made to feel ashamed of their thick lips, kinky hair, and different skin color. Puerto Rican children are made to feel like strangers in their own land, mainly because of language differences.

To add to these problems, minority children can hardly be shielded from the way their role models are treated. Black and Spanish-speaking children often see members of their own ethnic groups depicted negatively on television, in the movies, in magazines, books, and newspapers. Minority children, unless given special encouragement, will quickly lose the feeling that they are adequate and, therefore, not think of themselves as able to function as supervisors and leaders.

The key to opportunity is found in society's attitudes. If there is confusion and misconception about a particular group, it is almost impossible for members of that group to successfully reach the supervisory level. Such is the problem facing white women and minorities. Many of the myths, misconceptions, and double standards that plague these groups have been around longer than American society itself.

Negative or Positive Forces

It is important to examine the forces that work negatively or positively for women and minorities in relationship to their ability to supervise.

The Media

One such powerful force is the mass media. Most often, the effects

---

[1] U.S. Department of Commerce, Bureau of the Census, *The Social and Economic Status of the Black Population in the United States, An Historical View.* 1970-1978.

are negative for minorities. Newspapers, for example, seldom print good news about minority groups, perhaps because good news does not increase circulation. The same is true of television. Minorities on television will either be involved in some problems with the law or will be portrayed in non-serious roles. Programs featuring minorities usually depict them as stupid and unable to understand simple things. Often minorities are shown in a subservient role. The movie industry, from its inception, has cast minorities in a poor light. For example, Bill Robinson, who was one of the finest tap dancers that the industry has ever known, could only find success in Hollywood by entering through the back door. He could only dance on the screen as a servant to a little white girl, Shirley Temple. Radio is equally guilty of depicting minorities unfavorably; Amos and Andy is a prime example. The American Indian must not be forgotten when reflecting on the treatment of minorities by the media.

Myths

The many myths embedded in our society affect both dominant and minority races. However, negative effects tend to be more pronounced with women and minorities than with white males. Myths may be defined as ideas that are imaginary and have no verifiable existence. These ideas are passed down from generation to generation. In many instances, myths have been a part of societal belief for so long that they are simply taken for granted. For example, the myth that white males make better supervisors than white females and minorities has more or less become a societal belief. Likewise, the myth that black people are innately inferior to white people or that women are inferior to men. Unfortunately, once these myths are embedded in the beliefs of society, they become truth for many people.

Preconceived Notions

Another force in society that works against women and minorities is the many preconceived notions they encounter. Preconceived notions are opinions formed prior to gaining knowledge or experience. Such notions can be positive forces, as they typically are for white males. Many preconceived notions are so much a part of society that women or minorities use them against one another.

The following incident is an example of a preconceived notion: Two black males earned college degrees in the late 1940s. No doubt, the preconceived notion at that time was that blacks were poor risks in business and law. This notion was probably due to the fact that no one had given blacks an opportunity to prove their ability and few, if any, people were willing to take the chance. Consequently, it was easier to just not employ them. Since these men were not able to open their own business and law firm, they had to seek employment elsewhere. Today, the man who has the business degree is employed as a window-washer at Cook County Hospital and the man with the law degree is a scale mechanic at the main U.S. Post Office in Chicago. By the time the notion that blacks were too risky to hire in business and law was partially dispelled, those two individuals were too old to consider a change of employment. Since they had not had any experience in their professions, their skills are now obsolete.

Preconceived notions can inhibit or enhance one's opportunity to reach the supervisory level. For many women and most minorities, they are a negative factor.

Mind-Set

Still another force to consider is mind-set. Mind-set can best be described as deciding that something has to be done in a particular way. It may also mean that something can or cannot be a certain way, despite evidence that it may be just the opposite. In relation to supervision, mind-set most often works in a negative manner for females and minorities. Mind-set, like myths and preconceived notions, is deeply rooted in society and must be combatted in order for members of these groups to move to the top. The following incident is an example of mind-set.

A white female university professor went to work in a rural school district as a consultant. She invited a white male colleague to accompany her. On arrival, the project director suggested that both be introduced to the principal. The project director introduced the female as ''our new consultant, Dr. King.'' The principal immediately reached for the hand of the male, only to be told that the male's name was Mr. Lane.

One might surmise that this was not a mind-set, but rather an honest mistake since the principal did not know if the consultant was male or female. On the other hand, it is customary in this society that if a male and female are being introduced at the same time, the female is introduced first. Normally, one would expect the Principal to extend his hand to the female. Obviously, the principal had been conditioned to associate Ph.D. degrees and leadership roles with white males.

Double Standard

Still another problem embedded in our society is the age-old double standard. Double standard is defined as a set of principles that apply differently and more rigorously to one group of people or circumstances than to another. Double standards have been encountered by most people in society in one way or another. For minorities, the effects of the double standard are usually negative. Just being female causes many white women to encounter double standards in employment, education, politics, religion, as well as many other vital areas.

This brings to mind an incident witnessed by the author in a large elementary school that was committed to the team teaching concept.

The teacher's watch was five minutes fast because she wanted to get started for work a little early that morning. She got busy during the day and forgot to set it back. Consequently, she inadvertently left the science laboratory five minutes early. The next day she found a long note in her mailbox berating her for being uncooperative and inconsiderate to other teachers and children because she brought her class back to the area early. The teacher, who was a minority, continued to observe one of her white colleagues leaving the science laboratory six to eight minutes early on many occasions. One day, the minority teacher decided to follow the white teacher to determine what was being said about her. Both teachers walked past the team leader. Immediately, the team leader came over and reprimanded the minority teacher. When the team leader was reminded that the white teacher came down first, the team leader commented that she did not see the other teacher.

Prejudice

Perhaps the oldest and most pronounced problem embedded in society is prejudice. Young children, both white and minority, are born free of prejudicial feelings. However, it does not take long for children to learn prejudice through identification with adults and, as a result, prejudice becomes a vicious cycle in society. Of all the societal forces encountered by women and minorities, prejudice is, no doubt, the most destructive to one's self-concept.

Prejudice is defined as "injury or damage resulting from some judgment or action of another in disregard of one's rights." No doubt, almost every individual who is old enough and in a rational frame of mind has experienced some form of prejudice. Likewise, one should be suspicious of the individual who states, "I don't have a prejudiced bone in my body."

It is a fact that minorities have suffered greatly because of prejudices exhibited by whites, but they have also suffered due to prejudices exhibited by other minorities. Few white people who have dealt with minorities have not encountered the sting of prejudice. Whites, like minorities, also demonstrate prejudices toward each other.

The author contends that this one societal force is more detrimental to one's access to supervisory positions than any of the others. It must be admitted that most often discrimination exhibited by minorities towards whites has little influence on the ability of whites to move up the career ladder. However, it is a different story with the prejudicial influence of many whites. Oftentimes, such influence can prevent a minority's access to top level supervisory positions.

Most people recognize prejudice when they confront it. Nevertheless, the following incident is indicative of how it works.

Four university professors from Chicago were traveling together to an educational meeting. They stopped at a prominent hotel in a large southern city. One of the minority professors, being the first to register, asked the clerk about the discount for educators and was told that there was no such discount. Even after the minority professor produced proof that there was, the clerk still refused to grant it. A short time later, one of the white professors registered and was promptly given the discount. When told that the parties were together, the clerk still refused to give the minority professor the discount. The manager had to intervene before the problem was settled.

There is irony in the display of prejudice in educational organizations. Though theoretically conceived on the rational premise of equal opportunity and the criterion of expertness for advancement without regard to background issues such as race and sex, prejudicial contradictions abound. Women and minorities have indeed suffered the most but like most diseases, prejudice strikes all groups. How many men, for example, are heads of research and training programs that focus on the problems of women? Rare indeed is the white who heads an Afro-American or Latino study center. To suggest that whites cannot possibly understand the problem of minorities or that men cannot understand the problems of women and thus in each case should be excluded from such leadership posts gives credence to similar arguments given by white males with regard to the more mainstream leadership positions in society.

Prejudices, preconceived notions, myths, and stereotyped ideas about men, women, and minorities have infiltrated all aspects of American society. They are particularly significant in their effect on opportunities for women and minorities. Perhaps one day these forces will no longer influence opportunities for the less powerful citizens of this country.

The Educational Process

An examination of the American educational system will probably yield evidence that many of its practices are antiquated and infused with myths, preconceived notions, and the double standard. Moreover, the system still contains separate but *unequal* schools almost three decades after such schools were outlawed by the highest court in the land.

There are double standards for males and females just as there are for whites and minorities. In the ghettos of large cities, there are separate but *unequal* schools for minorities. In those schools, minority children are subjected to the following misleading assumptions:

1. They cannot be expected to do well in school because there is no father in the home.

2. The children's ability for future success can be predicted by their I.Q. scores.

3. These children are in need of sympathy because they have been deprived.

4. Black parents are not interested in their children.

5. Because children are from deprived homes, they come to school with problems that interfere with their ability to learn.

6. Black children are innately inferior to white children.

According to Kenneth B. Clark, such assumptions are really alibis for educational neglect and not a reflection of the education process. Rather, such assumptions have the insidious consequences of self-fulfilling prophecies for minority children.[2]

Educational institutions are guilty of programming females into certain areas of the curriculum and males into other areas. Males tend to have grave reservations about becoming involved in areas that have been traditionally dominated by females. Until recently, males would not consider positions in kindergarten/primary education, nursing or secretarial training, and other fields dominated by females. Though there is a slight increase in male participation in these non-traditional areas, they are still not popular. Traditionally, economics, sports, mathematics, science, and the trades have been considered male territory. Recently, however, females started entering these areas in greater numbers and with fewer reservations. Perhaps, they have finally discovered that future economic gains tend to be greater in these areas.

The anticipated practice that females should take certain courses and males should take others has penalized white women in their quest for top level supervisory positions. Minorities, on the other hand, most often attend separate and *unequal* schools. These schools are unequal by virtue of the courses offered, teacher ability, physical plant construction, and equipment. In many cases, the students are not offered much more than the three R's. Consequently, both males and females fail to gain skills that will adequately prepare them to function in top level positions.

Usually, white females are educated for such low paying, low prestige jobs as sales clerks, secretaries, homemakers, and teachers. On the other hand, most minorities are not being educated and therefore, not trained for specific trades and professions.

Institutions of higher education reflect the discriminatory practices that exist in public schools toward education of minority students and white women. Financial assistance enables minorities to attend institutions of higher education. There is usually not enough money to go around for all of those in need. Many minorities who are able to secure grants find that funds provided are small. Part-time jobs secured by minorities pay less than those obtained by white males. This probably accounts for the fact that as recently as 1978, about one out of ten black

---

[2] Kenneth B. Clark, *Dark Ghetto* (New York: Harper and Row, 1965).

men and women, ages 25 to 34 years, had completed four or more years of college, whereas, one of every four white men and women had completed four or more years of college.[3] In 1976, for example, the attainment of a college education was beyond the reach of most American Indian/Alaskan natives, blacks, Mexican Americans, and Puerto Ricans.[4]

Should Minorities Supervise Other Minorities When They Become the Majority in a School System?

Schools in the United States were established for the purpose of teaching each individual to read. When assessing the entire population, it is recognized that the schools failed to fulfill their original mandate. A large segment of the population still cannot read well enough to file a job application or understand the want-ad section of the newspaper. Certain members of all ethnic groups fall into this population, but the problem is greatest among blacks, Hispanics, and American Indians.

Many whites are leaving large urban areas in search of better schools, thereby leaving most big city school systems with an enrollment that is almost totally minority. Community leaders in these areas are calling for minority educators to head the school systems.

Chicago is an example of a city where the call for a minority educator is prevalent. Community leaders insisted that a recent superintendent's vacancy be filled by a black educator. As a result of this demand, whites asked such questions as:

Why is it that once minorities become the majority in a school system, they demand a minority educational leader?

Should not the best qualified person rather than the best qualified minority person be hired as the superintendent?

Is it the consensus among black people that once they become the majority in a school system, whites can no longer educate them?

Is not the demand for a minority to head the school system an expression of racism by blacks?

Minority leaders responded by noting that a black superintendent would be as capable of running the Chicago School system as a white superintendent. Further, they argued that a black superintendent would serve as a model for minority youth and give them an incentive to aspire to leadership positions. It was also believed that a black educator in a leadership position could better understand and relate to the problems faced by minorities since he or she would have faced similar problems in the past.

Albert Briggs, a veteran black Chicago educator summed up the demand for a minority superintendent as follows:

[3] U.S. Department of Commerce, Bureau of the Census, *The Social and Economic Status of the Black Population in the United States, An Historical View.* 1970-1978.

[4] *Ibid.*

We ought to have a black superintendent because it's our turn.... If we aren't going to get one when we have 80 percent minority enrolled, then when will we?[5]

In answer to the question as to whether white educators can still educate minorities once minorities become the majority in a particular community, it is the consensus among black leaders that it is possible. They are aware that white educators have the experience, the know-how, and the academic background necessary to educate all children regardless of their ethnic makeup. However, these leaders also know that the vast majority of uneducated people are blacks, Hispanics, and Native Americans.

Minority leaders accept the fact that white educators may have had the good intention of educating all children to their maximum potential. They know that such intentions were to be carried out regardless of racial or ethnic make-up. Thus, leaders are also aware that white educators traditionally maintained separate but *unequal* schools for minorities for more than 100 years. It might be interesting to see what history will record concerning the hiring of a black superintendent in the Chicago school system and the trend toward hiring black superintendents in other large, predominantly black, cities.

Conclusion

There are widespread problems in relation to equal access to supervisory positions for women and minorities throughout American society. Many of the myths and preconceived notions are imaginary and have no verifiable existence. Many of the ideas, opinions, and attitudes are often formed without prior knowledge or experience in a particular area. Yet, these inconsistencies continue to penalize certain members of society and hamper their opportunities for equal access to top level positions.

Because of the pressure exerted by affirmative action programs and women's liberation organizations, some strides are being made toward dispelling the myth that the white male is right. The practice of hiring white males first, and then a token number of minority males next, for supervisory positions will have to be eliminated. So too, will the practice of relegating white women and minorities to low paying, low prestige positions. This problem is so widespread and the myths, preconceived notions, and double standards are so deeply entrenched in society that it will take years of constant work to eliminate them. The job is so enormous that it will take the efforts of all who are concerned. The author recognizes that there is no panacea for the problem, but offers the following suggestions, nevertheless.

1.   All aspects of the media need to develop the policy of portray-

---

[5] *The Chicago Defender Newspaper,* June 17, 1980.

ing minorities in positive as well as negative roles. They should be given fair coverage, the same as members of the dominant group. Minority children need to know that members of their race are not all bad.

2. The television and movie industry need to put forth an effort to cast minorities in serious rather than mainly comical and subservient roles.

3. Societal institutions should be committed to the development of a climate that is conducive to dispelling the many myths, preconceived notions, mind-sets, double standards, and prejudices that hinder women and minorities from equal access to top level supervisory positions.

4. All individuals should work at respecting individual differences. They should work hard at trying to respect people for their self-worth, rather than the color of their skin.

5. Women should be given equal opportunity to participate in all aspects of American society. This opportunity should be based on their ability and not on their sex.

6. There needs to be a concerted effort on the part of those individuals who are in charge to eliminate the inequity that exists in the nation's schools.

7. Minority children need to be exposed to role models who are in top level supervisory positions to assure them that it is possible for minorities to ascend to that level.

8. Institutions of higher education should put forth a special effort to give women and minority employees equal opportunity to gain access to top level supervisory positions.

9. Women and minorities should have the opportunity of preparing for trades and professions that will afford them a decent salary, as well as access to top level positions.

10. Elementary and high schools should abandon the practice of programming females and males into separate curricular areas, since females are most often programmed into areas that prepare them mainly for low level positions.

11. The concept that people advance in this country on the basis of preparation and ability regardless of sex or racial background should apply equally for minorities, females, and white males.

12. There should always be an air of mutual respect between those who are designated as supervisor and those who are being supervised.

References

The Chicago Defender Newspaper, June 17, 1980.

Clark, Kenneth B. *Dark Ghetto.* New York: Harper & Row, 1965.

Goodman, Mary Ellen. *The Culture of Childhood.* New York: Teachers College, 1970.

Grant, Carl A., ed. *Multicultural Education: Commitments, Issues, and Applications.* Alexandria, Va.: Association for Supervision and Curriculm Development, 1977.

Grove, Cornelius Lee. *Communications Across Cultures.* Washington, D.C.: National Education Association, 1976.

Hornsby, Alton, Jr. *The Black Almanac,* 4th ed. New York: Barron's Educational Series, 1975.

Hunter, William A. *Multicultural Education Through Competency Based Education.* Washington, D.C.: American Association of Colleges for Teacher Education, 1974.

Longstreet, Wilma S. *Aspects of Ethnicity.* New York: Teachers College Press, 1978.

Stone, James C., and NeNevi, Donald P. *Teaching Multicultural Populations.* New York: Van Nostrand Rinehold Co., 1971.

Part IV.
Hidden Dimensions in Supervision

ADMINISTRATORS AND SUPERVISORS IN SCHOOLS look to management and organizational theories for insights into how schools should be structured and operated. Implicit in these management and organizational theories are certain ideologies, beliefs, and assumptions about the nature of humankind. These assumptions are typically manifested in the provisions for supervision and control that are implicit in the theories. In schools conceived as ad hocracies, for example, the issue of teacher control is viewed as emerging naturally from the necessity teachers feel for working cooperatively as members of ad hoc groups. On the other hand, in schools conceived as classical bureaucracies the issue of teacher control is viewed as one best handled by defining details, policies, procedures, and expectations to which teachers must respond. In the image of the classical bureaucracy the organizational structure of the school tends to act as a surrogate, albeit impersonal, system of supervision by expanding or constricting teacher prerogatives, narrowing or opening teacher options, and restricting or freeing teacher behavior. Bureaucratic accounting such as the Carnegie unit, bureaucratic scheduling such as the 50-minute class period, and bureaucratic hierarchal arrangements such as the chain of command require conformity from teachers who often wish to respond uniquely to particular student needs. Teachers can respond to such needs only in ways that fit the organizational pattern.

Paul Pohland and James Cross in their chapter "Impact of the Curriculum on Supervision" analyze several curriculum and instructional approaches showing that each represents an ideology that affects teacher behavior in the classroom. Curriculum and instructional formats, they argue, are not independent dimensions but represent highly developed models of teaching, supervision, and evaluation. They raise the questions: can a supervisory strategy or approach be developed separate from a particular curriculum and instruction design, or is the supervisory system really a dependent dimension controlled by the more dominant assumptions implicit in the curriculum design and the instructional system?

Gerald Firth and Keith Eiken provide a comprehensive and critical examination of the schools' bureaucratic structure in their chapter "Impact of the Schools' Bureaucratic Structure on Supervision." They seek not only to chart the relationship between structure and supervision, but point out as well those aspects of structure that are dysfunctional to supervision. They suggest ways in which structure might be changed to accommodate a quality supervisory program.

"Since schools serve as our primary socializing agent, they mirror the crises of the moment" argues Louis Rubin in the final chapter of Part IV, "External Influences on Supervision." Maintaining that supervisors are typically committed to humanistic values and to a broad concept of quality education, Rubin describes the stress they experience in accomodating to current pressures to emphasize teacher effectiveness research, increased student accountability, and other expressions of scientific-rationality in supervision. Rubin provides suggestions as to how this movement might be used to one's advantage and concludes optimistically that current crises are not likely to result in the erosion of long-standing values.

Chapter 10.
Impact of the Curriculum on Supervision

Paul Pohland and James Cross

THERE IS A CERTAIN SEDUCTIVENESS to the title "Impact of the Curriculum on Supervision." It is seductive at the outset in presupposing that curriculum indeed has an impact on supervision. Based on this presumption a research agenda for determining the nature and/or magnitude of that impact is suggested. Further, the direction of impact is specified: curriculum (the independent variable) impacts on supervision (the dependent variable). But are these assumptions justifiable? Is it possible, for example, that supervisory theory and practice impact on curriculum rather than vice versa? Even more extreme, is it possible that the basic premise itself is insupportable and there is no impact at all?

There is another sense in which the title is seductive. Within the professional literature, the terms curriculum and supervision tend to be associated so readily as to form a unity — curriculum supervision. In the parlance of everyday speech they go together like ham and eggs, mother and child, war and peace. Each phrase conveys a commonsense image of unique and sometimes quite disparate elements bonded to form a new relationship. Yet as we learn from chefs, pediatricians, and political scientists, those new relationships are complex and rarely fully understood.

If the cautions indicated here are meaningful, the title is not only seductive but sensitizing. It is sensitizing in the first instance by suggesting focused attention to each member of the pair independently. Second, it suggests examining the pair as an entity, exploring the patterns of relationships that may exist while initially suspending judgment about the functional consequences of the relationships. Such sensitizing also provides a rubric for organizing this chapter.

1. Curriculum

Curriculum theorists are scarcely of one mind. McNeil (1977) summarizes the "state of the field" thus:

Paul Pohland is Professor of Educational Administration and Supervision, University of New Mexico, Albuquerque. James Cross is Principal, Southwest School, Evergreen Park, Illinois.

The search for bibliographical references conveying the "state of the field" in the curriculum yielded both the expected and unanticipated. The expected, of course, is the utter lack of agreement among educators, curriculum developers, curriculum analysts, evaluators and policy makers on the question of what schooling is about. The surprise is the richness and complexity of the disagreement. The field of curriculum is so fluid, so enmeshed in funding and politics, that diverse and even contradictory paradigms exist and jostle each other for dominance in the professional literature (p. 627).

It would be patently impossible within the confines of this chapter to wade through, much less synthesize, all the "diverse and even contradictory paradigms" that exist in the conceptual holding company called curriculum. Yet some start on that task is required. Hence in a modest way we have attempted a comparative analysis of five conceptions of curriculum. We have approached that task by asking the broadest question possible, that is, "What is the underlying conception of curriculum?" Our rationale for phrasing a question of such magnitude is simply the belief that how a phenomenon is initially perceived structures its subsequent development. Clearly, the question as posed carries with it some self-limiting features, for example, restrictive attention to such crucial curriculum issues as purpose, selection and organization of content, and the like.

A second self-imposed limitation is restricting the analysis to five conceptions of curriculum. In large part this decision was guided by the relative recency and easy availability of a somewhat similar attempt by Elliot Eisner and Elizabeth Vallance to differentiate among conceptions of curriculum (see *Conflicting Conceptions of Curriculum*, 1974). Like Eisner and Vallance we have treated the conceptions as "classes" or exemplars, recognizing full well that variations within classes may be as extreme as variations among them.

A third limitation is noticeable in our decision to limit the number of variables in the analysis to five. While in our judgment those selected appear to have high discriminating power, the arbitrariness of choice is recognized. The summarized analysis is presented in Figure 1.

Even a cursory scanning of Figure 1 provides ample evidence of the diversity of thought within the field of curriculum. Class titles alone indicate the absence of a governing paradigm. And, in our judgment, the absence of a governing paradigm can be attributed initially to basic philosophic disagreements relative to the purpose of schooling. These diverse orientations to schooling we have labeled utilitarianism, efficiency, liberalism, confrontation/adaptation, and scholasticism, respectively.[1] More important, we would argue that each in turn shapes and drives the conception in use.

Cognitive Processes curricula proceed from the belief that there exists a basic set of intellectual skills that are fundamental and generalizable

---

[1] Our debt to Eisner and Vallance is large and recognized. However, conceptual categories like "utilitarianism" have been derived by the present authors and any argument should be with them.

across a wide range of intellectual and experiential problems. It is in this sense that a cognitive processes orientation is utilitarian. It is (as are the others) also compelling. Who can argue against the necessity of acquiring "basic skills" (Bereiter, 1974) or proficiency in problem solving (Burns and Brooks, 1974).

Anchored as it is in utilitarianism, the remainder of the "model" logically follows. Developmental psychology, most heavily influenced recently by the work of Piaget, suggests the appropriate time for introducing particular intellectual processes to the student. Equally, since human development and experience is individualistic, the client is the individual learner. Further, since intellectual processes are generalized, the curriculum is content-independent, that is, not limited to a specific discipline. Bloom's taxonomy (cognitive domain) is as applicable to agriculture as to zoology. Logically, a central, continuously active role is ascribed to the teacher in the identification of the intellectual processes to be mastered, the assessment of the readiness of the learner to acquire them, and the provision for such learning to take place. Clearly, such conceptions place heavy role demands on teachers and supervisors alike.

Curriculum as Technology proceeds from a very different philosophical orientation. Schooling is seen as non-problematic insofar as it assumes consensus on goals. In a sense, then, the curriculum simply "is," and the major task of the curriculum developer therefore is to devise the instructional delivery system. It is "efficiency" oriented: no doubt exists that there is a "best way." The task, of course, is to find it. And it may be found in a variety of sources: hardware, such as computer assisted instruction (Bushnell, 1967); in software, such as programmed learning (Glaser, 1965); in the careful "engineering" of an instructional sequence (Gagné, 1967); in the careful application of psychological theory, such as the "S-R Reinforcement Model" (Silverman, 1974).

Like their cognitive processes brethren, technologists take a content-independent stance. Technology can be applied to any domain of human knowledge. Domains differ, however, with respect to client and teacher role. For technologists the client is only incidentally the individual learner. Their target is larger: the individual school or school system that intends for whatever reason to "adopt" a new curriculum; a community; a nation as a whole. Hence the intrusion of the language of the economist in curriculum, for example: "The public school curriculum, viewed in its entirety, appears to the economist as a community-purchased and distributed bundle of teacher-pupil interactions carried out over a carefully defined period of time" (Goldman and others, 1974, p.81). At the national level, this orientation becomes apparent in the concern for "planned variation" (Rivlin, 1971).

The technology and cognitive processes orientations differ also in the role ascribed to the teacher. As previously stated, the latter ascribes

Classes / Descriptors	Cognitive Processes	Technology	Self-Actualization	Social Reconstruction-Relevance	Academic Rationalism
Philosophic Orientation	Utilitarianism	Efficiency	Liberalism	Confrontation/Adaptation	Scholasticism
Goals/Objectives/Focus	Intellectual autonomy; development of a repertoire of generalized intellectual skills	Determination of "best" means of knowledge transmission; development/packaging of curriculum materials, processes, and technology; "engineering"	Human fulfillment and wholeness; celebration/liberation of the individual cognitively and affectively	Social reconstruction	Understanding and appreciation for the distinctive, public modes of thought (concepts and patterns of relationships)
Content (Substance)	Content independent	Content independent	Inter- and multi-disciplinary; "the human experience"	Issues of social relevance	Discipline specific
Psychological Basis	Developmental psychology	Behaviorism	Humanistic psychology	Engagement ("Learning by doing")	Faculty psychology, cognitive rationality

Client	Individual	School/community/society	Individual	Society (the "relevant and preferred utopia")	Civilization
Role of Teacher	To identify intellectual processes and make provision for their development; continuously active	Initially active in diagnosis and prescription; moves toward passive monitoring and "fine-tuning" pupil progress	Role model for learner	Social critic to social activist; adaptation agent	Central in focusing, clarifying, conveying, and portraying disciplinary-rooted phenomena; major, active role in instructional setting

Figure 1. Conceptions of Curriculum

a continuously active and central role. Not so the technological. The curriculum as "engineered and packaged" drives the process. In the main, the teacher's role is limited to an initial set of decisions regarding which curriculum ("package"?) to select. Thereafter it is largely limited to monitoring and "fine tuning." The latent consequences of this alteration in the teacher's role are only dimly perceived (Brod, 1972).

Self-Actualization, or Curriculum as Consummatory Experience, the third conception of curriculum identified by Eisner and Vallance, differs systematically from the prior two. The magnitude of the difference is immediately noticeable in the philosophic orientation. As we have noted, cognitive processes are rooted in utilitarianism which, by extension, suggests that individuals take a reactive stance toward coping with an existent world. Technologists, too, take the world as a given and are consequently reactive. In contrast to both, self-actualization implies a creative, proactive, initiating stance. Hence we suggest that self-actualizing conceptions of curriculum are philosophically rooted in classical liberalism.

At its best, liberalism is a celebration of life. Human perfectibility is seen as not only desirable but possible. The whole of human experience consequently becomes the subject matter of the curriculum. Hence, the development of attitudes, beliefs, and values are as important as the development of cognitive skills. Humanistic psychology provides an intellectual base; however, this slides easily and quickly into phenomenology and existentialism.

The language system reflects this orientation. Absent is the language of "behavioral objectives," "input-output," "criterion vs. norm-referenced tests." In its place is the language of poetry and philosophy: "transcendence," "spirit," "hope," "wonder, awe, and reverence" (Phenix, 1974). And the language system carries over into the role of teacher. One does not find "developers" (except in a very different sense), "facilitators," "decision makers," "diagnosticians"; instead one finds "dramatists" and "social critics" (Junell, 1974). More generally, the teacher is the living witness to the celebration of life who in every act of being provides an exemplary adult role model for the young.

Social Reconstruction-Relevance perspectives of curriculum distribute themselves along a continuum from radical reconstructionism to maintenance of the status quo. More frequently, however, they tend to cluster around two intermediate points: confrontation and adaptation.

Confrontation models are closely allied philosophically, conceptually, and operationally with Self-Actualization curriculum perspectives, albeit with a major change in focus. Both, for example, call for confrontation of socially relevant issues; both require the learner's active involvement; both require the teacher to assume the critic's posture. There are, however, differences initially cued in the terms "self" and "social." Whereas the former predictably focuses on individual perfectibility, the latter focuses on the perfectibility of society at large or, to quote Metcalf and Hunt, "the relevant and preferred utopia."

There are other differences. At the extremes, the self-actualizationist's concern with "transcendence" has little in common with the radical reconstructionist's strident call for unleashing political power. Commitment to inquiry rooted in "opposition to all outlooks that presuppose a fixed content of knowledge, beliefs, or skills" (Phenix, 1974, p. 130) is hardly consonant with advocating "a massive political effort" (Mann, 1974, p. 150). At such points Self-Actualization and Social Reconstruction-Relevance diverge widely.

The second major point on the Social Reconstruction-Relevance continuum is adaptation. Located here are curricular approaches that seek to prepare students to adapt to the social order rather than to reconstruct it. At first blush such approaches appear to be totally inconsistent with the concept of reconstruction. However, advocates of the adaptation stance maintain otherwise, arguing that social institutions are not static but dynamic, continuously "reconstructing" themselves in response to an ever changing environment. Consequently they perceive the school's curriculum as a socially legitimated means of preparing students to live in a naturally evolving world. Given this orientation, the teacher's proper role is to facilitate adaptation — cognitive, social, attitudinal, and behavioral.

Academic Rationalism, the fifth of the Eisner and Vallance conceptions, is probably the most familiar although it appears in various guises. The term conjures up images of schooling ranging from the cloistered halls of ivy and graduate programs to the little red schoolhouse and the 3 R's; from demands for "intellectual rigor" to demands for "basic skills" and "accountability." Whatever the particular image, the common thread is cognition, and for this reason we have associated it philosophically with scholasticism. Further, it is because of its concern for the "cultivation of the intellect," or those "desirable states of mind with which education in its specific sense is centrally concerned" (Hirst and Peters, 1974 p. 178), that we have identified a "faculty psychology" or "cognitive rationality" as operative.

Given this orientation it logically follows that the focus of the curriculum is properly the "structure" and "syntax" of a discipline (Schwab, 1974). In the Hirst-Peters formulation it becomes comprehension of those "distinct, public modes of experience and knowledge which man has achieved (p. 178)." Clearly, then, the curriculum becomes content specific. As Hirst and Peters argue," . . . within the domain of objective experience and knowledge, there are such radical differences of kind that experience and knowledge of one form is neither equatable with, nor reducible to, that of any other form" (p. 182). Indeed, Hirst and Peters identify precisely seven such "areas" of experience and knowledge.

Embedded in this conception of curriculum is that of teacher as scholar. Surely no one can elucidate the structure and syntax of a discipline unless one is thoroughly conversant with it. Teaching takes an active, central role in the instructional process, and teaching is

. . .a process of focusing on points of contact and connection among things and ideas, of clarifying the effect of each thing on the others, of conveying the way in which each connection modifies participants in the connection — in brief, the task of portraying phenomena and ideas not as things in themselves but as fulfillments of a pattern (Schwab, 1974, p. 169).

In brief, the most common image of the teacher conveyed is that of the stimulating lecturer.

Even in our foreshortened analysis, one problematic area remains with respect to academic rationalism. The issue at hand is the identification of the client. To be sure, Hirst and Peters talk in terms of "the pupil" and the necessity to "educate a person." Yet reading the academic rationalists suggests more of a concern with preserving and extending the best of human thought than with the individual's intellectual autonomy or individual self-actualization. "Cultural transmission" ("Great Books") seems to be the metaphor in use. Hence in our schema we have identified civilization itself as the client.

This, then, is a thumbnail description of five conflicting conceptions of curriculum. They move on a continuum of alike to different in a variety of ways. They are alike insofar as all are internally consistent. They are substantively different insofar as they are derived from initially disparate philosophical stances. Stated another way, each conception is energized by a "This I Believe" statement about the purpose of schooling, but the "This I Believe's" differ. They are partially alike (or different) in their position on content, client, and ascription of teacher role. Clearly, McNeil's (1977) assertion relative to the diversity of curriculum paradigms is supported.

2. Supervision

McNeil's observations relative to the "expected and unanticipated" status of the field of curriculum are equally applicable to the field of supervision. Again one finds substantial lack of agreement, complexity, fluidity, and diverse and competing paradigms. Part II of this Yearbook suggests the extent of that phenomenon. Equally, as in the curriculum field, claims of comparative superiority abound, yet in the absence of empirical support such claims are more a function of private than public knowledge.

Our approach in this section is similar to that of the last. We briefly present a comparative analysis of four major conceptions of supervision: Administrative, Instructional Processes, Counseling, and

Performance-Based. Clearly, the number of extant conceptions is considerably larger, for instance, those anchored conceptually in value development (Zahorik, 1977); in interpersonal relations (Blumberg, 1968); in community relations (DeWitt, 1977); and so forth. Further, variation may be found within class (conception). We indicate the extent of such variation by detailing three instructional processes conceptions — Clinical, Technological, and Artistic. Further elaborations are possible; for example, the clinical perspectives advanced by Cogan (1973), Goldhammer (1969), Mosher and Purpel (1972), and Acheson and Gall (1980) are not identical in all respects. Finally, we note that our analytical descriptors are both limited and in some sense arbitrary. Our analysis of selected supervisory conceptions is presented in Figure 2.

Administrative models of supervision are pervasive. In no small part this can be accounted for by the fact that by law, tradition, or default principals assume the major responsibilities for supervision. More important for present purposes, however, is the fact that most principals tend to be managerially oriented. As has been pointed out elsewhere (Pohland and Higbie, 1978), that orientation has a long and consistent history. Further, as it has been promulgated in graduate programs in administration, managerial orientations tend to place high value on such organizational imperatives as rational planning, order, conformity, coordination, maintaining organizational equilibrium, and the like. The increasing size and complexity of schools exacerbate this condition. This combination of factors, we argue, leads to a press for efficiency and we have so indicated in Figure 2.

The evidence of this orientation is equally pervasive though not well documented. We note, however, some common indicants of managerial orientations to supervision: (1) the location of supervisors in administrative offices, whether at the central office or the school site; (2) the tendency of supervisors *vis à vis* curriculum to press for districtwide plans, adoptions, and so on; (3) the linking of teacher evaluation with personnel decision making; and (4) the tendency to equate instructional supervision with student assessment. With respect to the latter, a managerial orientation would call for routinely and easily administered standardized tests for selected classes, grades, or schools that would "profile" the district. This is precisely what occurs in most school districts.

Clearly, managerial perspectives can be manifested in widely divergent ways, spanning the entire spectrum from Theory X to Theory Y (McGregor, 1960), from task-focused to people-focused, from behavior anchored in an optimistic view of people to that anchored in a pessimistic view.[2] But however manifested, administrators are,

---

[2] For a managerial perspective on the Theory X end of the continuum, see J. Shuttlesworth and N. Evans, "Why a Principal Must Be a Supervisor," *School Management* 18, 5 (May 1974).

Classes / Descriptor	Administrative	(Clinical)	Instructional Processes		Counseling	Performance-Based
			(Technological)	(Artistic)		
Basic Orientation	Managerial	Empiricism	Efficiency	Aesthetics	Individual growth and development	Pupil learning outcomes
Goals/Objective/Focus	Organizational efficiency and effectiveness	Teacher mastery through knowledge acquisition	Teacher mastery through skill acquisition	Teacher mastery through appreciation	Self-actualization	Pupil mastery of curriculum content
Knowledge Base	Administrative theory and practice	Pedagogy	Behaviorism	Criticism	Personality theory	Curriculum theory
Concept of Teaching	Bounded set of organizational role expectations	An intellectual and social act	Patterned teacher/pupil interactions	Creative performance	Enactment of a personal role definition	Technology
Role of Supervisor	Administrative superordinate	Analyst	Change agent	Critic	Counselor	Monitor/adjustor/evaluator
Supervisor-Teacher Relationship	Superordinate-subordinate	Teacher-learner	Master-apprentice	Critic-performer	Counselor-counselee	Evaluator-evaluatee

Figure 2. Conceptions of Supervision

organizationally speaking, superordinates, and that shapes their beliefs and behaviors; similarly, teachers are subordinates and that shapes their beliefs and behaviors. The resultant tensions have been well documented (Corwin, 1965).

Mediating the tensions, however, between teachers as practicing professionals and administrators as supervisors are several factors. We note them only briefly since a full explication would carry us too far afield. First, though certainly not a new idea, teaching as a "lonely profession," that is, with limited opportunity to interact with other adults, provides a context where professional interaction may be welcomed whatever the source. Second, the teacher's long socialization into the profession tends to make administrative supervision normatively acceptable. Third, increasing standardization and consensus decision making, for example with respect to curriculum determination, serve to minimize the potential for conflict. In brief, one might argue that administrative supervision is perceived as latently functional for supervisors and teachers alike.

Clinical supervision, as befits its recent prominence, is treated at length in Chapter 3 of this Yearbook. Hence the discussion here is limited and is included primarily to demonstrate its relationship with and to other supervisory conceptions.

In Figure 2 we suggest that clinical supervision's basic orientation is toward empiricism. This appears to be consistent with Mosher and Purpel's (1972) stance that "teaching, as an intellectual and social act, is subject to intellectual analysis" (p.79); the conception of supervisors and teachers as "hypothesis makers" (p. 82); the accent on inquiry into causal relationships; and the "idiosyncratic analysis of behavioral data" (Goldhammer, 1969, p. 54). "Search," "analysis," and "understanding" tend to be central constructs. The high emphasis on intellectual activity leads us to identify its goals as teacher mastery through knowledge acquisition. Its intellectual base is similarly identified as "pedagogy" — an unfelicitous term but one intended to capture what is known about teaching, learning, and curriculum. The central, active, and "clinical" role of the supervisor in this process suggests identifying the supervisor as analyst. The consequent relationship between supervisor and teacher is one of teacher and learner with, however, strong efforts toward collegiality through collaborative planning, problem solving, and the like.

A second variant of instructional processes conceptions of supervision is what we have labeled *technological*.[3] Unlike clinical models which emphasize improvement of instruction through the acquisition of a broad knowledge base, technological models seek improvement through the acquisition of discrete skills. In large part this difference in orienta-

---

[3] Our label is derived from B. F. Skinner's *The Technology of Teaching* (New York: Appleton-Century-Croft, 1968).

tion springs from divergent assumptions relative to knowledge. For the clinicians, the current knowledge base is inadequate to the task, hence the hypothesis testing. Technologists take the opposite stance; that is that both the knowledge base applicable to teaching and the technologies derived therefrom are sufficient. Consequently, improvement of instruction is predicated on teacher mastery of that technology or what is referred to in Figure 2 as efficiency.

Our analysis further indicates that technological approaches are derived from behavioral psychology. From this perspective, teaching is learned and patterned behavior and consequently subject to modification or change. The supervisor is therefore correctly perceived as the agent of change and the teacher (or more precisely, specific teacher behaviors) as the object of change. Operationally this requires the supervisor to engage those technologies that will most efficiently modify teacher behavior, that is, improve instruction.

The evidence of this mode of thought is easily found. Microteaching as a technology (Koran, 1969) is widely used as a supervisory strategy in enhancing a wide variety of teaching skills. Holistically, carefully designed and sequenced micro-teaching experiences can constitute the major portion of a "competency-based" teacher education or certification program. One might further point to the legions of teachers who have been taught to control their verbal behavior through such mediums as Flanders Interaction Analysis. Similar strategies have been developed for improving questioning skills (Sanders, 1966) or constructing behavioral objectives (Mager, 1962). In brief, what we have called technological approaches to the improvement of instruction are widely used in the supervisory process.

A third sub-category of instructional processes conceptions of supervision has been labeled *artistic*. Such conceptions are almost uniquely the contribution of Elliot Eisner to the field of supervision and are discussed at length by him in Chapter 4 of this Yearbook. Hence our presentation is brief and, like our discussion of clinical models, is included only to show its relation to other conceptions.

Like other instructional processes conceptions of supervision, artistic conceptions focus on in-class teacher activity and depend heavily on detailed observational data. However, the approach to the act of teaching and data utilization is quite different. Teaching tends to be perceived as a creative performance (the analogue with the performing arts is deliberate) and the guiding rubrics for the supervisor are drawn from aesthetics rather than pedagogy or behaviorism. This orientation leads the supervisor to adopt the stance of the connoisseur privately ("appreciation") and the stance of the critic (as in art critic) publicly. In the public world, criticism implies the act of disclosure, of heightening awareness of the intrinsic and extrinsic beauty of a creative act. "Thick description," interpretation, and illumination become both the goals and the medium of expression.

The rationale for *counseling* conceptions of supervision is articulated by Mosher and Purpel (1972): ". . . what the teacher is personally affects what he does and what pupils do (i.e., learn)" (p. 114). Focusing on "what the teacher is personally" clearly differentiates the thrust of counseling conceptions from administrative and instructional processes conceptions. The latter two focus either on *who* the teacher *is* (subordinate, role incumbent, low level line officer, and so on, from an administrative perspective), or on what the teacher *does* ("behaves," assigns, lectures, questions, and so on, from an instructional processes perspective.) Further, "what the teacher is personally" suggests a definition of teaching as the enactment of a personal role definition rather than enactment of a set of role expectations, patterned behaviors, or "performance." Finally, it indicates grounding in a human growth and development metaphor rather than in acquisition or construction (Skinner, 1968).

It should be fairly obvious that the number of possible variations on this theme is quite considerable, ranging from gross "human relations" models to sophisticated approaches drawn from such diverse theoretical formulations as Freudian psychology, ego-counseling, motivation psychology, and non-directive counseling. Underlying all such perspectives is the goal of assisting individuals in "becoming what they might be," and what, after Maslow, we have termed self-actualization.

Under this conception of supervision, roles and relationships are fairly straight-forward. The supervisor plays out the role of counselor and the teacher the role of counselee. More generally, this orientation provides the prime set of conditions for the "client relationship" that is frequently advocated in the supervisory literature. However, in the judgment of the authors, counseling models are potentially fraught with more danger than those sketched thus far. The dangers/difficulties are several-fold. First, counseling models tread in the most sensitive domains. Second, the establishment of the intimate bond between supervisor and teacher required in counseling models is no simple task. Third, few supervisors whom we know possess adequate counseling skills, much less sophisticated psychoanalytic skills. Fourth, teachers might well view this approach with suspicion, feeling they are being manipulated by supervisors. For all these reasons, Mosher and Purpel's (1972) advice that supervisors with a counseling orientation limit themselves to the secondary ego processes of planning, logical thinking, and problem solving appears to be well-founded.

Our final class of supervisory conceptions, *performance-based*, is fundamentally different from the others in that the focus of attention is less on teachers than on students. Stated another way, pupil learning outcomes ("terminal pupil behavior") rather than on-going, in-class teacher activity (or being) is the principal supervisory concern. In brief, this is what we mean to suggest by a criterion of "effectiveness."

The roots of this conception are long indeed. They are easily traceable to the spelling bees and other forms of public examinations of colonial days. In this century they become formalized in the early work of Bobbitt (1918) and others in developing curriculum objectives; were institutionalized and legitimated by Ralph Tyler (1950, the "Tyler Rationale"); and more recently have been popularized by Mager (1962), Popham (1969), and others. Further, such a conception is immediately and socially responsive to demands for accountability and the concern over Why Johnny Can't Read (or write, or compute, or think logically, ad nauseum).

Analytically, we have anchored this orientation to supervision in curriculum theory. We have done so with some trepidation given our previous discussion of competing conceptions of curriculum. Our intent, however, is to draw attention to the concern for the detailed specification and ordering of objectives (learning outcomes), the crafting of instructional units geared to the accomplishment of the same, and the development of instruments to measure pupil achievement. Given this orientation, the supervisor enacts an essentially technological role in the formulation of objectives, designing a program of learning experiences specific to those objectives, monitoring the processes, and assessing the outcomes. It is this latter activity that persuades us to describe the supervisor-teacher relationship non-pejoratively in terms of evaluator-evaluatee.

Performance-based models of supervision currently enjoy broad-based appeal, especially among hard-pressed administrators. Further, designing an objectives-based program can be a rewarding and effective inservice activity for those teachers serving on curriculum committees. Such advantages, however, must be balanced against potential disadvantages. For example, difficulties may be encountered in transferring the experiences and learnings of teachers engaged in program development to those not included. Further, the approach is time-consuming and expensive. Because of this, individual schools or small districts can rarely adopt this approach. Even larger units are seldom able to design the total package of objectives, instructional units, and assessment devices. As a result supervisors may find themselves spending their time and energies designing alternative strategies to help teachers cope or bridging the gap between intentions and developed components. Clearly, such a condition provides high stress for teachers and supervisors alike.

In sum, we have presented briefly four major conceptions of supervision: Administrative, Instructional Processes, Counseling, and Performance-Based. Further, we suggested the variation within classes by identifying three sub-classes of instructional processes conceptions: clinical, technological, and artistic. We noted that, similar to curriculum conceptions, all were driven by a basic orientation to the task that ordered its goals, roles, activities, and relationships. Finally, all perspectives are oriented toward a basic goal of improving instruction. In that sense all supervisory roads lead to Rome. None are without their pitfalls and potholes, but some focus more directly on instruction (for example, clinical) than others (for example, administrative).

3. Curriculum and Supervision: Impact and Interaction

"Perspective," write Katz and Kahn (1966, p. 171), "is everything." That terse but insightful observation by two eminent social psychologists suggests a way of determining the impact of the interaction between curriculum and supervision. In this final section we shall identify and discuss three quite different perspectives: an historical perspective, a perspective from the viewpoint of the teacher, and a perspective drawn from research that we have labeled "planned variation."

McNeil's (1977) observation that there is no "rigorous historical analysis of curriculum and its shaping" (p. 646) is quite accurate. Nonetheless, the broad outlines of large scale curriculum movements can be plotted over time. Granting certain liberties, and reversing the order of Social Reconstruction-Relevance and Academic Rationalism conceptions of curriculum, Figure 1 provides a crude 20th century curriculum time-line. A reading of Figure 1 from this perspective might go something like this.

Very early 20th century curriculum thinking was dominated by a liberal arts orientation. The curriculum was "classical" (notably but not exclusively at the university level) in the sense of ascribing primacy to history, philosophy, mathematics, language, literature, and the like. The goal of such an education was not totally dissimilar from that which we described earlier relative to a cognitive processes orientation to curriculum, that is, equipping an individual with a set of generalized intellectual skills sufficient to cope autonomously with the world.

The liberal arts (cognitive processes) orientation crumbled under the press of the Industrial Revolution and in the main gave way to technology. Callahan's (1962) *Education and the Cult of Efficiency* is the classic documentation of that shift in perspective. Technology in turn gave way to Human Relations ("self-actualization"), largely as a function of the Great Depression and its associated social phenomena. However, World War II and the launching of Sputnik in 1957 altered the national perspective. "Academic rigor" (Academic Rationalism in Figure 1) became the slogan of the 50s and spawned "new math," Project Physics, NDEA, and the like. The Vietnam War and the endemic social upheaval of the 60s diverted attention quickly from Academic Rationalism to Social Reconstruction-Relevance. Sit-ins, alternative schools, ethnic studies programs, open education, and the like were all manifestations of this phenomenon. But like other movements, the curriculum upheavals of the 60s passed. How historians of the future will classify the 70s is indeterminate, but it is not unthinkable that given a currently depressed economy and a demand for accountability that they may well classify it as the re-emergence of an efficiency cult.

From such an historical perspective curriculum clearly affected supervision. The liberal arts orientation required a "head teacher" who could serve both as a role model of the educated person and who could engage explicitly in teacher training of a like kind. The Age of Efficiency brought forth both the "empirical" and "technological" orientations to instructional processes orientations to supervision as we have described them earlier. Similarly, the Human Relations movement provided the impetus for conceptualizing supervision as counseling, and the turn to academic rigor called for exquisitely trained subject matter specialists in the supervisory role. Finally, who would deny that such phenomena as open and/or alternative schools with their new patterns of groupings, unique clientele, experience-oriented curricula, and frequently dispersed students and faculty did not require new and different modes of supervisory thought and action? Clearly, then, from an historical perspective curriculum has had a substantive impact on supervision.

A radically different perspective on the impact of curriculum on supervision is from the viewpoint of the teacher. This "view from below" varies along a host of dimensions. It tends to be highly personal, situationally specific, essentially holistic (particularly in the sense that teachers tend not to differentiate between curriculum and supervision), and more affective than analytical. Moreover, from this perspective the direction of impact appears to be reversed; that is, supervision (largely drawn from administrative perspectives) tends to impact on curriculum—if there is any impact at all. The latter point is not insignificant. As Cuban (1968) noted a decade ago, most teachers find instructional supervision "irrelevant," and more recently Blumberg (1974) has observed that suggesting to teachers that supervision should play a significant role in their professional lives is most likely to elicit smiles and snickers.

Some support for the negligibility of impact/irrelevance thesis has been obtained from studies done at the University of New Mexico. Over the past several years, students in a graduate course in supervision have been asked to write a brief account of an experience with a supervisor. The vast majority of accounts have been of the following order:

Thirty years ago I began my career as a teacher in a small town near the Mexican border. . . . At that time one could bring a gallon of liquor across the border at a bargain price, especially rum. Each month my supervisor and sometimes several others felt the need to pay me a visit, usually bringing materials a beginning teacher would need, but little time was spent with me in a classroom situation. There had to be time to cross the border and pick up their quota and mine. So much for supervision.

Such sentiments suggest rather forcibly that teachers perceive the locus of responsibility for instructional improvement and day to day decision making relative to the curriculum as lying within themselves. Further, such sentiments establish and reinforce norms of individualism and collegial sharing of technical knowledge (Lortie, 1975). "Self-supervision" and "peer supervision" become the standard modes of operation.

While the historical and teacher perspectives are substantially different, they are, however, similar in one important respect. Briefly, insofar as can be determined, curriculum and supervision appear to be independent entities, "loosely coupled" at best. Obviously, the condition suggests an alternative, a "planned variation" to use another in-vogue term, in which the articulation between a particular conception of curriculum and a particular conception of supervision is consciously and deliberately planned. We present an example of this as our third perspective.

In a series of reports and papers, Niedermeyer and his colleagues at the Southwest Regional Laboratory describe the development of an articulated prototype curriculum-supervisory system (Niedermeyer, 1970; 1972; 1977; Sullivan and Niedermeyer, 1973). The curriculum component was essentially technologically oriented (see Figure 1); that is, it focused on the development and production of "exportable" instructional units. Further, the curriculum was "outcomes-based" (constructed around a limited set of pre-specified behavioral objectives). For example, the SWRL Beginning (Kindergarten) Reading Program had as intended pupil outcomes

(1) reading 100 words by sight, (2) saying the sound of eleven initial consonants and digraphs and twelve vowel-consonant ending phonograms, (3) sounding out and reading new words composed of word elements learned in the second outcome, and (4) reading each letter by its name in either upper or lower case form. (Niedermeyer, 1977, p. 36).

Subsequently, instructional materials based on these objectives were designed and produced.

In order to most effectively implement the curriculum, a parallel outcomes-based supervisory system was developed (see Figure 2, Performance-Based). The two major elements of that system were (1) "instructional information" procedures designed to be of assistance to teachers in the development of performance standards, and (2) "instructional improvement" procedures designed to be of assistance in the analysis and remediation of observed pupil deficiencies. Both components relied heavily on the production and utilization of technological resources like filmstrips, cassettes, training manuals, and measuring/charting/reporting instruments.

The curriculum-supervisory system just described was adopted by 24 schools. The results as reported by Niedermeyer (1977) are quite dramatic. In the schools when the system was fully implemented (21 out of 24 schools), students clearly out-performed control group peers on such measures as end-of-year reading tests and number of instructional units completed. Equally important for present purposes, students in the fully implemented system out-performed their peers in those schools where for whatever reason the supervisory component was under-utilized or broke down!

It is quite true that the supervisory requirements in the system just described were fairly modest; clinical conceptions are far more demanding. It might also be argued that a kindergarten reading curriculum with limited, pre-specified, and easily measurable objectives is quite simplistic in itself and hence makes few supervisory demands. Further, it might be argued that experimental conditions are a distortion of reality. However valid such arguments might be, the SWRL planned variation clearly demonstrates (1) that close rather than loose coupling between compatible conceptions of curriculum and supervision is possible; (2) that curriculum can indeed impact on supervision through energizing a particular set of supervisory processes; and (3) that a planned, articulated curriculum-supervisory system can enhance student achievement. From some perspectives, that, after all, is what schooling is all about.

Summary and Concluding Observations

In a provisional way, this chapter explored the impact of curriculum on supervision. Mindful of Isaiah Berlin's (1969) observation that "The first step to understanding of men is the bringing to consciousness the model or models that dominate their thought and action . . . [and] to analyse the model itself . . . (p. 19)," we began in Part 1 by delineating five models ("conceptions") of curriculum—Cognitive Processes, Technology, Self-Actualization, Social Reconstruction-Relevance, and Academic Rationalism along with their respective descriptors (Figure 1). In Part 2 we did the same for supervision, identifying and describing four major classes—Administrative, Instructional Processes, Counseling, and Performance-Based. Within the Instructional Processes class, three discrete perspectives were chosen for analysis, Clinical, Technological, and Artistic. In Part 3 we inquired more closely into the relationship between curriculum and supervision. Consistent with Parts 1 and 2, such relationships were viewed from three perspectives—historical, teacher, and deliberate intent ("planned variation"). What general observations can be made?

Observation 1. Our reading in the fields of curriculum and supervision suggests that each has developed largely independently of the other. However productive this strategy may have been for the maturing of the separate disciplines, it has been equally limiting in its joint impact on the teacher's world. The history of innovation in schools, for example, the "new math" experience, would surely suggest a greater need for articulation.

Observation 2. The interactive impact of curriculum and supervision is a function of the degree to which one or the other or both is "open" or "closed." By "open" or "closed" we mean the extent to which one is amenable to influence by the other. Programmed learning curricula, for example, are on the closed end of the continuum. Supervisors functioning within such contexts may need to be content with seeking to influence the external aspects of teacher/learner interactions. Similarly, closed supervisory models, for example, personnel evaluation, are unlikely to influence curriculum in a significant way.

Observation 3. The interactive impact of curriculum and supervision is likely to be increased if both are approached from compatible perspectives. We are not prepared to argue at this time that the extent of compatibility must constitute a "planned variation." Intuitively, however, disjunctures in perspective are unlikely to create a climate conducive to productive teacher/supervisor interaction.

Observation 4. The interactive impact of curriculum and supervision is equally a function of a set of organizational factors (March, 1966). While this is not the time or place to delve into the organizational context of curriculum and supervision, it is clear that the structural characteristics of schools exert major influences on curriculum and supervision. "Open" curricula, for example, have difficulty surviving in "closed" organizational structures. Similarly, organizational role definitions that imply that teachers "do" curriculum while supervision is something "done to" them are unlikely to facilitate the development of "organic" teacher/supervisor relationships. In sum, concern for the educative process requires simultaneous attention to a wider set of phenomena than taken into account heretofore.

References

Acheson, K., and Gall, M. *Techniques in the Clinical Supervision of Teachers.* New York: Longman, 1980.

Bereiter, Carl. "Elementary School: Necessity or Convenience?" In *Conflicting Conceptions of Curriculum.* Edited by Eisner and Vallance.

Berlin, I. "Does Political Theory Still Exist?" In *Philosophy, Politics, and Society.* 2nd series. Edited by P. Laslett and W. G. Runciman. Oxford: Basil Blackwell, 1969.

Blumberg, A. "Supervisory Behavior and Interpersonal Relations." *Educational Administration Quarterly* 4 (1968): 34-45.

Blumberg, A. *Supervisors and Teachers: A Private Cold War.* Berkeley: McCutchan, 1974.

Bobbitt, F. *The Curriculum.* Boston: Houghton Mifflin, 1918.

Brod, R. *The Computer as an Authority Figure: Some Effects of C&I on Student Perception of Teacher Authority.* (Technical Report #29) Palo Alto, Calif.: Stanford Center for Research and Development in Teaching, 1972.

Burns, Richard W., and Brooks, Gary D. "Processes, Problem Solving, and Curriculum Reform." In *Conflicting Conceptions of Curriculum.* Edited by Eisner and Vallance.

Bushnell, D. "On Using Computers to Individualize Instruction." In *The Computer in American Education.* Edited by D. Bushnell and D. Allen. New York: Wiley, 1967.

Callahan, R. *Education and the Cult of Efficiency*. Chicago: University of Chicago Press, 1962.

Cogan, M. *Clinical Supervision*. Boston: Houghton Mifflin, 1973.

Corwin, R. "Professional Persons in Public Organizations." *Educational Administration Quarterly* 1 (1965): 1-22.

Cuban, L. "The Powerlessness of Irrelevancy." *Educational Leadership* 25 (1968): 393-396.

DeWitt, W. "Instructional Supervision." *Educational Leadership* 34 (1977): 589-593.

Eisner, E., and Vallance, E., eds. *Conflicting Conceptions of Curriculum*. Berkeley: McCutchan, 1974.

Gagne, R. "Curriculum Research and the Promotion of Learning." In *Perspectives of Curriculum Evaluation*. Edited by R. Stake. Chicago: Rand McNally, 1967.

Glaser, R., ed. *Teaching Machines and Programmed Learning II: Data and Directions*. Washington, D.C.: National Education Association, 1965.

Goldhammer, R. *Clinical Supervision*. New York: Holt, Rinehart and Winston, 1969.

Goldman, Ralph F., and others. "Some Economic Models of Curriculum Structure." In *Conflicting Conceptions of Curriculum*. Edited by Eisner and Vallance.

Hirst, P. H., and Peters, R. S. "The Curriculum." In *Conflicting Conceptions of Curriculum*. Edited by Eisner and Vallance

Junell, Joseph S. "Is Rational Man Our First Priority?" In *Conflicting Conceptions of Curriculum*. Edited by Eisner and Vallance.

Katz, D., and Kahn, R. *The Social Psychology of Organizations*. New York: Wiley, 1966.

Koran, J., Jr. "Supervision: An Attempt to Modify Behavior." *Educational Leadership* 26 (1969): 754-757.

Lortie, D. *Schoolteacher*. Chicago: University of Chicago Press, 1975.

Mager, R. *Preparing Instructional Objectives*. Palo Alto, Calif.: Fearon, 1962.

Mann, John S. "Political Power and the High School Curriculum." In *Conflicting Conceptions of Curriculum*. Edited By Eisner and Vallance.

March, J. G. "Organizational Factors in Supervision." In *The Supervisor: Agent for Change in Teaching*. Edited by J. Raths and R. Leeper. Alexandria, Va.: ASCD, 1966.

McGregor, D. *The Human Side of Enterprise*. New York: McGraw-Hill, 1960.

McNeil, L. "Bibliographical Essay." In *Curriculum and Evaluation*. Edited By A. Bellack and H. Kliebard. Berkeley: McCutchan, 1977.

Mosher, R., and Purpel, D. *Supervision: The Reluctant Profession*. Boston: Houghton Mifflin, 1972.

Niedermeyer, F. "Developing Exportable Teacher Training for Criterion-Referenced Instruction Programs." Los Alamitos, Calif.: SWRL Educational Research and Development, 1970.

Niedermeyer, F. "Differential Effects of Individual and Group Testing Strategies in an Objectives-Based Instructional System." *Journal of Educational Measurement* 9 (1972): 119-204.

Niedermeyer, F. "The Testing of a Prototype System for Outcomes-Based Instructional Supervision." *Educational Administration Quarterly* 13 (1977): 34-50.

Phenix, Philip H. "Trancendence and the Curriculum." In *Conflicting Conceptions of Curriculum*. Edited by Eisner and Vallance.

Pohland, P., and Higbie, V. "Formal Expectations and the Principalship." Paper presented at the annual meeting of the American Educational Research Association, San Francisco, 1978.

Popham, W. J. "Objectives and Instruction." In *Instructional Objectives*. Edited by W. J. Popham, E. Eisner, H. Sullivan, and L. Tyler. Chicago: Rand McNally, 1969.

Rivlin, A. *Systematic Thinking for Social Action*. Washington, D.C.: The Brookings Institution, 1971.

Sanders, N. *Classroom Questions*. New York: Harper and Row, 1966.

Schwab, Joseph J. "The Concept of the Structure of a Discipline." In *Conflicting Conceptions of Curriculum*. Edited by Eisner and Vallance.

Skinner, B. *The Technology of Teaching*. New York: Appleton-Century-Crofts, 1968.

Silverman, Robert E. "Using the *S-R* Reinforcement Model." In *Conflicting Conceptions of Curriculum*. Edited by Eisner and Vallance.

Sullivan, H., and Niedermeyer, F. "Pupil Achievement Under Varying Levels of Teacher Accountability." Los Alamitos, Calif.: SWRL Educational Research and Development, 1973.

Tyler, R. *Basic Principles of Curriculum and Instruction*. Chicago: University of Chicago Press, 1950.

Zahorik, J. "Supervision as Value Development." The Wisconsin Elementary School Principals' Association *Bulletin* 42 (1977): 13.

Chapter 11.
Impact of the Schools' Bureaucratic Structure on Supervision

Gerald R. Firth and Keith P. Eiken

DESPITE THE ADMONITION THAT FORM SHOULD FOLLOW FUNCTION, supervision often conforms to the organizational context in which it operates. The impact of the bureaucratic structure of the school district on the supervision of instruction is direct, strong, and, in many instances, immediate. Often such influences are obvious and formal. Even in more subtle and informal ways, however, the effects of the organization bend the official supervisory system out of shape in actual operation.

In a school or district, the choice of organizational structure provides the linkage between the views regarding administration and the expectations for supervison. If changes are sought in supervisory practice, the values and assumptions implicit in the organizational structure of schools must first be altered.

It is unnecessary and perhaps impossible to catalog the various configurations by which supervisory services are delivered throughout the nation. Seven of the more common bureaucratic models for supervision of instruction will be briefly examined: staff consultant, line authority, multiple central office support, decentralized area support, performance assessment, local school support, and intermediate service agency support.

The advantages and disadvantages of each of these structures for supervisory services are described in reference to leadership, technical skills, communication, decision making, morale functions, curriculum responsibilities, and organizational roles.

A. Staff Consultant Roles

The most common type of supervisory role is that of a chief instructional leader in the office of the superintendent. The individual functioning in such a position may have a number of titles, including curriculum coordinator or instructional supervisor. Although usually

Gerald R. Firth is Professor and Chairperson, Department of Curriculum and Supervision, University of Georgia, Athens. Keith P. Eiken is Coordinator of the Advance Program for Instruction, Jefferson County Public Schools, Louisville, Kentucky.

considered a staff position that carries no authority, incumbents frequently accrue power because the actions they recommend are supported by superordinates and/or unchallenged by subordinates. Repetition of this process establishes decision making authority that is not reflected by an organizational chart.

In larger school districts, the efforts of this generalist are supplemented or supplanted by subject specialists, such as in mathematics, reading, or media, who operate on a K-12 basis. In some situations, the responsibilities are divided among grade levels with respective supervisors for the elementary, middle and/or junior high, and high schools. Subject specialists emphasize the vertical relationship of particular programs and seek articulation from one grade or school level to another. School level specialists emphasize the horizontal relationships of various programs and seek coordination at the same grade level within and among schools.

Supervision of instruction through a staff consultant structure is based on the assumption that an effective organization distinguishes and separates those who advise and counsel from those with power who direct.

The success of supervisory leadership in this structure is a function of the value placed on instructional improvement by the administration. If the superintendent and the principals are committed to management and maintenance, the influence of the supervisor is diminished. However, the staff consultant has the opportunity to shape the priorities of the organization and to enhance the importance of instructional improvement by determining the allocation of resources.

As a staff consultant, the supervisor relies on a combination of human, managerial, and technical skills to influence both faculty and administration. Although all such skills are important, it is the technical competencies requested by teachers directly or indirectly through principals that gain initial entry for the supervisor to classroom or office and sustain his or her presence there. The supervisor is expected to possess teaching experience, to model appropriate behavior, and to provide necessary assistance.

In communicating ideas, requests, and responses as consultant to both teachers and principals, the supervisor becomes an information broker. Linkages are established within and among schools and the centrality of the supervisor enables him or her to become an information gatekeeper. In addition to such internal activities, the supervisor often must communicate trends or interpret data from external sources to faculty and administration. However, access to official communication channels is available only through the organizational structure. If such communication is rigidly monitored (for example, three signatures required for each memorandum), the process slows considerably under the burden of administrative control.

For supervisors serving as staff consultants, decision making is restricted to creating awareness, persuading, and advising. Effective supervisors in such roles must be highly informed about programs and instruction in the schools. The information they provide can influence the quality of administrative decisions by minimizing precipitous or unwarranted solutions proposed in the name of expediency. However, the supervisor must offer alternatives knowing that the administrator may come to a decision by using other legitimate criteria.

Those in staff consultant roles can enhance morale of teachers by becoming a professional ally who is not required to make decisions regarding their future. However, this situation may deteriorate and result in frustration when supervisors sympathetic to the teachers' cause are impotent to alter the conditions necessary for improvement. The supervisor likewise is frustrated when he/she is unable to provide the circumstances teachers need for success.

Legislative mandates and public outcries for improved student learning have forced supervisors to become more involved in curriculum planning, implementation, and evaluation. However, commitment of the supervisor's time and energy to areas in which they are not well prepared limits opportunities for staff consultants to respond to teachers and principals when problems of instructional improvement and staff development emerge.

The effectiveness of the supervisor as a staff consultant depends on the functions assigned to the position in the total bureaucratic structure of the school district. If program design and program implementation are conceived as rigidly separate responsibilities within the organization, the influence of the staff consultant role is limited. The potential of the role for affecting change is related to control of resources directly by the supervisor or indirectly through influence on the principals. Therefore, the nature of the informal relationships between the supervisor and the principals is of prime importance.

B. Line Authority Roles

The vesting of responsibility for supervision in an administrative position with the title of assistant or associate superintendent for instruction is typical. In many school districts, principals are responsible to this individual, at least for curricular and instructional matters. However, complications often arise when the principals are also responsible for all duties except instruction to an assistant, associate, or even a deputy superintendent for administration.

Some school districts distribute supervisory responsibilities among directors of elementary and secondary education while other districts have the similar position of director of junior high/middle schools. This pattern has the advantage of coordinating all programs within the respective school levels at the expense of articulation between school levels.

Supervision of instruction through a line authority structure is based on the assumption that an effective organization combines authority and responsibility for various operations in the same position.

The concentration of leadership in line positions is often a mixed blessing. While this structure enables the individual responsible for instructional supervision to act in a number of related areas, it represents a superior-subordinate relationship many believe interferes with effective supervisory practice. It also forces supervision to compete with various managerial tasks and other concerns for the time, energy, and attention of the line administrator at the district or school level.

As a qualification for appointment to a line position, supervisory skills are often given low priority. Consequently, technical skills essential for improvement of instruction often must be developed on the job. It is human nature to emphasize the managerial skills called on by other responsibilities while tending to avoid situations that require the technical skills of supervision.

Communication is clear and direct but is often authoritative rather than consultative. Because the supervisor is a line officer, messages from him or her are assumed to be directives. More important, information considered potentially detrimental to teachers, but that a supervisor would need in order to assist teachers with their problems, might not be transmitted to the supervisor in a line authority position in fear that the supervisor would use it against teachers in his or her dual role as administrator.

Difficulty frequently arises in maintaining both perspective and balance in decision making for the supervisor in a position of line authority. Matters of program and personnel, generally considered to be the prerogative of this role, must compete with matters of finance, facilities, and student services. Conforming to existing administrative policies or organizational procedures may take precedence over improving instruction. Therefore, supervisory responsibilities assigned to a line authority position may be compromised by management decisions made by the same individual.

Although teachers may view the individual occupying a line authority role as able to resolve their problems, morale may be influenced negatively if he or she is considered unwilling or reluctant to do so. The absence of a separate position devoted fully to supervision limits the amount of specialized assistance teachers can hope to receive in improving instruction and restricts the willingness of teachers to identify problem situations that may expose their real or perceived weaknesses.

Curriculum responsibilities can be readily assigned to an individual in a line authority role. Carrying out such responsibilities, however, illustrates a significant disparity between authority and ability. The requirements stated in job descriptions for such positions often demand even less preparation and/or experience in the area of curriculum than in the area of supervision. Line authority positions are usually filled on the basis of qualifications in administration and management, rather than either curriculum or supervision.

The allegiance of the individual in a line authority role to the organization that created his/her position limits the probability and perhaps the possibility for extensive change in the current structure. However, it is likely that the supervisor in a line authority role will ultimately recognize the importance of and significant relationships among curriculum, instruction, and administration. He/she can then use line authority to remove barriers within the present structure or modify the organization to accommodate program innovations.

C. Multiple Central Office Units

Another common pattern of supervision consists of multiple assignments at the central office level. In some districts, the size, complexity, or funding of certain programs, particularly for vocational education, special education, and career education, prompt the appointment of supervisors to serve each area. Such arrangements are sometimes established to foster collaboration among teachers scattered throughout several schools and engaged in the implementation of the same innovative project or practice; for example, teachers involved in a particular approach to reading. Dissatisfaction with the traditional structure for providing supervisory services has led some districts to create an alternative and competing structure to meet new and special needs. The gamble here is that the new organization will circumvent, outlast, and ultimately replace the original organization.

Supervision of instruction through a multiple central support structure is based on the assumption that an effective organization fully utilizes specialization.

The uneven and broad distribution of supervisory leadership to individuals in specific content areas often promotes the formation of coalitions. Supervisors representing related programs (art and music, for instance), frequently join forces—at least informally—to obtain a greater share of resources than those in other coalitions, such as industrial arts, home economics, and vocational education. Striving to preserve parochial interests then frequently becomes more of a driving force than does the effort to achieve organizational goals.

Supervisors serving each unit have highly specialized technical skills that they apply to their particular fields. However, their very specialized vocabularies and approaches interfere with cross-fertilization among programs or the use of supervisory personnel in other portions of the program. As a result, although some general supervisory skills may be refined and strengthened through continued use, others needed to support organizational goals may decline due to inactivity.

Communication is far more likely between individuals in a particular field because of their common vocabulary and interests. Members of a unit seek mutual assistance through communication with peers. As the interdependence of those within an area increases, however, there is often a corresponding decrease in communication with members of other units.

Supervisors of multiple central office units often consider several alternatives before making a decision. Their judgments about improvements though tend to be unduly influenced by the effects of the proposed change on the area they represent as supervisor. The determination to "guard the turf" often fosters political negotiations rather than educational leadership.

Morale within each separate supervisor's group may be high and the commitment to teamwork strong. However, members of one unit may become suspicious of another unit simply because no understanding develops between them. Successes or gains by one group are interpreted as failures or losses by another.

Commitment to curriculum is restricted to those programs represented by members of the unit. Beliefs common to the group will be reinforced while those of other specializations will be ignored. Such convictions will be held so strongly that conflict among units is likely to result when a total curriculum is considered. Any departmentalization stresses articulation within the particular program while coordination with other programs is neglected.

Multiple central office units within an organization can bring about duplication of effort, divided loyalties, role ambiguity, and territorial disputes. The mere existence of more than a single supervisory unit in the same school district threatens coordination, cooperation, and communication. Collaboration among such units is essential if supervision is to assist rather than disrupt instruction. Yet this is extremely difficult to obtain because specialists prefer to stress the distinguishing characteristics that support retention of their separate units.

D. Decentralized Area Support Roles

Large school districts, particularly in metropolitan centers, have sought to decentralize in an effort to increase responsiveness to subcommunities. Some members of the central office staff may be assigned to the offices of assistant superintendents in their respective areas. Those who remain in the central office may be viewed as senior specialized resources to supplement, upon request, those available in the area offices. In other metropolitan districts seeking to decentralize, the functions of those in the central office may be redefined to focus on planning, implementing, and/or evaluating for the district as a whole.

The decentralized model may necessitate a diffusion of staff members with technical skills and knowledge into regions where responsibilities are more general in nature. Depending on the overall organizational plan, the specialist-turned-generalist frequently becomes a "problem-solver" with responsibility for arranging logistical support to the local school, rather than providing specific technical assistance in program developments.

Supervision of instruction through a decentralized area support structure is based on the assumption that an effective organization assigns responsibility close to the operational level.

The diffusion of leadership among the regions can foster a variety of staff relationships, ranging from competitive to interdependent. Depending on the leadership style evident in each region, supervisory tasks can be co-opted into purposeless directives, such as fund-raising campaigns for the United Way, or result in the imaginative sharing of specialized knowledge, such as the application of mastery learning principles across the curriculum.

The attempt to establish duplicate supervisory units in each decentralized area results in spreading the pool of leadership personnel thinly across a broad front, with a corresponding decrease in the number of specialized resources available to any area. It is unlikely that veteran supervisors, previously identified with narrow specialities, can completely alter their roles to become expert across-the-board planners and that they can avoid the tendency to seek opportunities to apply skills with which they have been successful in the past.

Advantages exist, however, in smaller administrative units. Supervisory personnel become better informed about the general school operation and more aware of local instructional problems. And the sense of isolation from the central school authority commonly felt among the school staff lessens as communication increases. If the supervisory roles are not defined to prevent it, however, and if strong communication links are not forged with the central authority, the area supervisory staff may focus on operational tasks and neglect program development priorities.

Decision making can be enhanced in this decentralized model by providing a broader base of involvement for determining priorities and deploying resources. Sub-communities can be involved in advisory capacities related to current problems. In reality, however, decision making may become narrower in focus if the immediate needs of the local situation obscure the long-range goals of the school district or subvert the consistency of general policies that provide integrity to the district as a whole.

The morale of supervisors is influenced by the functions required of them under the decentralized model. If resources are available to accomplish realistic goals and if results can be achieved, then morale is increased. Both program planning and inservice training are major supervisory tasks in a decentralized district; these functions are necessary for progress and contribute to morale. Task commitment decreases and morale is lowered, however, if supervisors simply facilitate administrative changes.

Decentralization is designed to increase responsiveness to and involvement in curriculum in each region. Lacking a districtwide plan, each region may view curriculum differently; for example, which subjects to be learned, objectives to be achieved, or minimum competencies to be mastered. If program development receives less attention than program implementation in the overall structure, curriculum changes become mere expedients to satisfy the demands of current policy makers and are subject to frequent change. Program development should receive conscious attention to provide continuing direction.

Although a separate leadership team is established under the decentralized area support structure, the credibility of the supervisor may be reduced. Since line authority is a dominant characteristic in a decentralized organization, the district teams may be dominated by administrators who are concerned solely with implementing directives. Supervisors then become "go-betweens" responsible for negotiating with individuals and groups who may support or subvert the directives. Unless the local school staff and the sub-community perceive supervisors as technically competent to resolve problems related to curriculum and instruction, their role becomes merely another bureaucratic layer that hinders any meaningful action.

E. Performance Assessment Roles

Trends toward competency-based education and professional accountability have created a variety of roles concerned with the assessment of teacher performance. Many of the individuals engaged in this activity are not considered supervisors as that term traditionally has been applied within the school context. However, they use procedures associated with instructional supervision and the results of their efforts have significant impact on both teachers and supervisors.

A prominent feature of the assessment process is the classroom observation conducted by individuals specially trained in a particular technique. Emphasis is placed on using recently developed instruments and gathering objective data. Teachers would not, however, expect assistance from those who collect data. Moreover, those who provide supportive supervision to teachers must not be required to render judgments regarding the teachers' retention in or dismissal from employment.

In some situations, teams comprising teachers, supervisors, and administrators collect data, develop profiles, and analyze competencies. These reports are then shared with the observed teacher in a nonthreatening atmosphere by a member of the assessment team and/or by a supportive supervisor. Individualized plans for improvement are prepared by the teacher in cooperation with the supervisor. In this model, responsibilities for performance assessment may be assigned to a teacher evaluator and those for staff development to a teacher educator.

Supervision of instruction through a performance assessment structure is based on the assumption that an effective organization separates responsibility for evaluation from responsibility for support.

Leadership is focused on "correction" of factors assessed as below acceptable minimum according to the standards applied. Although the responsibility for improvement clearly is vested in the regular supervisory staff, their efforts are directed by the requirement of demonstrating progress within the particular system. In effect, the assessment both determines the nature of the assistance to be rendered and the assignments of those who are responsible for assisting.

The technical skills of supervisors that are called upon most frequently are those associated with the standards on which teachers receive the lowest ratings. Conversely, the skills with which supervisors are most qualified may not be utilized because the assessments do not indicate need for them. As a result, supervisors find that their technical skills must conform to the assessment standards.

Communication between supervisors and teachers is focused on the results of the assessment and little else. Supervisors confer with assessors on those same topics. Other needs felt by the teachers and/or perceived by the supervisor are seldom considered because of the importance of the standards and the press of time for demonstrating improvement.

Even when teachers have contributed to the development of the standards to be imposed—rare in these days of accountability—their attitude toward the application of such assessment procedures is consistently negative. Teachers typically believe no standards can be universally applied to all situations without modification for particular conditions. Moreover, they feel they are invariably placed at a disadvantage when trying to convey an accurate picture of their performance.

Curriculum change occurs as a result of the assessment process, but changes are incremental, haphazard, and incidental to the numerous instructional changes made based on the performance ratings. Even though no overall curriculum change is intended, the results in each classroom are idiosyncratic to the particular teacher and reflect the local situation. In effect, the assessment standards that were intended to produce similarity in performance actually contribute to greater, more unstructured diversity in school program.

Although unintentionally, performance instruments shape the organization in which the assessment is made. In particular, the performance assessment structure shifts the locus of responsibility for supervision. The relationship between teacher and observer takes on greater importance than the relationship between teacher and students or supervisor. The teacher anticipates the behavior to be recorded on the particular assessment instrument while, in effect, the observer assumes the role of supervisor. When the instructional supervisor dilutes his/her attention to classroom performance under the press of other duties, he/she contributes substantially to this redefinition of the supervisory role.

F. Local School Support Roles

Another step in decentralizing authority and responsibility for supervision is the development of specific roles to support the improvement of instruction in each school. Such local school support roles may be performed by a single individual; the assistant principal for instruction is a familiar example in the high school. Or, in some districts, local school support is provided by several individuals. Traditional department heads in the high school, team leadership in the junior high/middle school, and lead teachers in the elementary school are examples of this plural form. Although some elementary schools are large enough to assign a lead teacher at both the primary and intermediate levels, a single resource teacher in an elementary school is more common. Recently peer or collegial supervision by teachers themselves has been encouraged as the source of support at the local school level.

All such local school support roles increase opportunities for response to teacher problems. A single individual may act in a capacity similar to the generalist operating districtwide. The assistant principal for instruction or resource teacher, for instance, must view a particular classroom in the perspective of coordination within the program. In the form of plural roles, the characteristics displayed are similar to the subject or school-level specialists operating districtwide. The department head in the high school, team leader in the junior high/middle school, and lead teachers in the elementary school must view a particular classroom in the perspective of articulation among levels of particular subjects.

Supervision of instruction through a local school support structure is based on the assumption that an effective organization uses people immediately available and familiar with the situation.

The existence of local school support roles shifts responsibilities for leadership in supervision, instruction, and curriculum from the principal to one or more designated deputies. As these individuals are called on more frequently by members of the faculty or are directed by the principal to respond to requests, the principal has in fact delegated to a subordinate responsibility for the most important aspects of the school. The converse of this situation is that some faculty will perceive that supervision, instruction, and/or curriculum are accorded lower priority than some management duties because the former are assigned to the assistant principal or resource teacher while the principal attends to the latter. When plural support roles exist in a school, responsibility is dispersed among several individuals each of whom is expected to provide leadership in a limited sphere. Although a department head or team leader is responsible for only a single portion of the school program, he or she often exercises substantial authority over its direction. The effect is that while communication among those involved in a particular program increases, so do the problems of coordination throughout the school by the principal.

Technical skills of those serving in local school support roles often must be developed on the job. As their effectiveness in improving instruction increases, they emphasize those skills while allowing other skills, even the teaching competencies that may have earned them the job, to diminish. At the same time, the administrator relieved of the direct supervision of faculty devotes attention to managerial activities.

The existence of local school support roles tends to interrupt the communication network between teachers and principals regarding matters of supervision, instruction, curriculum, and, often, personnel. The single form, such as assistant principal or resource teacher, typically becomes an intermediary. The advantage of this situation is that the principal is provided a comprehensive view of the program from a single source. The accompanying disadvantage is that the principal relies on a subordinate's perspective for this most important aspect of the school. Moreover, direction of communication on such matters to the assistant principal or resource teacher increases the proportion of communication regarding managerial affairs reaching the principal. Plural support roles at the local school level create a lateral communication network among such individuals. This diffuses communication to and from the principal so that neither the principal nor the department heads or team leaders possess all of the information on a particular topic at a given time.

It can be argued that the principal ultimately makes the final decision even when matters of supervision, instruction, and curriculum are the primary responsibilities of a subordinate. Experience demonstrates the fallacy of this argument, however. If the principal has confidence in the assistant principal or resource teacher, the principal will encourage that individual to exercise judgment and initiative. By consistently confirming the recommendations of the subordinate, the principal effectively places the decision making process at the next lower level. Many decisions made by department heads or team leaders which in themselves appear routine and even innocuous combine to shape a program. The support approved or denied ultimately may determine a total configuration that would never have received acceptance if examined in its entirety. Perhaps the most significant decision made by the subordinate is not to decide. In such a case the subordinate not only fails to support the teacher's request but effectively eliminates the opportunity for the teacher to appeal to the principal.

The morale of the faculty is disrupted if confusion exists in regard to appropriate allegiance within a school. Although teachers may appreciate the delegation of responsibility for supervision, the parameters of local school support roles are often ill-defined. As a result, teachers may consult the assistant principal or team leader on matters that the principal feels should have been referred to him or her. Conversely, they may bring to the principal matters that the principal feels should be handled by the subordinate.

It is paradoxical that the local school support role in its single form is likely to increase the potential for curriculum change while in its plural form may inhibit such change. The key to improvement is the encouragement of an innovative teacher at the crucial early stages of planning and development. An assistant principal or resource teacher willingly devotes attention to an activity that appears to enhance his or her role in supervision, instruction, and/or curriculum. The same activity may be burdensome to a principal who has a broad spectrum of responsibilities. Lack of active support, albeit unintentional, may be interpreted by the innovative teacher as a signal to decelerate or to abandon a promising project. In contrast, the plural roles operate against the marshaling of sufficient resources—time, material, funds, and/or personnel—to support an innovation. In this case, several departments or teams must be convinced of the favorable consequences of a proposed change. Moreover, the criteria applied to such proposals often are based on perceived benefits to the department or team rather than to the total school enterprise.

The establishment of local school support roles for supervision, instruction, and curriculum intrudes a structural level between the principal and teachers. In its single form, responsibility for specified duties is concentrated in an assistant principal or resource teacher and the principal's time is freed for responsibilities in other areas. Whether the principal can appropriately function in such an organization remains a matter of conjecture. In schools with plural support roles, no such concentration occurs and loyalties to the department or team are created with corresponding diminution of allegiance to the total school. The official recognition of plural roles, although often essential to the effectiveness of the program, nonetheless establishes structures that impede reallocation of resources. Such structures not only compete with each other but with the total school for shares of a finite supply of resources. Larger departments or teams possess greater internal flexibility but may be less willing to adapt to the needs of the total school.

G. Intermediate Service Agency Roles

Supervision is frequently included among the varied functions of intermediate service agencies established between the state education department and local school districts. The differing designations applied throughout the country, such as intermediate unit, board of cooperative educational services, or cooperative educational service agency, often reflect the particular governance structure. Irrespective of title, these organizations were formed to share services on a collective basis among school districts that independently could not justify them because of limited size, programs, and/or funding.

Supervisory services available through such intermediate agencies may include generalists, subject specialists, grade level specialists, coordinators of special programs, and/or consultants for innovative projects. The range of services provided by a "second layer" of supervision tremendously complicates delivery of assistance to an individual teacher in a particular school. Relationships among supervisory personnel from the state education department, the intermediate service agency, and the local school district frequently lack clarification. State supervisors typically work directly with supervisors in the central office of the school district, by-passing staff members of the intermediate service agency. Moreover, staff members from the intermediate service agency typically work directly with leadership personnel or teachers in a local school, by-passing supervisors in the central office of the school district. A further complication is introduced by the preference of some teachers to call upon supervisors from the central office of the school district because of acquaintance and/or confidence, ignoring expertise provided or responsibility assigned elsewhere in the organization. It is usually more difficult for a supervisor operating on an inter-district basis to establish such relationships or to maintain responsive service.

Supervision of instruction through an intermediate service agency structure is based on the assumption that an effective organization shares specialized services rather than duplicates general resources.

Leadership at the local school and district office level is crucial to the success of the intermediate service agency structure for supervision. The particular blend of assistance to teachers in the improvement of instruction is a function of proper selection among available resources. The more individuals involved in the supervisory process at different levels, the greater the importance of the organizational structure regarding the delivery of such services to the classroom teacher. Supervisors from the central office and from the intermediate service agency may be utilized by a particular school while neither source of assistance may be called upon to assist another school in the same district.

An intermediate service agency selects its supervisory personnel with the intention of supplementing skills available from the central office staff of the respective school districts in the geographic area. However, the larger number of supervisory personnel available may be an inaccurate index of the assistance that can be brought to bear on a given situation. The staff recruited by the intermediate agency to serve the general needs of several school districts may be inappropriate to meet the specific needs of a particular district. In fact, some services in-

Decision Making	Minimizes rash solutions with alternatives but dependent on persuasion of administrators	Clarifies prerogatives for supervision but compromises by management responsibilities	Permits consideration of varied alternatives but encourages protection of parochial interests	Encourages broad basis of involvement but risks loss of district policy integrity	Contributes to improved performance but limits attention to items in assessment	Encourages initiative by subordinates but removes decision from principal	Retains local prerogatives but questions loyalty of agency staff
Morale Functions	Provides sympathetic ally but dependent on others to alter circumstances	Possesses ability to resolve teacher problems but considered reluctant to do so	Promotes teamwork within unit but fosters suspicion between members of different units	Increases opportunities for assistance but dependent on resource availability	Establishes standard for assessment but distrusted due to general application	Enhances opportunities for assistance but confuses teacher allegiance	Enhances importance of supervision but requires request for assistance
Curriculum Responsibilities	Contributes to program development but limits opportunities to assist teachers	Accepts assignments readily but lacks appropriate qualifications	Encourages attention to each subject area but restricts consideration of total program	Increases responsiveness to local program needs but threatens total district direction	Promotes change for similarity but produces unstructured diversity	Increases potential for change but restricts marshaling of resources	Addresses particular concerns but may compromise district goals
Organizational Roles	Potential related to resource control but limited to relationships with principals	Possesses power to modify situation but holds allegiance to existing structure	Distinguishes particular characteristic but threatens collaborative efforts	Provides team for particular area but increases tendency for supervisors to become part of management	Shapes organization to assessment but shifts responsibility for supervision	Frees principal for other duties but intrudes additional level of structure	Promises mutually supporting structure but requires clear distribution of responsibility.
Value Assumption	Advise and counsel should be separate from power and direction	Power and responsibility for related operations should be combined	Specialization should be fully utilized	Responsibility should be assigned close to the operational level	Responsibility for evaluation and support functions should be separated	Sources of support should be immediately available and familiar with local situation	Resources should be shared rather than duplicated

variably will duplicate the skills of supervisors in a particular district.

Communication becomes complicated at every level when an intermediate agency support structure is established. It is perhaps most confusing in the local school. Some teachers are saturated with divergent, and perhaps contradictory, views offered by supervisors representing several levels of organization. Other teachers receive little or no assistance from any organizational level. If services from the intermediate agency are directly available to the principal, other options open to the supervisor in the district may not be considered. If such services can be called upon only by the district supervisor, two explanations are required.

Decision making on the part of staff members of the intermediate agency are limited to recommendations since they are "once removed" from the district supervisory operation. There is always a question of loyalty to the teacher and to the district in which a supervisor serves. A further complication occurs for the supervisor who "works for" an intermediate agency that "works for" the district that employs the teacher in need of assistance.

Morale will be affected, if only because of the additional personnel involved in the process of instructional improvement. Principals often view a call for assistance, whether for themselves or for a teacher, as an admission of inadequacy. The problem is compounded when supervisors in the district office hold the same view concerning the use of staff members from the intermediate agency.

Unless the staff members from the intermediate agency are well acquainted with the total curriculum of a school district and the direction of its development, their assistance with particular instructional concerns may in fact compromise the long-range goals. Time is unlikely to allow the necessary familiarity that would provide such perspective. If improvements are to contribute to total programmatic thrust, monitoring must be done by supervisors within the respective districts.

Organizational roles must be clear if the services provided by the intermediate agency are to be effective and efficient. Confusion in responsibility, role ambiguity, and territorial disputes results in service that is both uneven and inequitable. Unless roles are clear, previous modes of operation are likely to continue and supervisory services will be requested from the intermediate agency only when time and/or circumstances dictate. It is possible to develop a mutually supporting structure that will allow the intermediate service agency to benefit several districts which retain their particular integrity and sovereignty—political, geographic, and programmatic. The greatest obstacle to the evolution of such an organization is the reluctance of the local school districts to release supervisors already in their employ to serve other districts within the area served by the intermediate support agency. This is particularly true if partial control over such services would be surrendered to the intermediate agency by a local school district that also expects to call upon it for assistance.

Summary

The delivery of supervision to schools is influenced by the type of bureaucratic structure in which such services must operate. The many and complex variables involved in each situation preclude a single definitive description. However, it is possible to indicate the likely consequences of the seven organizational patterns for supervision selected for examination in this chapter. The accompanying chart presents the major advantages and disadvantages of staff consultant, line authority, multiple central office support, decentralized area support, performance assessment, local school support, and intermediate service agency support roles.

It is possible to select among these alternatives for the delivery of supervisory services the pattern most compatible with the values and assumptions upon which the bureaucratic organization of a school or district is based. Perhaps even more significant is the option of restructuring supervisory practice on the basis of changing values and assumptions regarding organization. The pattern selected can serve to make supervision more informal, make evaluation more formative than summative, reduce authority relationships, or involve teachers more directly in the supervisory process. Only a change in priorities for the school or district will permit working with teachers directly in instruction and in classroom improvement to become the primary concern of administrators and of supervisors.

Chapter 12.

External Influences on Supervision: Seasonal Winds and Prevailing Climate

Louis Rubin

LIKE ANY OTHER ENDEAVOR IN THE PUBLIC ARENA, supervision is subject to the ebb and flow of policy and politics. Educational goals and instructional priorities habitually are readjusted to fit the changing times. Thus, schooling—and therefore supervision—invariably reflect social concerns and societal trends. In the 40s, for example, we witnessed a strong drift toward greater socialization efforts; in the 50s the tides turned to modernization of subject matter; in the 60s humanistic values took on renewed importance; and in the 70s the focus again shifted to teacher effectiveness in achieving specified learning outcomes.

The present scene is no different in that it is characterized by its own spate of external pressures. The continuing growth in teachers' political strength, the persistent interest in cooperative as opposed to administrative management, a new posture on the education of handicapped children, and the ubiquitous preoccupation with accountability and "basics" have all had their impact. Currently, moreover, supervision must also contend with the aftermath of prolonged educational criticism in the media, a somewhat new troublesome phenomenon known as teacher burn-out, budgetary reductions, and the implications of recent research in teaching and learning.

Sustained media emphasis on declining test scores, as an illustration, has resulted in a wholesale attempt to raise—at virtually any cost—student achievement on standardized tests. Many supervisors, in fact, are now forced to spend the whole of their professional energies on bettering student performance. At least temporarily, therefore, the traditional supervisory goal of good general education has been displaced.

In addition, the nature of the time has sharply diminished teachers' sense of well-being. As the neo-conservative mood deepens, a broad conception of well-balanced curricula has given way to a constrained, more fundamentalist, educational program. Worse, collective bargaining coupled with teacher strikes have eroded the long-standing esteem in which teachers have been held. Today's practitioners are

Louis Rubin is Professor of Education at the University of Illinois, Urbana-Champaign.

viewed more as members of a self-serving craft than of a helping profession. As a result, the customary impediments confronting supervisors have been greatly compounded. Job insecurity brought on by extensive school closings, salaries decimated by inflation, lack of parental support, and plain violence making teaching an increasingly dangerous vocation, have had a cumulative effect. It is not surprising, therefore, that many supervisors must cope with teachers who are disillusioned and embittered.

The machinations of Washington have also had an impact. As various federal programs are curtailed or terminated, there is a corresponding alteration in supervisory responsibilities. Recently, for example, national policy has bent in the direction of school-based reform, greater principal responsibility for school improvement, more parent participation, and increased collaboration among educational agencies. Concerned about possible redundancy, federal program officers have sought to promote cooperative networks that yield greater efficiency. More specifically, supervisors have been called upon to diagnose school weaknesses, project correctives, and help implement desirable changes. If these endeavors prove beneficent, it is probable that more and more supervisor time will be devoted to such activity. If, on the other hand, they are not particularly efficacious, it is predictable that supervisory energy will be directed elsewhere.

The products of research and development, too, have their consequences. Current theory argues that the direct pursuit of a learning goal is more efficacious than an indirect approach; that the level of student achievement is, foursquare, related to the amount of time spent on the objective; that considerable portions of the school day often are not devoted to learning; and that even well-behaved children may be inattentive or uninvolved in the teaching going on. Beyond all these things, the principles of effective teaching are gaining greater and greater acceptance among practitioners and, as a result, supervisors are being asked to deliver inservice programs that familiarize teachers with alternative instructional methodologies and ways of increasing student engagement.

To sum up these circumstances, then, since schools serve as our primary socializing agency, they mirror the crises of the moment. As particular problems move to the forefront, the curriculum shifts and supervisors must make corresponding realignments. At any given point, therefore, supervisors are likely to be involved in immediate (and often transient) objectives, as well as with long-range goals. An elementary school consultant, for example, may find it necessary, temporarily, to set aside his or her passion for greater emphasis on aesthetic experiences in order to help improve test scores in reading proficiency. Once the scores have reached the desired level, however, the teacher will again return to instruction that gives children adequate exposure to the arts.

Deviations of this sort, even when sensible, can give rise to a kind of professional schizophrenia—a fragmentation of commitment that generates a sense of impotence and frustration. Worse, when the required deviation is senseless or irrational, rage and despair may also develop.

Most supervisors are dedicated to given principles and beliefs. Their work is based on deeply-entrenched values regarding the function of education, the process of learning, and the role of teachers. Nurtured over time and refined by experience, these convictions become the hallmark of the supervisor's professional ethos. When they are interfered with or distorted by external pressures, a degree of alienation is virtually inevitable. If not countered in one way or another, this alienation may eventually take a fearsome toll. Few of us, after all, readily embrace false gods, or submit to the prostitution of our ideologies.

Consider, by way of illustration, the reversals of the recent past: the open classroom has, for all practical purposes, closed; humanism has almost become a lost cause; the arts are in danger of being reduced to a token gesture; heuristic learning has given way to rote preparation for tests; and the cognitive curriculum once again dwarfs the affective. All of this is not to suggest, obviously, that drill is unnecessary, or that acceptable performance on standardized measures is not essential, or that "fundamentals" should be slighted. Rather, it is to underscore the fact that a vast number of able supervisors have been forced to abandon, if only for the moment, important aspects of their professional creed in order to accommodate pressures from outside sources.

Devoted, by training and intent, to teacher welfare, supervisors tend to resent anything that undermines their efforts. Countless high school department heads, as a case in point, have agonized over the need to terminate staff because of declining student enrollments, or to assign teachers to subjects for which they lacked sufficient training. All externally imposed changes, to be sure, are not bad. Many, in fact, are advantageous. Where, however, the required alterations are not congruent with the supervisor's aims and beliefs, steps must be taken to counter a potential disintegration of spirit.

Countering Disintegration of Spirit

What, then, can be suggested in the way of antidotes? For one thing, we would be well-advised to caution against a mind-set of despair. To the extent that our attitudes are conditioned by our outlook, three things should be kept in mind. First, many of the obligatory changes, stemming from external demands, are time-bound and will, sooner or later, give way to something else. As test scores rise, for example, other urgencies will take precedence. Hence, some difficulties may eventually resolve themselves.

Second, through imaginative tactics, it may be possible for supervisors to meet current impositions and, at the same time, also sustain at least some focus on their earlier objectives. An emphasis on systematic achievement assessment, for instance, does not preclude exercises in problem solving. Similarly, ensuring adequate time-on-task and respectable standards need not prohibit some attention to the learner's well-being.

Third, teachers are not capricious in their professional convictions: strong beliefs, if set aside by circumstance or necessity, tend to be resurrected when opportunity permits. A practitioner who has discovered, through adept supervision, the power inherent in particular methods or topics is likely to find ways in which they can be used. Thus, revisions compelled by outside forces do not undo well-ingrained values.

Fourth, the maturation of educators is a good deal more drawn-out and complex than one might suspect. Professional seasoning goes well beyond the basic orientation acquired in preservice training. Teachers and administrators alike are shaped over time by their continuing experiences. For this reason, skillful supervisors frequently have a lifelong effect on those with whom they work and inspire. These effects, needless to say, outlast the vagaries of periodic fluctuation. The patient efforts of dedicated supervisors, it might be observed, pay their own peculiar rewards.

The supervisor's crafts have both scientific and artistic dimensions. There are time-honored principles, tested techniques, and useful rules-of-thumb to be passed on. But there are other dimensions of supervision that are guided by perception, creativity, and intuition. The ineffectual leadership sometimes denigrated by teachers is attributable—in most instances—not to theoretical sterility but to malpractice. It is the ability to adapt theory to the unique requirements of the situation, as well as the capacity to call forth the best teachers have to offer, that separate good supervision from bad. During the course of their careers, most supervisors work on a great many different tasks and themes. Programmatic changes, as we have seen, come and go. The supervisor's true contribution, however, lies more in the professional evolution of a good teacher than in a short-term revision of instructional content. It is in this sense that expert supervision transcends the small revisions required, now and then, by changing political currents.

Perhaps, then, the fulcrum of balance between external pressures and the supervisor's internal values lies in the human rather than the curricular element. Teaching units are developed, programs organized, textbooks selected, and methods demonstrated but—at bottom—it is the supervisor's impact on the teacher's professionalism that lives beyond its moment in time.

Conditions of Professional Development

In this regard, four conditions surrounding professional development are worth noting:

One, professional development stems from interpreted experience. However, the individual internalizes only those ideas that are personally relevant. A teacher, for example, may at various points participate in a workshop, observe the procedures of a colleague, and listen to a talk by a supervisor. The utility of each, however, depends almost wholly on its immediate bearing on the teacher's work situation: whatever is not applicable is eliminated by a perceptual filter.

Two, professional development is both cumulative and correlative. Maturation continues throughout the course of a career. As the individual experiences new events, yielding different insights and visions, subtle modifications in practice take place. Successful supervision, in short, gives birth to new understanding which eventually is incorporated in the individual's professional credo.

Third, professional development is eclectic. It encompasses all phenomena that even tangentially relate to the work scene. Virtually any event or occurrence that bears upon schooling may have an effect. A television program depicting teachers as excessively permissive, a newspaper article on classroom vandalism, a chance remark by a parent at a social gathering, a salesperson having difficulty with basic arithmetic, the behavior of children playing in the street can all influence the teacher's attitudes.

Fourth, every professional is the unique product of a collective personal history. There are infinite variations in family patterns, life encounters, education, and so on that make every practitioner different. Hence, the work habits of teachers and administrators are highly individualized. While supervision can model generally accepted techniques and procedures, the impress of diverse backgrounds causes each professional to use them in different ways.

Supervision's contribution to professional development, whether directly through staff development or indirectly through program reorganization, provides our only protection against fruitless reform. To wit, consider the curricular peregrinations of the past two decades. The potency of the innovations was diminished by a variety of factors. To begin with, we attacked the revisions piecemeal, failing both to synchronize our energy and to consolidate our gains. We tinkered, as the saying goes, rather than remodeled. The tinkering covered a wide front: we introduced new forms of mathematics, added courses in black culture, altered the presentation of grammar, broadened the structure for teaching social studies, fabricated teaching methods that facilitated individualization, and pressed, generally, for more sophisticated instruction. We forgot, however, that schools are monolithic institutions, deeply set in their ways, and as has often been the case in the past, many desirable improvements are defeated by an unanticipated passive resistance to change.

In the late 1950s, for instance, educational television was heralded as the salvation of the school. Through its magic, we were told, the world's most gifted teachers could be brought to every child in the land. Forceful lessons, prepared with infinite care, could be given again and again. But when the final evidence was in, educational TV, like its forerunners the phonograph and the radio, failed to revolutionize the teaching industry. The difficulties instructors faced in bridging the gap between the televised and the live lesson were seemingly insurmountable.

Team teaching was heralded as another panacea. But the spectrum of its cure proved, alas, to be narrow. Even when teachers worked with the same instructional materials, labored toward the same objectives, and used the same procedures, they often interpreted their functions differently. And in an all too human way, each deferred to the idiosyncrasies of personal style and belief. Thus, team teaching was victimized, not by its own inherent shortcomings, but by the inability of the teams to work together.

More recently, behavioral objectives and accountability have become popular goals of reform. Both have a logical rationale. Yet neither has been able to penetrate the establishment to a point of reasonable saturation. Apart from the current fixation on test items, teaching toward a behaviorally-specified goal—one in which the student's learning is measured by what he or she can do—is still a long way from becoming common practice throughout the curriculum. And the movement toward accountability—determining the extent to which objectives have been achieved—has not yet resolved the critical questions: accountable to whom, and for what?

Beyond tinkering, the reform movement was debilitated by our tendency to be caught up in the thick of thin things. In a sudden interruption of its usual dedication to tradition, education found a Promethean spirit and faddism became the hallmark of the times. In the aftermath, however, it became clear that in toying with the decorative elements, we avoided fundamental modifications in the system itself. It could have been no other way, perhaps, for historically social institutions have always defended themselves against the intrusion of change that threatened the existing order. The best of these defenses, in most instances, has consisted of altering the conditions that matter least.

The notion that everything new is desirable has become one of the most seductive myths of our culture. We are maligned by consumer trends in education fully as much as in our other marketplaces. There seems to abound in society a feeling that technology curdles if left unused. A few years back the schools were said to be walking the edge of error because of their old-fashioned ways. Then, like Detroit, they became recklessly fascinated with seasonal remodeling. It is not, of course, that innovation in itself is without value. Indeed, the search for something better ought to go far beyond our present endeavors. We would do well to remember, however, that a change is an authentic improvement only when it brings superior outcomes. Mindless substitutions are far worse than no change at all, if only because unfulfilled promises are hard on the consumer's spirit. If educational reform is to be the categorical imperative of the day, it is essential that we recognize its boundaries, for there are no quick cures and no final solutions. As Dewey suggested, each end can only launch a new beginning.

All of this is to say that the hoped-for reformation of schooling was diminished, partly because some of the attempted innovations were not really innovative at all, being essentially a matter of new gloss on old ideas, and partly because even in those instances where an authentic modification was initiated, the goals were of secondary rather than primary importance.

The greatest failure of all, however, lay in our underestimation of the teacher's role. We assumed, with astonishing naivete, that if a prospective innovation was logical in its conception and fertile in its potential, successful improvement would occur as a matter of course. And so, in our zeal, we overlooked the human in the system. We searched at the end of a non-existent rainbow for a fail-proof curriculum and discovered, in retrospect, that the quest was only an illusion.

The Role of Supervision

Supervision, obviously, played a part in these attempted innovations. They were spawned externally, for the most part, but supervisors were expected to oversee their implementation. The major flaws in this expectation were, first, that supervisors were not given sufficient time to prepare teachers for the changes—to establish an appropriate mind-set—and second, there was a simplistic assumption that teaching can be performed according to formula and transformed at will. In short, the real power of supervision—to shape pedagogical values—was disregarded.

Lesson plans, visual aids, and a course of study are no more than tools in the hands of an artist. If they are to be of practical worth, the artist must like them, value their utility, and master the intricacies of their use. In teaching, as in most other human arts, a tool is no better than the talent of its user. The teacher, therefore, is *the* indispensable curriculum agent. However good the instructional materials, and however rich the learning environment, the cause is largely lost if the teacher's performance is defective. Whereas a skilled practitioner can take a lesson well beyond the visions of its designer, a poor one can destroy even the best-laid plans.

Even if the organization of schooling was totally overhauled, it is doubtful whether we could diminish the power of the teacher to affect the kind of learning that takes place. Apart from the fact that teachers cannot help but reflect their own values in their teaching, a child's response to a lesson can never be accurately predicted. Hence, if we were to devise tightly structured lessons and specify an exact teaching methodology, we still would be heavily dependent on the teacher's ability to adjust the lesson to the particular student.

To sum up, then, in view of the limited gains derived from recent curriculum reforms, the failure to prepare teachers for the innovations that emerged from the theoretical drawing boards, and the impossibility of devising a school that is free from the teacher's influence, it seems entirely reasonable to argue that the improvement of education depends, in the main, on our ability to make superior teachers available to children. Almost three million teachers are involved in the overall educational enterprise. Whatever modifications we seek must—whether provoked externally or internally—be accomplished primarily through their efforts. It seems clear, then, that the continuing re-education of the teacher now in service is a central ingredient in the process for reform.

Peripheral influences on supervision, therefore, like those arising within the craft itself, have their moment of truth when supervisors affect teachers. The ultimate significance of both, consequently, is to be found in what supervisors actually do with teachers. Presently, for example, many supervisors draw from instructional research and urge teachers to use learning time more effectively. In response to the test anxiety that has developed among students, they suggest greater emphasis on adequate preparation. Aware that dollar austerity may increase the student-teacher ratio, they show teachers devices that make work with large classes easier. Worried about the mounting tensions afflicting educators, they sponsor workshops in stress-reduction. And fearful that the itch for high test scores will pervert the curriculum, they remind practitioners that a humane school is also important.

Whether supervisors look outward or inward, it is their perception of events that governs their intent. In "Essays of a Humanist" Julian Huxley remarks that "it is the general idea system, the ideological pattern of ideas and knowledge, values and beliefs, which essentially characterizes human societies and cultures."[1] All of us seek an ordered universe—a workable relationship within the circumstances of our lives. These circumstances may differ from person to person, but everyone, nonetheless, must have a system that explains the world and directs behavior. If the goal of supervision is to develop worthy teachers and administrators, then supervisors must help people to formulate an ideological framework. Before this can happen, however, supervisors themselves must have a personal conception of their professional destiny and work style.

Our vision of order comes to us in fragments. Lessons learned in training are vital pieces of a puzzle that will eventually become a complete picture. It is therefore important that all practitioners acquire these pieces. Yet, over the last two decades we have become increasing-

---

[1] Julian Huxley, *Essays of a Humanist* (New York: Harper and Row, 1964).

ly aware that many facets of pedagogy can only be grasped after one has entered service. Preservice training, in effect, is but prologue. A supervisor's educational convictions, for example, are likely to undergo a period of amendment during the transition between administrative training and practice. As experience accumulates, these convictions are refined by perceptions of the way things work. Such perceptions, it might be added, become deeply embedded and all-powerful. They control professional behavior more than anything else. Hence, they are not subject to quick mutation because of outside influence.

No one knows from what mysterious provenance comes the magical moment when a supervisory insight develops. A chance remark, a casual glance, or a frequent observation may set off a chain of apperception. An idea may grow slowly and methodically, as was the case with Einstein's field theory, or in quick penetrating instant, as when Helen Keller discovered that "everything has a name." In either case, understanding—the clarifying of confusion—creates its own special euphoria. Not only does it furnish the mind with new resources, it also enlarges functional capability in demonstrable ways.

It should be noted, as well, that the correction of misperceptions and misunderstandings whether of a child, a teacher, or an administrator is of equal importance. The repair of erroneous notions does not homogenize views with respect to schooling. Our attitudes regarding people and events, as we saw earlier, are influenced by personality and beliefs. Parents and their children sometimes want different things from school. Their desires—like those of teachers and supervisors—both influence and are influenced by their perceptions. Perceptual errors, consequently, often produce human action triggered either by false conceptions of reality or by distortions of its meaning.

It is because perception involves the *interpretation* of sensory data that we are so liable to perceptual mistakes. The basis for inaccuracy is compound: we may gather incorrect data (the teacher lacks commitment) or we may misconstrue the right data (the child is bored because he is too dull to grasp the lesson). Our perceptions tend to confirm what we *feel* or *think* to be so, leading us to believe that it *is* so. It is difference in perception that permits one person to regard an object as beautiful, and another to see it as ugly.

Perceptual errors are particularly significant in supervision. Criticism of the school is notable for its diversity and inconsistency. More, the periodic fluctuations that arise may be attributable to newly available improvements, experimentation, or discreet acquiescence to political expediency. Wrongly interpreted, they can diminish the supervisor's professional health considerably.

It is thus of great importance for supervisors to have accurate perceptions about the nature and intent of external demands. We are what our experiences have made us, and we tend to believe the world is exactly as we perceive it. In a sense, we are all "true perceivers."

Moreover, because there are many roads to good education—and many peddlers selling maps—every supervisor must have a personal feel for what is right and wrong.

By way of summation, it is safe to conjecture that supervision will always be afflicted by crises of one sort or another. For the most part, however, it is unlikely that they will result in the erosion of long-standing values. While supervisors must adjust to different points of focus as education accommodates alternating trends, outside forces are rarely inexorable. For the most part, supervision will continue to concentrate on the things that make irrefutable good sense.

Plainly said, supervisors do themselves and their clients the greatest good when they give free rein to their impulse and instinct. To do otherwise would be to court the disasters that occur when professionals violate their own values. Supervisors can hardly deny administrative mandates, but they can take solace in the fact that several factors mitigate against a prolonged interference with their professional objectives.

The decisive factor, in improving education, is better teaching. What supervisors have done in the past—and will do in the future—is of far greater consequence than a comparatively minor revision in policy.

In addition, the professional beliefs that underscore the efforts of teachers and administrators are the product of long experience and do not shift willy-nilly in response to one urging or another. And finally, effective supervision has its own power base with which to help guard against irrationality.

Supervision, because of its inherent dedication to betterment, has always had to fight against an uncongenial environment. Rather than defend the status quo, it has sought tirelessly to elevate the standards of good practice. In this regard, adversity is intrinsic to the art. So, the wise supervisor will avoid misreading the signs and see an optimistic—not pessimistic—future.

Part V.
The Future

To Chapter 13 and its author, Robert H. Anderson, is left the most difficult task of pulling together the major strands of thought highlighted in this Yearbook and of assessing their implications for further development of supervision as a field of study and practice. "Creating a Future for Supervision" is more a beginning than an ending, a harbinger of the future than a summary of chapters.

Building on the optimistic note that substantial progress has been made on both scholarly and professional fronts Anderson calls for a massive new effort to bring the field of supervision to full stature. He believes a new set of standards is needed in both the halls of state certification boards and among the college and university community responsible for preparing supervisors. Tougher in intellectual demands and more sensitive to actual needs of classroom supervision and practice, the new standards would require the development of high level skills in observation of teaching, data collection and analysis, conferencing, counseling, planning, and evaluation. These clinical skills would be complimented by demanding efforts to develop the human skills necessary for exercising successful leadership, and by the more traditional, albeit crucial, focus on matters of educational program planning and development and curriculum philosophy. Recognizing that state departments of education and universities are sensitive to the demands of the professional community they serve, Anderson suggests that *superintendents* and *boards of education* take the lead in this effort by adopting selection criteria for supervisors that exceed the now minimal and often trivial requirements of the states.

Anderson suggests further that the future of supervision rests in the hands of the supervision community itself and indeed a successful future will require more aggressive behavior by this community in the defense and nurturance of supervision. His chapter is not only a fitting conclusion to the 1982 Yearbook but represents a rallying banner under which the supervisory community might well pull itself together and move forward on a variety of fronts in establishing itself as a credible field of scholarly activity and a critical professional function in the development of excellence in our schools.

Chapter 13.
Creating a Future for Supervision

Robert H. Anderson

IN A FIELD THAT HAS RECENTLY BEEN BURSTING WITH ENERGY and generating a mature and exciting literature, this Yearbook will doubtless seem both a celebration and a prod. Both the unique importance of ASCD as an organization and the high quality of its resources come into focus as we consider these excellent Yearbook chapters and acknowledge the aggregate scholarship and influence of the contributing authors. Inasmuch as it was my privilege, along with editor Sergiovanni, to examine these chapters as they emerged as well as in their final form, I recognized early the enormous effort as well as the generosity of these experts whose ideas the profession may now assimilate and implement. I perceive that what is currently understood about the status and the potential of instructional supervision is cause for excitement and optimism, while at the same time a command to move forward. In this Yearbook, as well as in the rich experience and published material on which it draws, can be found ample clues to what we must know and what we must do if our future is to serve us well.

Every reader will have filtered and digested the previous chapters in his/her own way, and some will be either more or less willing at this point to believe that supervision *does* have a promising future. Obvious from several of the chapters is that supervision has a rather undistinguished history, a variety of sometimes incompatible definitions, a very low level of popular acceptance, and many perplexing and challenging problems. As Eisner in particular points out, even the terminology of super-vision causes discomfort and weakens allegiance. The inability or unwillingness of the society to develop and underwrite education as a legitimate profession has always had, and continues to have, a restraining effect on the development of educational supervision as the scientific, artistic, ad hocratic, humane, interpretive, inferential, appreciative, collegial, interactive, and multidimensional enterprise that the authors advocate.

Prevailing definitions and modes of teaching nurture resistance to supervision and even to the colleagueship so ably propounded by Alfon-

Robert H. Anderson is Professor and Dean, College of Education, Texas Tech University, Lubbock.

so and Goldsberry. The contextual framework within which most teachers and supervisors function is, if not actually hostile to effective supervisory arrangements, largely non-supportive. Limitations in the preparation, orientation, and skill of the existing supervisory force further reduce the prospects for excellent services, and racial and sex discrimination continue to complicate an already difficult situation. In the background, uncontrolled inflation and related political-social-economic problems meanwhile preoccupy the citizenry and government officials, so that the schools continue to suffer from neglect and to provide environments in which needed changes (such as in the quality and quantity of supervision) are extremely difficult to accomplish.

Despite all these difficulties, however, a mere decade has seen supervision emerge as a major force, perhaps we should rather say resource, in the significant improvement of educational services. Although the number of books and articles currently available on the topic of supervision may not be much greater than was the case in the early 1970s, there is no doubt that the quality and the usefulness of the newer materials are much greater. For one thing, scholars have produced sounder theory, especially with respect to the nature of effective organizations and processes of organizational change, and much more is understood about how the growth and development of adult human beings can be influenced and promoted within organizational settings. The emergence of *clinical* supervision as a central focus has greatly stimulated both theory and practice. The welcome revival, at a far higher level of discourse, of the old debate about science versus art in supervision has produced new insights into the many dimensions of supervision and helped us to see the need, as Sergiovanni approaches it in Chapter 5, for an integrated approach.

Throughout the volume, and indeed a dominant theme in convention and workshop discussions, is concern for the significant re-education of supervisors and for the promotion and advocacy of collaborative patterns of learning and of working. Although Valverde is clearly on target in proposing self-learning and the acceptance of full personal responsibility for growth, I am even more impressed with the need for embracing colleagueship in supervision and, by extension, the adoption of partnership patterns in both the practice of supervision and the pursuit of further knowledge and expertise.

Although the topic of team teaching has long since faded from the literature and from convention programs, and although teaming has not replaced the self-contained classroom arrangement as rapidly as its advocates would prefer, there is virtual unanimity on the values of professional role differentiation and sharing. In Chapter 7 are found several commentaries on the regrettable loneliness and isolation that generally characterize teaching; and in the discussion of peer supervision are found not only important advice about how teachers can help each other, but also clues to the ways supervisors can team up. Chapter

8 is similarly oriented toward a team approach. A very clear message in this entire volume is, as I perceive it, that the future of supervision as well as the future of teaching will depend largely on the willingness and ability of the personnel involved to join forces and to learn from and alongside each other.

The discerning reader may also have noticed how little reference is made in this volume to the various managerial, administrative, and even curriculum-development activities in which supervisors have traditionally been involved. Well known, and usually lamented, is the fact that many so-called supervisors are frequently conscripted by top administration to assist with maintenance functions, to deal with various crises that confront the school district, to put out fires for the benefits of the superintendents, and in general to serve as assistant line officers. While sometimes the diversion of supervisory personnel to administrative duties is a "necessary evil," often it reflects poor leadership and management in the central office or even at the level of the school board; and whether necessary or not, such diversion waters down the supervisory program and causes it to be less valued and appreciated by the corps of teachers.

Unfortunately, some supervisors are pleased to be diverted from direct work with teachers, either because they are not altogether comfortable in the supervisory role or because involvement with managerial duties seems more important and perhaps even endows them with higher status. Either way, this is a bad situation. More often, we hope, supervisors have fundamental loyalty to the helping role and are grateful when the top administration protects them from nonsupervisory duties and provides policies and resources to bolster them in the supervisory role.

Promoting Supervisors' Development

Happily, we have noticed a slight trend over the past three or four years in this positive direction. For reasons related to persistent questions of accountability and cost-effectiveness, and as a response to the greatly-decreased turnover in school districts and the longer tenure of teachers in service, school boards have lately called for a more intensive and sophisticated effort to evaluate teacher performance, provide growth (or remedial) opportunities, and in other ways attain a higher degree of quality control. As a result, the amount and the quality of supervisory assistance are being re-examined; and workshops, university courses, and training programs addressing topics such as teacher evaluation, clinical supervision, analysis of teaching styles, and related topics are increasingly well attended.

In these and related efforts to promote staff development inservice, supervisors represent not only the potential trainers, for example of principals and teachers, but also potential *trainees*. Again acknowledging

Valverde's admonishments to supervisors about their own responsibilities in this area, we note that superintendents and school boards
must become more conscious of their obligation to upgrade and maintain the multifaceted skills that are needed by supervisors. An emerging
and difficult question is "Who will supervise the supervisor?" We
perceive that leadership at the superintendency level must confront this
question and make sure that an appropriate organizational and procedural response is provided. It seems reasonable to argue that
everyone in the personnel chain requires and deserves both adequate
supervision of performance-in-role, and opportunity for inservice experiences that enhance and increase one's ability to perform at higher
professional levels.

This volume is rich in suggestions about the attitudes,
technologies, procedures, and skills in which expertise will be required
of tomorrow's supervisor. In Chapter 3, Garman examines four concepts (collegiality, collaboration, skilled service, and ethical conduct)
that in their explication embrace dozens of abilities or behaviors in
which the *supervisor qua learner* can be brought to higher levels of
familiarity and command. Eisner, in Chapter 4, proposes that supervisors be brought to states of sensitivity, awareness, and appreciation
that go well beyond conventional norms. The eight features of an artistic approach to supervision as described at the close of his chapter call
for persons whose selection, initial training, and inservice skill development must all be of a very high order. I found Rubin's argument, to the
effect that supervisors must feel more free to follow their impulses and
instincts, to be compatible with such thinking; and Rubin's four conditions that influence the evolution of a good teacher can best be nurtured
by the sort of supervisor that Eisner defines.

We have already noted the need of supervisors to increase their
skills of colleagueship and collaboration. Related to all these notions is
the almost unlimited need of supervisors for further skill in communication. We need note only the ways in which both body language and
word choices can cause conferences to go well or poorly, to appreciate
this need at one level. The comments by Pohland and Cross about some
of the risks in a counseling approach to supervision help to illuminate
the problem at another level. It is hard to imagine a supervisor, even a
distinguished veteran at the peak of his/her career, for whom the art-
science of supervisory communication does not pose further challenge
and mystery.

The implications for university preparation programs and for the
continuing inservice education programs of persons in supervisory roles
are enormous. The legal and statutory framework that specifies conditions for licensure and role access in most states is wholly inadequate,
and the expectation that supervisors will possess and maintain high-
level skills (such as in observation, data collection, analysis, conferencing, counseling, planning, evaluating) is not reflected in certification

regulations. As a result, universities feel little pressure to offer intensive and advanced courses in supervision. In fact, there are usually too few students in such courses to keep the courses alive in the catalog. The cadre of professors whose specialty is in supervision is a relatively small one, and even in ASCD circles it is often noted that the supervision people feel like a neglected minority. The same is generally true, in local school districts, with reference to inservice programs and the status of supervision people. As a result, the practice of supervision is only mildly influenced by what goes on in universities and in inservice programs, and most persons with supervisory responsibilities are ill-equipped to perform at a suitable level. Those who do develop the necessary expertise over time, usually have relied on their own resources along the way and have paid a heavy price for their hard-earned knowledge.

This situation can and must be turned around. Superintendents could and should adopt criteria for the selection of supervisors, directors, and building principals that go well beyond the trivial state requirements. In such a context, aspirants for supervisory roles would be put on notice that employment depends on evidence of excellent and comprehensive theoretical and practical training with a strong clinical emphasis, plus demonstrated supervisory skill at a substantial level of mastery. Teachers who have served on instructional teams, for example, and who have participated effectively in peer supervision or equivalent collaborative activities, would be given priority over those whose histories are barren of interactive experience and who have apparently preferred to function in self-contained isolation.

Superintendents also might well provide far more elaborate induction and orientation experiences in (clinical) supervision for newly-appointed supervisors and principals, through such devices as apprenticing future supervisors to proficient veterans-in-service, or sponsoring special clinics and workshops, or providing special supervisory services to the appointee during the first semester or two in the new role. Some superintendents have encouraged their supervisors and principals to work in teams, for example where three or four principals in the same general geographic neighborhood spend one morning or afternoon a week visiting each other's schools and practicing their clinical-supervision skills through full-dress observation cycles in the classrooms of volunteer teachers. Sometimes it is possible to engage university-based or other consultants to work with supervisors individually or in groups, on a retainer basis over time, so that expert coaching and monitoring can take place. Not only are such arrangements helpful at the moments of contact, but they tend to inspire principals and others to assign higher priority (in time allocated, and in emphasis) to supervision as they acquire more confidence in their supervisory skills and find more satisfaction in supervisory achievements. On the other hand, principals whose satisfactions are limited to dealing effectively with dysfunctional drinking fountains and ordering paper clips will very likely assign low priority to time spent in classrooms, especially if the superintendent and his or her staff pay more attention to the plumbing than to the pupils.

A Conceptual Framework for Effective Supervision

Gordon Cawelti has frequently pointed out to the ASCD membership that most educational leaders underestimate their potential influence, primarily for the reason that they have difficulty articulating a sense of direction for the schools. A quiet but important theme in this volume is that for supervision to become the force it deserves to be in improving schools, there must be a clear understanding of *and commitment to* educational goals on the part of supervisors. In seeking to conceptualize the operational essentials for effective supervision, therefore, we are obliged to connect all elements and activities to the goals that provide direction to everyone's work. In the accompanying Figure, the very center is the district's goal structure.

Sometimes a school's goals are at best implicit, or they are stated mostly as platitudes that have little operational meaning to either the teachers or the students. However, educators are fast coming to appreciate the importance of setting down clear and inclusive statements of the goals toward which everyone in the school district should be working, along with references to specific objectives, indicators of attainment, and performance standards that help to illuminate the way. Inasmuch as each school has its own culture and its own unique mission within the larger goal structure, it is important for the school staff not only to understand and embrace that larger goal structure but also to engage in a more particularized goal-setting process for themselves and to select foci and priorities for each year's efforts. Ideally, each school staff should also work out action plans, a performance management plan, and an assessment plan that will help in determining whether the goals are achieved. Within such a framework, each nuclear group of teachers (for example, a department or a teaching team) can select its own goal subset and performance plan; and at the grass roots each individual teacher ends up with his or her own particular targets and plans for accomplishment.

In Figure 1 the term Student Mastery has been chosen to symbolize the major concern of all school districts and of all individual teachers. It is hard to imagine a district goal that does not, ultimately, have some intended effect on the mastery by all students of the knowledge, skills, attitudes, and behaviors that are intended for them to learn.

Assuming the existence of a well-defined goal structure that is epitomized by student mastery, and further assuming that the teachers who work with students need, and deserve, assistance in the form of an effective supervisory program, what are the "operational essentials" of

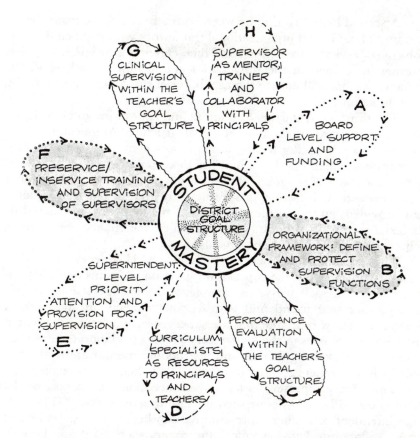

Figure 1. Operational Essentials for Effective Supervision

such a program? Eight such essentials or conditions are recognized, all of which are interactive and interdependent although there are four pairs that have especially close links with each other. The artist has connected them all to the student mastery core, in ways that suggest a circulating energy system. If one sees the district goal structure as the heart of that system (another possible analogy is the furnace of a home), then the goals are constantly providing new sustenance as attention (activity) is redirected to them. As energy orbits between points A and E, for example, one is reminded that an effective supervisory program must have the official blessing of the Board of Education, with both policy support and adequate funding, and also of the superintendent. Where school boards appreciate the need for teachers to receive continuous and expert supervisory service and set aside a sufficient budget for that purpose, the first essential has been met. It remains, however, for the superintendent to implement the policy and to give the supervisory program visible and enthusiastic support (for example through ways noted earlier).

A second loop, orbiting between points B and F, confirms the importance of having an organizational framework within which the functions of supervision are defined and then carefully protected, as well as training programs (in the universities and within the school district framework) that will ensure the capability of the supervisors to *perform* those functions.

The third loop, starting at point C and continuing to point G and returning, is geared to the teacher's goal structure. At one end, the importance of each teacher having in place, as a constant reference point, a performance plan that helps him/her to keep the year's goals in mind and be conscious of progress that is or is not being made toward them is acknowledged. It is within this frame of reference that supervision is best provided; and so in the other end of the loop we have placed the clinical supervision program through which the supervision function helps the teacher to reach those goals.

The remaining loop, between points D and H, refers to the various persons who carry out the supervision function. It seems realistic to indicate that principals play a major role, with the supervision specialist as a partner and friend and with various curriculum specialists as resources to draw on. Note that the supervisor is portrayed not only as one who participates in the supervisory process (collaborator), but also as one who provides guidance and instruction (mentor and trainer) to principals and others seeking to increase their helping technologies.

This Figure represents a tentative conception, and it may be that more needs to be said about such intriguing questions as (1) how the superintendent or his/her representative can best supervise (guide, instruct, collaborate with, evaluate) the supervisors; (2) if and how the system should acknowledge "peer supervision" as a legitimate influence on teacher growth-in-skill; and (3) how the role of the principal can be redefined so that there is less difficulty reconciling supervisory (helping) with administrative (evaluating) responsibilities. In sum, central attention to goals will invigorate the supervisory program, and put us in a better position to address these questions.

Aggression as a Virtue

Part of Rubin's heartening message is that, whatever in the current scene might tend to discourage us, a patient and steadfast loyalty to our best instincts will help us to survive — and perhaps even to prevail. I liked what he said about the importance of conceiving and perceiving one's professional destiny and work style. I also liked what he and several of the other authors touched on, to the effect that supervision is after all a form of teaching, and it calls for making such situational adjustments and adaptations as will call forth the best that teachers have to offer. Such decisions must of course grow out of a strong command of and commitment to the district goal structure and a sharp awareness of how various elements and forces impinge on the teacher's role in influencing student mastery. It follows, as indeed this entire volume proclaims, that supervisory work is among the highest callings available to educated men and women. It also follows that shoddy supervision in the schools, or the neglect of supervisory services for whatever expedient reasons, can have disastrous consequences for children and youth.

One does not, however, often hear that message in the various councils of educators, nor has there been much effort to persuade taxpayers and the shapers of national policy to that effect. On the contrary, the supervisory cadre has generally suffered its ups and downs without much complaint, and in a spirit of almost ungrudging submission to seasonal winds and prevailing climates. This submissive posture is, regrettably, in keeping with the historically unaggressive posture of educators in general; and it quite likely is explained by the fact that all supervisors were once teachers themselves and therefore were socialized into a compliant role before they moved into leadership responsibilities. Furthermore, supervision as a leadership role does not resemble either the principalship or the superintendency with respect to decision making and/or scrambling for resources. In supervision, a quiet and noncombative attitude is typical. Nor do superintendents tend to encourage or appreciate a more vocal and assertive stance on the part of their supervisory people, whom they prefer to view as assistants who help to keep the boat from rocking. As a result, neither the values nor the needs of supervisory programs enjoy much public attention or discussion.

It would therefore seem that the time has arrived for more aggressive behavior in the defense and the nurturance of our important work. There is room for initiatives to be taken in virtually every direction. Legal and fiscal policies in society do not acknowledge the importance of staff development as a dimension of improving school services. We are told that business and industry invest as much in the growth, development, and supervision of their workers as all of American education spends on educational programs for pupils. Why do we not suggest to these business leaders who serve on boards of education, that what they routinely do for their own employees makes just as much sense in the school business? Why do teachers and supervisors groups not lobby, as they are quite willing to do for better salaries, for better supervisory budgets and services? Why do not state and national ASCD units pass more forceful resolutions concerning such matters, and then pursue a full-court press toward their implementation? Why do not these groups join forces with universities in a serious effort to put excellent training in supervision at the very center of all graduate programs that purport to prepare educational leaders?

It is, in fact, critical to the future of supervision that university professors and administrators double or triple their efforts to understand the purposes and technologies of helping behaviors, and to implement such understandings in courses and programs. There is obviously no way for us to *command* supervisors to seek adequate formal as well as informal training and growth experiences, any more than we can *command* universities to step up their research activities and tighten up their course offerings in supervision. However, this volume will miss its mark if it does not cause both the producers and the consumers of supervision knowledge to acknowledge the need for more and better training. I am heartened by the apparent upsurge of interest in supervision research over the past two or three years, and I dare to hope that some of the exciting hypotheses that can be distilled from the foregoing chapters will be vigorously pursued. I am also encouraged by signs that textbooks in supervision (and, let us hope, the courses in which they are used) are paying much more attention to basic theories about supervisory purposes and processes, paying much less attention to the trivial topics that once cluttered such textbooks, and generally becoming more clinical in focus.

In sum, anyone with the audacity to participate in helping behaviors, or to pose as *teachers* of such behaviors, must match that audacity with aggressive advocacy of the roles with which such behaviors are practiced. That supervisors have deep convictions about the importance of their work is not usually evident to the general public, to boards of education and university trustees, or even to the administrators of school systems and universities within which supervisors ply their craft. That there is a rapidly-growing body of practical knowledge in supervision is evident in this Yearbook and is a source of inspiration to those inside the field, but in most respects it is a closely-guarded secret. As school boards place more and more pressure on superintendents to demonstrate that schools are sufficiently cost-effective and that pupils are learning, the initiatives being taken by supervisors to sketch out their role and show what might be done through their services are pitifully few. Supervisors seem almost helpless and paralyzed, whereas opportunity is not only knocking at the door, it is huffing and puffing enough to blow the house in!

Supervision is critically important, and the future of schooling could well depend on the adequacy with which supervisory functions are carried out. Supervision *deserves* a distinctive future, and a solid foundation of research, experience, and technical development already exists. I see this Yearbook as convincing evidence to that effect. If every Yearbook reader comes away with similar feelings, and if the aggregate of readers responds, with me, in a suitably aggressive mode, perhaps the time already lost can be recaptured and a new era can be launched.

ASCD 1982 Yearbook Committee

THOMAS J. SERGIOVANNI, Chairperson, ASCD 1982 Yearbook Committee; Professor and Chairperson, Department of Administration and Supervision, University of Illinois, Urbana-Champaign

ROBERT J. ALFONSO, Associate Vice President and Dean of Faculties, Kent State University, Kent, Ohio

JAMES CROSS, Principal, Southwest School, Evergreen Park, Illinois

DEANE CROWELL, Assistant Superintendent for Human Resources, Charlotte-Mecklenburg Schools, Charlotte, North Carolina

KEITH EIKEN, Director of the Advance Program for Instruction, Louisville Public Schools, Louisville, Kentucky

ELLIOT W. EISNER, Professor of Education and Art, Stanford University, Palo Alto, California

ETHEL GREENE, Professor and Co-Director, Race Desegregation Training Institute, Northeastern Illinois University, Chicago and Rockford, Illinois

LEONARD VALVERDE, Associate Professor of Educational Administration, and Director of the Instructional Supervision Program, The University of Texas, Austin

ASCD Board of Directors

Executive Council, 1981-82

President: LUCILLE JORDAN, Associate State Superintendent of Georgia Schools, State Department of Education, Atlanta, Georgia

President-Elect: O.L. DAVIS, JR., Professor of Curriculum and Instruction, University of Texas, Austin, Texas

Immediate Past President: BARBARA D. DAY, Professor of Early Childhood Education, University of North Carolina, Chapel Hill, North Carolina

GWYN BROWNLEE, Director of Instructional Services, Education Service Center Region 10, Richardson, Texas

ARTHUR L. COSTA, Professor of Education, California State University, Sacramento, California

RAYMOND E. HENDEE, Superintendent of Park Ridge School District #64, Park Ridge, Illinois

ALICE VIVIAN HOUSTON, Director of Curriculum Services, Oklahoma City Public Schools, Oklahoma City, Oklahoma

CAROLYN SUE HUGHES, Principal, Ludlow School, Shaker Heights, Ohio

STUART C. RANKIN, Assistant Superintendent, Detroit Public Schools, Detroit, Michigan

PHIL C. ROBINSON, Principal of Clarance B. Sabbath School, River Rouge, Michigan

MAIZIE R. SOLEM, Curriculum Coordinator, Sioux Falls Public Schools, Sioux Falls, South Dakota

RONALD STODGHILL, Deputy Superintendent of Instruction, St. Louis Public Schools, St. Louis, Missouri

BOB TAYLOR, Professor of Education, University of Colorado, Boulder, Colorado

Board Members Elected at Large

(Listed alphabetically; the year in parentheses following each member's name indicates the end of the term of office.)

Mitsuo Adachi, University of Hawaii, Honolulu (1983)

Martha M. Bequer, Dade County Public Schools, Miami, Florida (1982)

Gene Raymond Carter, Norfolk Public Schools, Norfolk, Virginia (1985)

C. Louis Cedrone, Westwood Public Schools, Westwood, Massachusetts (1983)

Milly Cowles, University of Alabama, Birmingham (1982)

Gloria Cox, Board of Education, Memphis, Tennessee (1984)

Mattie R. Crossley, Memphis City Schools, Memphis, Tennessee (1982)

Elaine McNally Jarchow, Iowa State University, Ames (1985)

Joan D. Kerelejza, West Hartford Public Schools, West Hartford, Connecticut (1983)

Marcia Knoll, New York City Public Schools, Forest Hills, New York (1984)

Betty Livengood, Mineral County Schools, Keyser, West Virginia (1985)

Elizabeth S. Manera, Arizona State University, Tempe (1983)

Gloria McFadden, Oregon College of Education, Salem (1984)

E. Gaye McGovern, Miami East School District, Casstown, Ohio (1985)

Blanche J. Martin, Winnebago/Boone County Schools, Rockford, Illinois (1982)

Marva Garner Miller, Houston Independent School District, Houston, Texas (1983)

Claire H. Sullivan, Secondary School Services, Clearwater, Florida (1984)

Laurel Tanner, Temple University, Philadelphia, Pennsylvania (1985)

William R. Thomas, Thomas Jefferson Elementary School, Falls Church, Virginia (1982)

Mildred M. Williams, State Department of Education, Jackson Mississippi (1984)

Unit Representatives to the Board of Directors

(Each Unit's President is listed first; others follow in alphabetical order.)

Alabama: Mabel Robinson, University of Alabama, Birmingham; Jim Condra, University of Alabama, Gadsden; Jim Gidley, Public Schools, Gadsden

Alaska: Denice Clyne, Public Schools, Barrow; Donald R. McDermott, University of Alaska, Anchorage

Arizona: Larry Kelly, Valley Cathedral Christian School, Phoenix; Pat Nash, University of Arizona, Tucson; Julie Strand, Public Schools, Tucson

Arkansas: Charles Adair, Public Schools, Harrison; Phillip Besonen, University of Arkansas

California: Helen Wallace, Public Schools, Cotati; Regina Cain, Public Schools, Tustin; Richard Ehrgott, Public Schools, Visalia; Bobbie Mulholland, Public Schools, Irvine; Doris Prince, Santa Clara County Office of Education, San Jose; Marilyn Winters, California State University, Sacramento

Colorado: Roxy Pestello, Public Schools, Boulder; James Curran, Public Schools, Englewood; Tom Maglaras, Public Schools, Aurora

Connecticut: Bernard Goffin, Public Schools, Monroe; Edward Bourque, Public Schools, Fairfield

Delaware: Joseph DeSalvo, Public Schools, Odessa; Melville F. Warren, Capital School District, Dover

District of Columbia: Irvin D. Gordy, University of D.C.; Romaine Thomas, Public Schools, Washington; Robert Walker, Title I Program, Washington

Florida: Daryl May, Jacksonville University, Jacksonville; Frank Farmer, Board of Public Instruction, Tampa; Jean Marani, Council of Secondary Education, Tallahassee; Hilda Wiles, Public Schools, Gainesville

Georgia: Joseph A. Murphy, Augusta College, Augusta; Gerald R. Firth, University of Georgia, Athens; Louise L. McCommons, Educational Service Agency, Thomson

Hawaii: William G. Cupit, Public Schools, Aiea; Larry McDonigal, Mid-Pacific Institute, Honolulu

Idaho: Patricia A. Wayland, Public Schools, Boise; David Carroll, Public Schools, Boise

Illinois: Kathryn Ransom, Public Schools, Springfield; Allan Dornseif, Public Schools, Matteson; Mary Anne Elson, Public Schools, Springfield; Richard E. Hanke, Public Schools, Arlington Heights; Sybil Yastrow, Educational Service Region, Waukegan

Indiana: Sue Pifer, Public Schools, Columbus; Donna Delph, Purdue University; Charles Mock, Public Schools, Bloomington

Iowa: Harold W. Hulleman, Linn-Mar Community Schools, Marion; Betty Atwood, Public Schools, Des Moines; Luther Kiser, Ames Community Schools, Ames

Kansas: Shirlie Hutcherson, Public Schools, Hutchinson; Gerald D. Bailey, Kansas State University, Lawrence; Jim Jarrett, Public Schools, Kansas City

Kentucky: Doris Mills, Davies County Board of Education, Owensboro; Jack Neel, Western Kentucky University, Bolling Green; Tom Taylor, Public Schools, Owenton

Louisiana: John Lee, Public Schools, New Orleans; Julianna

Boudreaux, Public Schools, New Orleans; Mary Kate Scully, Public Schools, Kenner

Maine: Joseph H. Capelluti, Public Schools, Auburn; Richard Babb, Public Schools, Auburn

Maryland: Richard J. Williams, Towson State University, Towson; Dennis Younger, Public Schools, Annapolis

Massachusetts: C. Burleigh Wellington, Tufts University, Medford; Gilbert Bulley, Public Schools, Lynnfield; Jacqueline Clement, Public Schools, Lincoln; Robert Munnelly, Public Schools, Reading

Michigan: James W. Perry, Public Schools, Muskegon; Rita Foote, Educational Center, Southfield; James E. House, Public Schools, Detroit; David Newbury, Public Schools, Hazel Park; Virginia Sorenson, Western Michigan University, Kalamazoo; George Woons, Public Schools, Grand Rapids

Minnesota: Les Sonnabend, Public Schools, Prior Lake; Tom Myhra, Public Schools, Fridley; Arnold Ness, Public Schools, St. Anthony

Mississippi: Jules Michel, Public Schools, Greenville; Juliet Borden, Public Schools, Plantersville

Missouri: Louise Culwell, Public Schools, Mexico; Frank Morley, Public Schools, Webster Groves; Anne Price, Public Schools, St. Louis

Montana: Kathy Miller, Public Schools, Helena; Henry Worrest, Montana State University, Boseman

Nebraska: James Davis, Public Schools, Bellevue; Larry Dlugosh, Public Schools, Springfield; Edgar Kelly, University of Nebraska, Lincoln

Nevada: Fred Doctor, Public Schools, Reno; Mel Kirchner, Public Schools, Reno

New Hampshire: Jack Robertson, Public Schools, Exeter; Fred King, Public Schools, Exeter

New Jersey: Paul Braungart, Public Schools, Moorestown; William Cuff, Montclair State College, Upper Montclair; Frank Jaggard, Public Schools, Cinnaminson; William R. Kieviet, Public Schools, Moorestown; Marian Leibowitz, Public Schools, Lawrenceville

New Mexico: Pauline A. Jones, Public Schools, Albuquerque; Zee Hunter, Public Schools, Roswell

New York: Donald E. Harkness, Public Schools, Manhasset; Anthony Deiulio, State University College, Fredonia; Stephen Fisher, Foxlane Campus, Mt. Kisco; Dorothy Foley, State Education Department, Albany; Timothy M. Melchior, Public Schools, Valley Stream; Mildred Ness, Public Schools, Rochester; Florence Seldin, Public Schools, Pittsford

North Carolina: Erma T. Scarlette, Public Schools, Salisbury; Lucille Basemore, Public Schools, Windsor; Robert C. Hanes, Public Schools, Charlotte; Marcus Smith, Public Schools, Salisbury

North Dakota: Richard Warner, Public Schools, Fargo; Quinn Brunson, University of North Dakota, Grand Forks

Ohio: Robert L. Bennett, Public Schools, Gahanna; Eugene Glick, Public Schools (retired), Medina; Ronald Hibbard, Public Schools, Akron; Robert Hohman, Public Schools, Avon Lake; Isobel Pfeiffer, University of Akron, Akron

Oklahoma: Rosa Belle Hess, Public Schools, Tulsa; Nelda Tebow, Public Schools, Oklahoma City

Oregon: LaVae Robertson, Public Schools, Albany; Jean Ferguson, Public Schools, Salem; Rea M. James, Public Schools, Portland

Pennsylvania: Anthony F. Labriola, Public Schools, McVeytown; Philip Boggio, Public Schools, Pittsburg; David Campbell, Department of Education, Harrisburg; Robert V. Flynn, Public Schools, Lemoyne; Joseph Kane, Public Schools, Devon; Jeanne N. Zimmerman, Public Schools (retired), Millersville

Puerto Rico: Lillian Ramos, Catholic University, Ponce; Etheldreda Viera, Catholic University, Ponce

Rhode Island: Guy DiBiasio, Public Schools, Cranston; James Turley, Rhode Island University, Providence

South Carolina: Karen B. Callison, Public Schools, Greenwood; Edie Jensen Public Schools, Irmo; Cecil Ward, Public Schools, Florence

South Dakota: Phil Vik, University of South Dakota, Vermillion; Janet V. Jones, Public Schools, Batesland

Tennessee: John Lovell, University of Tennessee, Knoxville; Marshall Perrit, Public Schools, Memphis; Everette Sams, Middle Tennessee University, Murfreesboro

Texas: Wayne Berryman, Public Schools, Kilgore; Robert Anderson, Texas Tech University, Lubbock; Edward Cline, Public Schools, Houston; Carol Kuykendall, Public Schools, Houston; Dewey Mays, Public Schools, Fort Worth

Utah: Dorthy Wardrop, State Office of Education, Salt Lake City; Florence Barton, Weaver State College, Ogden

Vermont: James M. Fitzpatrick, Public Schools, Hinesburg; Larry Ketcham, Public Schools, Charlotte

Virginia: Bob L. Sigmon, Public Schools, Richmond; Evelyn P. Bickam Lynchburg College, Lynchburg; Delores Greene, Public Schools, Richmond

Washington: Peggy O'Connor, Public Schools, Tacoma; Francis Hunkins, University of Washington, Seattle; Monica Schmidt, Department of Public Instruction, Tumwater

West Virginia: Ann C. Shelly, Bethany College, Bethany; Helen Saunders, State Department of Education, Charleston

Wisconsin: LeRoy McGary, Public Schools, Menomonie; Arnold M.

Chandler, Department of Public Instruction, Madison; John Koehn, Public Schools, Oconomowoc

Wyoming: Phyllis Messer, University of Wyoming, Laramie; Donna Connor, Public Schools, Rollins

ASCD Review Council

Chairperson: CHARLES G. KINGSTON, Principal, Thomas Fowler Junior High School, Tigard, Oregon

DELMO DELLA-DORA, Professor and Chairperson, Department of Teacher Education, California State University, Hayward

PHILIP L. HOSFORD, Professor of Education, College of Education, New Mexico State University, Las Cruces

ELIZABETH S. RANDOLPH, Associate Superintendent, Charlotte-Mecklenburg Schools, Charlotte

GLENYS UNRUH, Public Schools (retired), Clayton, Missouri

ASCD Headquarters Staff

GORDON CAWELTI/Executive Director

RONALD S. BRANDT/Executive Editor

RUTH T. LONG/Associate Director

ROOSEVELT RATLIFF/Associate Director

KATHY L. SCHAUB/Assistant Director for Program and Research

JOHN BRALOVE/Business Manager

Sarah Arlington, Joan Brandt, Gayle Crossland, Anne Dees, Delores Dickerson, Anita Fitzpatrick, Virginia Flynn, Daniel Jones, Jo Jones, Teola Jones, Jacqueline Layton, Indu Madan, Deborah Maddox, Clara Meredith, Frances Mindel, Nancy Modrak, Nancy Olson, Robert Shannon, Carolyn Shell, Betsey Thomas, Barbara Thompson, Anita Wiley, Colette Williams